12121

The Story of
North Way Christian Community

Alexander Hettinga

with Dr. Jay Passavant

By Grace For Glory Publishing, LLC
Pittsburgh, PA
www.bygraceforglorylit.com

"Lord, your judgements are to be feared for your truth does not belong to me nor to anyone else, but to us all whom you call to share it as a possession. With terrifying words you warn against regarding it as a private possession, or we may lose it. Anyone who claims for his own property what you offer for all to enjoy, and wishes to have exclusive rights to what belongs to everyone, is driven from the common truth to his own private ideas, that is from truth to a lie."
Augustine. *Confessions*. Oxford University Press, 2008.

ISBN: 978-0-9987302-4-0

CONTENTS

FOREWORD
BY SCOTT MCCABE
MULTISITE AND CARE PASTOR AT NORTH WAY CHRISTIAN COMMUNITY

Once when I was a teenager, I took a road trip with my little sister Marcia (and our parents of course) to visit the state of Arizona. Our adventures included a stopover in Yellowstone, an Arabian horse ride in the desert, and a visit to the Grand Canyon. Pretty spectacular for us as kids. Still, few memories of that trip remain. Recently, however, my wife Missy and I got the chance to visit the Grand Canyon again, and this time our experience was not only memorable; at times it became deeply emotional, even bringing tears to our eyes.

Nearly 277 miles long, 18 miles across at its widest, and 1 mile deep, the Grand Canyon is one of the seven natural wonders of the world. Accompanied on this trip by our brother Mac, who is a geologist and Bible scholar, our appreciation for the things that our eyes beheld exploded into fuller view as geological history coupled with explanations of God's irrefutable handiwork were meticulously explored and explained.

We began to understand and appreciate the causes behind the diverse, beautiful colors reflecting off the distinctive rock formations. We learned about the canyon's history, how the

Colorado River shaped the enormous chasm we were seeing, and why the rock squirrel is the canyon's most dangerous animal (they're everywhere and might bite you, just because!). We moseyed along several miles of the mile-high rim that day, taking in an aerial view of the canyon without ever taking to the air.

In *12121*, Alexander Hettinga invites you to experience an aerial view of a truly remarkable spiritual wonder, the formation and evolution of North Way Christian Community. He takes you places you have never been before, and he shows you things you have probably never seen. You'll go back in time exploring elements of North Way's foundation that have heretofore been observed by only a few. Your view of the church is about to explode into countless elaborate details!

As someone who has been a part of this church from its beginnings, I was quite surprised by the number of *aha!* moments that I had in my reading. After all, I thought I knew everything about North Way. But *12121* is loaded with fun facts and rarely told stories, including the FBI's role in Pastor Jay's calling to ministry, the impact 4,000 turkeys can have on a city like Pittsburgh, and how profoundly the book of Acts shaped and continues to shape the personality of the North Way community.

Reading North Way's story in *12121* has given my personal story more meaning, and I'd be willing to bet that it's going to affect your story in the same way. You will discover how God put certain patterns and processes in place from the very beginning that He continues to use today to define our church and to transform each of us into disciples more deeply devoted to Him.

As you turn these pages, you will learn the real story of how North Way was formed and how its name was chosen: why it is called a "community," not a "church." Your affection and pride for how God faithfully formed this church will deepen as you discover how many brilliant, humble leaders God has developed within and sent out from North Way to fulfill the Great Commission, changing the world.

As for Missy and myself, it's been nearly 40 years since we became a part of the North Way family. Metaphorically, we have spent all these years winding our way down this miraculous gorge — partnering hand in hand with other sojourners as God continues to give shape and purpose to this breathtaking, spiritual wonder. It's been refreshing to see North Way from an "aerial view" in *12121*, and I pray that you are as refreshed as I was in your own reading.

I encourage you to read carefully and reflect deeply on the practices and principles laid out in these pages. If you will do this, your perspective will most certainly change. Your appreciation for what God has done and is doing now will deepen. And perhaps most importantly, many of you will see more clearly how important your own story is to North Way's story and how important North Way's story is to God.

4

CHAPTER ONE:

PREPARATIONS

On March 29th, 1981, a new kind of church held its first Sunday service in Wexford, Pennsylvania. Advertised only by word of mouth, the service drew 240 people. Those in charge suspected this number would see a drastic drop the following week, but when over 200 returned, they knew something real was happening.

For the preceding three months, nine men and their wives had been meeting in a basement several times a week to brainstorm, study, and pray about what this new church should look like. Getting back to the basics of family-style fellowship and support, these brothers and sisters in Christ did life together and explored how they could realize a 1st century church model in the late 20th.

Decades before the first inkling of their idea formed, key experiences had begun to mold these couples into leaders and develop the values that would guide them. In mysterious ways, through extraordinary circumstances, they were being equipped for a specific vision and ministry. With thousands of lives to be changed in the future, countless needs to be met and prayers to be answered, there was much more at work behind the preparations for this experiment than anybody involved could have imagined. In fact, the story of North Way Christian Community begins generations before its founding pastor was even born.

JAY & CAROL

"I am the result of the prayers of my forefathers," said Dr. Jay Passavant, as he and I began meeting to record his stories of the founding of North Way. When he went on to let me borrow a heavy 1906 clothbound book from his library titled, *Life and Letters of W. A. Passavant,* I could see what he meant. Jay's family ties, not only to Pittsburgh, but also to the work of church planting and church leadership, are profound.

William Alfred Passavant was born in 1821 in Zelienople, Pennsylvania, a town near Pittsburgh which was named for his mother, Fredericka Wilhelmina Basse, "Zelie". Though he was from a wealthy family, W. A. was captivated by the gospel at an early age and wanted to be a pastor. He traveled across the mountains to Jefferson College in Canonsburg, Pennsylvania and went on to Gettysburg Seminary, beginning a pastoral career that would lead to the founding and administration of churches, colleges, missions, hospitals, orphanages, homes for epileptics, and nursing homes. He also established a publishing career as a writer, editor, and printer of Lutheran pamphlets, magazines, and hymnals. He served as a chaplain for the Union Army in the Civil War and fought slavery as well as discrimination against immigrants.

The accomplishments and establishments of W. A. Passavant are many and not hard to find — I passed by UPMC *Passavant* Hospital on my way to each interview with Jay — but it is of particular importance for this story to note that he was a true trailblazer in the Pittsburgh region as a missions-minded church builder. He did not simply plant churches; he was a pioneer of fresh ideas and new programs in these churches. W. A. reformed how church services were held, brought new Lutheran movements to the United States, and directed the attention of his denomination to the importance of firm doctrine coupled with unwavering service and care for people of all colors, creeds, and denominations. In *Life and Letters of W. A. Passavant*, author G. H. Gerberding describes W. A.'s formative role in the Lutheran church in America as that of "searching, sounding, and sifting;" seeking how to best adapt the church to new surroundings, without losing her character and life.

Though Jay did not read the whole 604-page book about his predecessor until well into his own pastoral ministry, it is clear that he came from good stock as a leader of mission-minded, people-loving, gospel-centered ministry. The future ideals of the North Way Christian Community would carry on the legacy of W. A. Passavant in more ways than could possibly be accounted for by the reading of a book. W. A. was a man of prayer, and his earnest prayers for the continuation of the ministry to which he dedicated his life would not be wasted.

Gerberding ended *Life and Letters* with this prophetic call:

Why are such men so rare? Why has our Church in America produced but one Dr. Passavant? We need such men. The Kingdom of God needs them. Let our young men in college, seminary, in the active ministry, make the same unconditional surrender of self, self-seeking, and self-glorifying. Let them empty themselves of all reliance on the arm of flesh; submit themselves under the Word and lean upon that will; let them trustfully follow that leading; let them hold mystic fellowship and communion with Him; trust Him as implicitly, love Him as ardently, and love their fellow men with the same abandon as did this saint of God, and the Church shall have other Passavants. (603-604)

The most significant spiritual influence in W. A. Passavant's early years was his mother. The lessons young William learned from Zelie showed up all through his life and are told throughout *Life and Letters*. Generations later, young Jay Passavant grew up with a similar relationship to his mother Elsie, but with one key difference: his mother was a devout Catholic.

Jay's father Jack considered himself a Lutheran, following the Passavant tradition, but did not have a problem with his three young children being raised Catholic. Jay was the oldest and had a brother Glenn, three years younger, and a sister

Susan, four and a half years younger. Jack drove his young family to St. Bernard Church in Mt. Lebanon, close to their home.

It had been over a century since a member of the Passavant family had entered full-time church ministry. Instead, Jack provided for his family as a traveling salesman with Mobil Oil Company and Strick Trailers. He covered a territory of West Virginia, Northern Ohio, and Western Pennsylvania. When Jay was six years old, Jack moved his family north of Pittsburgh to rural Beaver, a better location for his sales territory.

As Jay's mother was looking for a church to attend in their new area, a friendly neighbor reached out to her and invited her to a women's Bible study in a nearby home. Elsie had never experienced this kind of group, but she gave it a try. The women she met there were engaging, and though they were not of her own Catholic faith, it was clear to her that they were very devout people.

Over the course of just a few months in this small group, Elsie came to know and believe in Christ in a new and dynamic way. She encountered Him personally and began a relationship with Him. From that point on she became much more intentional about growing in her faith and about leading her family on this journey. This pivot in Elsie's spiritual life would be life-changing for Jay as well because Elsie was now on a mission to have her children meet Christ.

The Passavants found a Presbyterian church where the Bible was preached on a weekly basis. Another way she sought to lead her children was through attending evangelistic camp-meetings. W. A. would have been proud; he took part in the same kind of meetings back in the 1840s!

When Jay was 13 years old, the family attended one of these meetings in Toronto, Ohio at Camp Hollow Rock. As one of America's very first meeting grounds of the Second Great Awakening, Hollow Rock had (and has) been holding revival meetings continuously since 1818. Countless families came to this historic ground for its powerful preaching and singing, but Jay was rather reluctant about being dragged along. He could not have guessed he was about to become one of the countless converts to repent and receive Christ there.

As the preacher talked about sin, his words resonated deep in Jay's heart. Jay knew he needed to change, and he went forward, repenting in tears. People gathered around young Jay and prayed for him, and he received Jesus. In the car on the way home, Jay wondered how his life would change after accepting Christ; *how he would be different?* He knew he had been touched, but he was not sure what to do next.

Arriving back to the same friends and the same church and with no follow up, nothing very different did happen. He could tell that his moral compass had been reset such that he now knew when something he did was wrong, but he didn't feel that he was living a particularly indulgent life and wondered if there was more to being a Christian than just being a "pretty good kid."

Jay's church did not have a dedicated youth minister, and he did not connect with anybody who could show him how to grow. His mom would ask how he was doing in his walk with

God from time to time, but overall, something seemed to be missing. For the next five years, Jay felt stuck in neutral. He knew that his encounter with God at Hollow Rock had been real, but he did not feel he was changing much in response. His conversion had been emotional and dramatic, yet it was somehow inadequate in setting him on a steady spiritual journey.

Leaving his small hometown of Beaver at age 18, Jay attended Washington and Lee University in an even smaller town: Lexington, Virginia. He majored in Chemistry with the plan of someday obtaining his PhD and working for a large company like DuPont Pharmaceuticals. Washington and Lee was an all-male student body, and Jay played on the school's basketball team. Small town or not, God had set divine appointments for him to grow and to have his mind opened to the powerful possibilities of fellowship and ministry.

One day, after an unremarkable basketball practice, as the team finished washing up and the locker room emptied out, something profound happened. John, one of Jay's freshman teammates, asked if Jay had a few minutes. Jay responded that, of course, he did.

"Well, ya know, I'd like to share something with you that happened in my life," said John. Slightly nervous at first, but succinctly, he shared his testimony about how he had received Christ and come to know Him personally.

As John shared, Jay had the dramatic realization that John did not see him as a believer. Jay did not see himself as an overtly foul or vulgar person, but he had to consider that perhaps neither was he demonstrating qualities of Christian character that would make it obvious to others that he knew Christ.

"I've been getting to know you, and I'm wondering if this is something you might like to do," John finished.

Here Jay responded that he had already received Jesus. "John, I asked Jesus into my life five years ago, and nothing really happened."

John paused.

"Well," he said finally, "Then what we need to do is we need to start following Jesus. And I can help you to do that. Do you want to get to know Christ and really build a relationship with Him? Are you willing to do that?"

With the seed of faith in his heart from Hollow Rock and feeling emotionally convicted by the way John talked about a relationship with God, Jay said, "Yeah, I'd like to do that!"

Jay knew he needed a different level of relationship with God, and he wanted to pursue it. He figured this might mean that he and his new friend John would go to church together or that perhaps there was a Christian fellowship on campus he could join. His mind went through his busy schedule with classes and basketball and he figured he could find some time on Sundays, perhaps.

John's response was slightly different than Jay expected: "Okay, let's start tomorrow."

"What's tomorrow?"

"Well, it's Wednesday... how about lunch time? I'll come

over to your dorm, and we'll just do a few things and then go to lunch."

Sure enough, at 11:59 a.m., Jay heard three sharp knocks on his door, and it was John White. Together, John and Jay read from the book of Mark and then prayed. Jay mostly listened. In Mark Chapter 1, they read how Jesus called the first of His disciples and told them He would make them fishers of men. It wasn't a long meeting, and after just about 15 minutes, John said, "Okay, I'll see you tomorrow, then."

"What?" said Jay.

"Yeah, we need to do this pretty much every day."

This guy meant real business! As Jay began to realize how serious his new friend was, he thought, *I don't know if I'm ready for this.*

John kept showing up at Jay's dorm room every day at noon to pray and read the Bible for 15 to 20 minutes. Jay's carnal side knew this wasn't good. What the Bible calls the "new man" in Jay knew he should do what John was talking about, but the "old man" knew that if he sought this new level with God, he might distance himself from his other friends. They might think this was a bit freaky or think he was becoming a religious fanatic! The campus did not have a Christian fellowship or any kind of Christian group to join like a normal person would do. This one-to-one relationship with transparency and persistence was going to lead him to depths he wasn't sure he wanted after all.

But John persevered. *Knock, knock, knock.* Jay could have set his clock by John showing up every day at noon. For several weeks, Jay felt a tug-of-war going on in his heart, but John was diligent. Sometimes Jay wouldn't answer the door. "I know you're in there," John would say and keep knocking.

As the weeks passed and John persisted, Jay's heart softened. The two grew closer as friends, and the words they read together in the gospels worked a change in Jay. He began to discover how to read the Bible for himself. To this day, he has kept the copy of the New Testament he read during that time. The binding is worn out, and at one point he had to put rubber bands around it to hold it together. The translation he used was by J. B. Phillips.

Jay found he could read and understand this translation. Phillips had first translated the New Testament for his youth group in the church of England, trying to capture the force of the gospel in modern English. Beyond being very readable, it was formatted more like a normal book, with a single column and the verses organized into paragraphs. The verse numbers could be found in the margins alongside the text, which kept them from breaking up the flow of the paragraphs. It was released for the public in 1960, over 30 years before translations such as the New Living Translation and the Message were published and over 50 years before the recent "Reader's Bible" formats were embraced by ESV and other translations. It changed Jay's life.

In John Chapter 1, it said:

A man called John was sent by God as a witness to the light, so that any man who heard his testimony might believe in the light. This man was not himself the light: he was sent simply as a personal witness to that light.

That was the true light which shines upon every man as he comes into the world. He came into the world — the world he had created — and the world failed to recognise him. He came into his own creation, and his own people would not accept him. Yet wherever men did accept him he gave them the power to become sons of God. These were the men who truly believed in him, and their birth depended not on the course of nature nor on any impulse or plan of man, but on God. (Phillips 180)

Though he wrestled with it at first, this friendship with John, this time in prayer, and this time in the Scriptures was what Jay had been missing for the past five years. This was *discipleship.* Over time, these sessions grew in length and depth. Jay began to discover what would become one of the building blocks of North Way — not because he read an inspirational book about it or attended a conference, but because he personally experienced it. John poured his life into Jay, and the daily prayer and time in the Word was just the beginning.

Next, John began to help Jay identify his leadership strengths and provided opportunities for him to develop those skills. Since they were still playing on the basketball team together, Jay and John started a chapter of the Fellowship of Christian Athletes for their school. They were the first two members, and soon a handful of other guys joined. Next, they started a chapter of InterVarsity Christian Fellowship. Jay didn't feel he had any outstanding spiritual gifts, but John kept encouraging him to discover and use them, stepping out of the way any time there was a chance for Jay to lead something.

By Jay and John's junior year, enough people were coming to the FCA meetings that they were able to engage a guest speaker for a special event. John let Jay take the lead on organizing. They put up signs around campus and an article in the school paper advertising their speaker, who called himself, "The Strongest Man in the World."

An Olympic Gold Medalist and World Champion in weightlifting and powerlifting, Paul Anderson was indeed one of the strongest humans in history. He had broken multiple world records at official championships at an early age and continued breaking these records unofficially at his shows and strength exhibitions. Anderson and his wife were devout Christians. The couple founded a home for troubled youth and supported it by an average of 500 speaking engagements a year.

Jay didn't know if 20 people would show up or 200. The event was to be held over lunch hour in Lee Chapel, which held 600 people when full. The day came, and to Jay's complete astonishment, the chapel was packed. Every seat was taken, and all around the balcony there were people standing. Out of a student body of 2,000, close to 800 students were there.

When it was almost time for the event to start, Anderson was running late. With the full crowd waiting, Jay grew nervous. He breathed a sigh of relief when Anderson showed up, and the students welcomed him with enthusiasm. Anderson opened by saying, "You may wonder what I do that's so special — let me give you just one idea."

With his hand wrapped in heavy tape, Anderson took a 20-penny nail, nearly the size of a pen, and lifted it above his head. You could have heard a pin drop in that moment. He brought his hand down and drove the nail all the way through a 2x4. The chapel exploded in applause. Anderson performed several weightlifting feats for the students, and then he shared his testimony.

With John purposely playing a background role, Jay was able to feel the satisfaction of leading a successful event. It was wonderful for Jay to realize that he could initiate some things that would be of interest to other people, and it was an experience that marked him with the power of large-scale ministry. *Wow, people were affected!* he thought. *And it wasn't just feeling better about themselves — it was about GOD.*

Jay began to gain confidence in the leadership gifts John was helping him discover and develop. Jay's fraternity, Pi Kappa Alpha, made him president. He had stayed involved with this group since his freshman year, even though he did not partake in the drinking. When he was first stepping into committed discipleship, Jay had worried that he would lose his circle of friends — he not only kept them but was now able to lead and influence them because of his strong values.

In his senior year, PIKE told Jay that they needed somebody to represent them and raise their presence on campus by running for student office. Jay had no experience in politics of any kind and said that perhaps he could run for secretary. "Nope, we want you to run for student body president," they said.

"I have no idea what that even means," said Jay. There was a popular candidate running who had already been on the student council for three years and was considered the automatic choice. Jay ran anyway and, by the thinnest of margins, won.

This position opened up enormous opportunity for Jay to engage his spiritual values and to come to understand his own leadership strengths and weaknesses. Interacting with the student body in this broader circle, he found he was able to have a godly influence over administrative decisions and the school culture, even without announcing his convictions. He had never held a position with this much influence, and he found himself humbled and encouraged.

Throughout this year as student body president, Jay began to develop a deep sense of reliance on God. Jay knew he had peers with more experience than himself who were better equipped for this position, and yet he had a great year, even winning awards for instituting new ideas. While this process of being used outside his comfort zone helped dismantle his pride, it also helped him build a different kind of confidence for the things he would do in the future.

John continued to support and disciple Jay and invited him to spend occasional weekends with his family in Bethesda, Maryland. Together they visited John's thriving home church, Fourth Presbyterian, and Jay was impressed by its size and the teaching of the Rev. Richard C. Halverson, a famous author and pastor who would go on to serve as the Chaplain of the United States Senate from 1981-1994. "Wow," Jay thought, "There are some big, healthy churches out there."

When John and Jay graduated, John moved on to enroll in Fuller Theological Seminary in Pasadena, California. Jay stayed to work at Washington and Lee in a two-fold position as Assistant Dean of Admissions and Assistant Dean of Students, blessed to be the first student ever to be hired by the university right out of school. John and Jay would stay in touch for a number of years, but a key influence was already made. Jay had learned what discipleship was — not from a book but from three and a half years of personal experience. John's friendship was a spiritually formative one, vital to who Jay was becoming, essential to the core of the church he was being prepared to lead.

In June of 1969, Jay got an apartment in Lexington, VA, and looked to get involved in ministry at the church he had attended during college: Lexington Presbyterian Church. This was his first involvement in a local church ministry, shifting his focus from leadership of his peers on campus to a shepherding role of the church's youth. As volunteer student ministry pastor, Jay immediately sought to develop a more in-depth and consistent junior and senior high school ministry than the church had previously hosted.

Jay's job with Washington and Lee involved traveling on occasional weekends for recruitment, but Jay got a few college guys from Washington and Lee involved in volunteering with the youth program, and they were able to fill in when he was gone. The ministry grew from five students to forty-five in six months, an exciting number for a small-town church.

One junior high student in this program was named Vida Hostetter. Vida lived in the house right behind Jay's apartment and joined the youth group anytime they came over to Jay's. Besides her involvement with the youth group, Vida was in her school band and also enjoyed her PE class with a teacher named Miss Watson. Vida thought that Jay and Miss Watson should meet. At Christmas time, Vida invited Jay to the school band concert where she was playing, knowing Miss Watson would be there.

Jay was happy to come, as several kids in the band were in his youth group. At the intermission of the Christmas concert, in the hallway by the water fountain, Vida introduced the two. "Oh, I want you to meet my P.E. teacher, Miss Watson."

"Hi, how are you?" they said: just a simple meeting. Miss Watson caught that Jay's last name started with a P, but not being from Pittsburgh, she had never heard of it before and could not have told you what followed the P. Jay didn't make much of this short introduction and didn't suppose Miss Watson did either.

A few weeks later, Jay received a note from Miss Watson. It was a written but informal invitation to join her at a New Years Eve "Welcome the New Year" party. She said she was coming back from break early and suggested that if he was going to be in the area, perhaps he would like to join her.

Jay had to face the facts: he didn't have much else going on. *I guess, what do I have to lose?* he thought. Jay sent back his answer, at once cryptic and completely straightforward:

"Miss Watson, Affirmative. Jay."

As he got to know her, Jay realized that Miss Watson wasn't somebody who would typically have the boldness to ask a guy out. Thanks to Vida and to Miss Watson's willingness to give Jay P. a chance, Jay and Carol soon began a relationship.

Carol Watson grew up in Virginia with her older sister Mary Lynn and her mother. Her father died when she was seven years old, but despite being the only single-parent family on the street of their small community, nothing seemed abnormal about their family life. Carol's mother Loleeta raised her daughters while working as a full-time school teacher and was extremely involved in the local Presbyterian church. Whenever the church was open, she was there with her girls.

Carol accepted Christ at age twelve when an evangelist came and spoke, but her church was not geared very much toward the personal side of helping her grow in her walk with God. Her church had a youth group, and since she and her sister were the most faithful church kids, they led it themselves. Carol looks back and laughs at what lessons she and her sister might have come up with, admitting they had no idea what they were doing.

It wasn't until Carol went to college that church and God became a deeper and more personal pursuit. Attending Radford College (now University), Carol was about six hours from home, so she had to find a new church. This step allowed her to be responsible for attending church every week on her own, but it still did not go far beyond a good habit.

Carol majored in Physical Education with a minor in Biology, and after graduating, she took a job as PE instructor at Lexington High School. Getting to know Jay, she began to see the difference in what it was to have a personal relationship with Jesus. She started reading the Bible, and they talked about it together. "This is really new for me," she said.

Jay believed it was crucial for them to open the Word together, and as their relationship grew, he began to disciple Carol. She joined him at the youth group he was leading, and she remembers growing right along with the senior high students. Carol felt that Jay was bringing her along spiritually in a way she had never experienced. Jay often came to play basketball with the guys at the high school, so they saw each other frequently and in various contexts.

The same month Jay and Carol met at the Christmas band concert, something historical occurred in their wider context; the first draft lottery since 1942 for the United States military was held. The draft was for men born between 1944 and 1950 to be added to troops fighting the spread of communism in

Vietnam. Jay got a very low draft number of 62, so he knew he would be drafted within six months.

Rather than waiting to be drafted, Jay elected to join the Marine Corps Officer Program. He was scheduled to begin his training in Quantico, Virginia on February 1st, and having known Carol for only two months, he figured that it would be the end of their story. Then, five days before Jay was supposed to leave, he got a note that his start day had been pushed back a month to March 1st. Looking back, Jay sees the Lord's hand in this delay because it gave him and Carol another month to get to know each other and spend more time together.

March 1st arrived and Jay began his initial ten-week Officer Candidate School: the officer's equivalent of the notorious Marines boot camp. For the first three weeks of OCS, Jay saw no one except his fellow officer candidates and their drill sergeants. At the end of those three weeks, he had 30 hours leave from Saturday at 1 p.m. until Sunday at 7 p.m. He drove five hours to Lexington to see Carol and then made sure to leave early enough the next day to get back to Quantico. Brief visits like this every three weeks and handwritten letters in between totally comprised their relationship until Jay graduated from OCS in mid-May and received his commission.

Now a 2nd Lieutenant, Jay had gone from being "lower than dirt" in the eyes of his drill sergeants to being saluted by those who had only days before been able to order him to "drop and give them fifty." The next phase of his training was seven months of classes on every topic needed for leading Marines in the field, from logistics and strategies to calling in mortar fire.

He was under strict expectations six days a week from 6 a.m. until 3 or 4 p.m. but had more flexibility to be able to see Carol than during his initial 10 weeks of OCS. Additionally, he began to wonder if there was a way he could get involved in ministry on the Marine base.

Less than a month after finishing OCS, Jay met with the base chaplain and asked if there was any way he could start a youth group for students from military families on base. The chaplain said, "Well, that would be very nice; we need that. But, there's an ordinance: if you want young ladies to come, you have to be married. We do not allow single men to have contact with women like that."

Jay thought about this and said, "Well, uh, I might be able to fix that."

In late May, Jay took Carol up into the Shenandoah Mountains outside Charlottesville and proposed to her. She graciously accepted, and they got married July 25th of that same year, seven months after meeting. Jay and Carol both recommend that it is typically better to have a longer courtship and engagement, but despite the brief timeline, they felt God's hand and experienced His grace moving forward.

Jay had to be back on base at 7 p.m. the day following the wedding, so he and Carol only had time for a one-night honeymoon. By August, they started their youth program for the students of the Marine Corps Officers at Quantico. Though Jay jokes about asking Carol to marry him just so he could start a youth program, he says with a twinkle in his eye that this wasn't *exactly* true.

Jay's life plan — Chemistry to MBA to skilled work for a major firm — was still in his mind, but as he continued to seek ministry opportunities, he began to feel God leading in a new direction. He had to admit that he really loved these opportunities, and more importantly, he could see that God was blessing them. The things Jay did at college had been blessed above and beyond anything he could explain. The high school ministry in Lexington had grown and flourished under his leadership. And now, with Carol at his side, he watched a small outreach for the youth of the United States Marine Corps take off.

There was not very much for the kids to do on base, so the few that first discovered Jay's youth group soon told their friends. They met in a Quonset hut: a big, simple, metal building that looks like a 55-gallon drum cut in half. The group focused on the same foundational elements that Jay had learned in college with John: coming before the Lord together to read His Word, applying it to their lives, and praying together.

Over the course of three months, the kids involved became very committed to the group, which met two or three nights a week. The meetings were dynamic, and the kids were changing. By mid-November, some of the parents were wondering why their kids were suddenly so happy and so devoted to their faith. *What was happening at this Bible group?*

One day, Jay got called in by the company commander of his platoon of officers. The CO said he had received a letter about Jay. "I don't know what you did, but the Base

Commandant wants you and your wife to come up to his house." To get the attention of the Commandant, especially as a "lowly" 2nd Lieutenant, was a serious thing.

As they dressed to go to the Commandant's house, Jay and Carol had good reason to be nervous, but the weather made for a lovely evening. They arrived to meet the Commandant and his wife and two students from their youth group.

They soon learned that some of the parents of the students in the youth group had become suspicious of Jay when they saw a change in their children. It didn't make sense why their children would want to go to this religious group. The 16-year-old son of the Commandant had previously shown very little interest in school or in his mom and dad, but he was now on fire about God and excited about all the right things in life. When the Commandant found that several of the other officers were noticing the same changes in their students, they together concluded, "There's no explanation for this other than drugs."

At that point, the Commandant decided to investigate — to have his friend, the head of the FBI, investigate, to be precise. The FBI headquarters shared a boundary with the Marine base, so he called on his friend and said, "I have this problem, and it's out of my jurisdiction, but could you send people and do a full check on John (Jay) E. Passavant and Sue Carol Watson..."

The FBI sent people back into Jay and Carol's lives, their hometowns, and their schools. They checked everything they were involved with and everything about them, trying to find where the drugs could have gotten into their lives. The report came back, and the FBI said in summary, "We didn't find a thing." Whenever Jay tells the story, he jokes that they found a couple things on Carol, but that his record was perfectly clean.

The FBI Agent in Charge reported back to the Commandant of the Marine Base and said, "We have checked this out the best we know how, and all I can say is, if this guy was going to start something like this on our campus at the FBI, I'd send my kids to it." The Commandant had to realize that the change in his son had to be real.

The dinner with Jay and Carol was, in the end, one to show appreciation for what they were doing. At the end of the dinner, Jay was presented with a Certificate of Commendation from the United States Marine Corps: for Investment in the Spiritual Lives of the Students of the Officers of the Marine Corps Base at Quantico. There was no medal for such a designation, but the certificate was a similar and sincere way of honoring Jay for his distinguished service.

This Commendation would be used in Jay's life as a dramatic confirmation of God's calling. Jay has had conversations since with many young people who ask, "How do you know when you're called to ministry?" In these conversations Jay says, "Sometimes you know it because of revelations that come through reading Scripture. Sometimes you know it because circumstantially God makes it inescapable — sometimes, it's just implausible any other way."

Reflecting on his own journey, he can say, "Some people's confirmations to ministry come from reading passages like Ephesians 2:10 and hearing God say to them, 'I've created you for works that I have already prepared,' or whatever — *we* were part of an FBI investigation."

Carol remembers their time leading this group as a positive introduction to ministry together. She thinks it was a good thing that Jay didn't have aspirations to be a pastor at the time, even though with her church background she was open to the idea. Jay is the first of many in this book who by the time they received their call to ministry could be found doing the work of the ministry already. Jay didn't start looking for ministry opportunities once he heard a call to be a pastor; he was called to be a pastor while faithfully serving along life's way.

It was impossible for Jay to receive something like that Commendation without thinking, "Is this God getting my attention?" He began to pray fervently, "What am I supposed to do?"

Jay's chaplain from the Marines was enthusiastic in recommending that Jay pursue a seminary degree, but Jay's plan until now had been business school. Then he got a call out of the blue from an old friend. Jay hadn't stayed in close touch with John White since college due to the grind of the Marines and the simple nature of long-distance communication at the time, but his old discipler reached out just as Jay was wondering where he should go next. John had not been picked for the draft, so he was finishing his second year at Fuller Seminary.

"You have to check this place out!" John said, after hearing about what Jay had been up to in youth ministry. He said that Jay should fly out to visit Fuller's campus in Pasadena to see it for himself, and since the military was willing to pay for his flight, Jay figured that it couldn't hurt.

Reading about the school and even hearing about it from John might not have been quite enough to consider such a change in his life's course, but stepping out in faith — literally putting his feet on the ground at this campus — was what he needed to do. As he walked around the school with his old friend and got a feel for the student body, Jay felt that this might be the place where he was supposed to go next.

Jay and Carol decided together that he should apply to both seminary and business school. Carol remembers being at peace with either direction. The fact that seminary might mean she would be a pastor's wife did not bother her; it had never crossed her mind as something she wouldn't want to do. Jay and Carol placed Jay's applications to Fuller Seminary and Wharton School of Business in the same mailbox, together. "Let's throw them out there and see what comes back," they agreed.

Upon acceptance to Fuller, Jay and Carol felt certain that God was telling them to pursue this path. Jay appealed his assignment with the Marine Corp, asking for reserve status so he could pursue theological education. This was granted, and in early June of 1971, Jay and Carol packed up to start full-time seminary life.

Jay's parents came to Quantico to say goodbye. His father took one look at the truck they had loaded and said, "Okay, we have to unpack all of this because you will never arrive with anything in good shape." As he helped unpack and repack Jay and Carol's one truckload of belongings, he voiced some more serious concerns to Jay. "Do you know what you're doing here?

Moving to California for four years?"

Despite the grand Passavant pastoral legacy, Jay would be the first to pursue the ministry in several generations. Leaving for seminary instead of business school was a true step of faith. However, Jay was confident this was the path God had him on and set off on the long drive with Carol and their tabby cat, Sam. Sam was a gift from the kids in the youth group, and they decided Sam was short for Samantha after she had four kittens.

Jay was thrilled by the student life at Fuller and thankful to be close to his college discipler again. John had also gotten married since college, and Jay and Carol got to know his wife and some of his friends. Carol found a job as an administrative assistant at the local hospital.

John had been attending a large local church in Pasadena called Lake Avenue Congregational Church. This was a different kind of church than Jay or Carol had ever been a part of, but they quickly started volunteering there. Jay had been excited when he grew the youth group at his church in Lexington to 40 or 45 kids, but now he was witnessing a church with a youth group of 400 to 500!

Jay's paradigm for ministry began to be shaped in a dramatic way, not only by the theology he was studying, but by witnessing powerful, vibrant ministry at Lake Avenue. God, and what He was able to do, was much bigger than Jay had ever imagined. The size of the church wasn't everything, but the way it helped him understand the bigness of God was key.

Foundations were being laid for his future ministry in every way. By serving in this church, Jay was learning vital things about relational ministry, even during the time when he was filling his mind with all of the intellectual challenges of Biblical Theology and Systematic Theology. Having been discipled by John and then learning to disciple others, he was seeing first-hand how leaders multiply leaders. He learned how to truly pray for people and how to be well-organized for effective ministry.

Jay could not have found himself in a more happening place in terms of church ministry than Southern California in the early '70s. Fuller's location put Jay right in the middle of the birth of the contemporary Christian worship movement. The Maranatha! Singers record label launched in 1971 out of Calvary Chapel in Costa Mesa. The first Vineyard church began meeting in 1975 in Beverly Hills. Jack Hayford, someone who would greatly influence Jay, was also beginning his pastoral ministry at Church on the Way. Jay would find Hayford to be intellectually honest *and* open to the Holy Spirit. Jay saw and understood for the first time how those two things were not contradictory.

After the first year, Carol got a teaching job at Pasadena Christian School, which she greatly enjoyed. Carol loved living in California, and she and Jay wondered why they might not just stay there after school. Yet, the summer before Jay's final year of seminary, he was offered an opportunity to lead the youth group at Memorial Park Presbyterian Church in Pittsburgh. Jay and Carol thought it would be nice to be back in Pittsburgh, just for a summer. The position was as an intern and there was no long-term opening, but it would give them some time close to Jay's parents and not so far from Carol's mom. It would also give Jay more practical experience with everything he was learning at seminary.

When Jay took the internship, the youth group at Memorial Park grew, and he quickly became known as Mr. Yuk — always ready to "yuk it up" and have a good time, according to members of the youth group. After a good summer, Jay and Carol went back to California, and Jay completed his degree, a Masters of Divinity. The MDiv at Fuller included in-depth Greek and Hebrew and was more focused toward pastoral ministry than the Masters of Theology. (Jay would eventually return to earn his Doctor of Ministry, which was similarly distinguished from a PhD in Theology as a consummate degree for pastors, rather than for teachers.)

Jay finished the four-year MDiv program early, in under three and a half. As he finished his degree and reflected on his ministry experience up to this point, Jay developed a key principle for his future, namely that it would be his job as a pastor not to simply *do* the work of ministry, but to *equip the saints* to do the work of ministry (Eph 4:12).

Jay and Carol were happy in California, and they wondered if they should stay long term after graduation. When Jay was offered the same internship as the previous summer at Memorial Park, he and Carol had to weigh it against exciting and tempting opportunities on the horizon in California. They decided once again that being close to family was most valuable and packed up for Pittsburgh.

MEMORIAL PARK

Upon Jay's return to Memorial Park, students in the youth group noticed a change. He was much more serious and had a different kind of focus. During his time there the previous summer, Jay had been loved for his charismatic personality: for his fun ideas, his skits, jingles, and games. Hundreds of kids who hadn't cared much for church had realized that youth group could be a great time. In fact, some of the kids felt a bit lost when Jay had gone back to seminary.

Now he was back, but instead of hitting the ground with fun ideas to get the group growing again, the group actually shrunk. *What's going on?* The students wondered. *What happened? Where's Mr. Yuk?*

Many of the students were confused, but two high school juniors named Bruce and Kathy leaned in to see what the change was all about. Sweethearts since tenth grade, Bruce and Kathy had developed their relationship and other close friendships at Memorial Park's youth group. Kathy had been assisting the youth pastor and teaching the middle schoolers. After a closer look, Bruce and Kathy realized that Jay had not lost his passion for ministry, but that he had actually gained a deeper heart for the Lord. "Jay had really been filled with the Spirit during that last year of seminary," says Kathy.

As the numbers waned, the depth of conversation grew. Jay taught them week by week what it meant to follow Christ, not just how to have a good time. Kathy says she will never forget one of the lessons he taught them: "Love is commitment, and

Jesus loved you enough to commit to come here and die for you — if He did that for you, what are you going to do for Him? Do we have to just be fun all the time? Or are we going to make a commitment to be disciples, and grow, and belong to the Lord, and love His word, and love to worship?"

"It was definitely a switch, and it was very meaningful," Kathy says. "We dwindled, but the lives of those who stayed were changed." The members of the youth group began to discover what it meant to have a relationship with Christ and found themselves attracted to the youth group for different reasons than the previous summer. They were learning how to plug into the transformational power of the gospel.

Reflecting on this time, Jay says, "I discovered that you can't compete with the world in terms of glitz and production, and so you shouldn't. You should really appeal to a deeper thing: knowing God — knowing God's plan for your life; what it means to serve, to care for others, and to make a difference."

Jay chose scriptures for the youth group to memorize together, and their first project was Psalm 1, which starts, "Blessed is the man who walks not in the counsel of the ungodly, nor stands in the path of sinners, nor sits in the seat of the scornful; but his delight is in the law of the Lord, and in His law he meditates day and night" (NKJV).

Jay had two assistants for the youth group during that second summer: Kathy and a high school senior named Amy. Amy remembers Jay caring about every detail of how the youth group was run, spiritually and practically. On one occasion, Amy and Kathy were tasked with picking up bananas for the youth group. When they came back with bananas that were all yellow, Jay said, "No, they should have this much green on each end," holding up his thumb and forefinger. They went back to the store.

Another day, Jay sent them to Home Depot to pick up some string and a box of metal washers. A simple necklace was made for each member of the youth group by putting a string through each washer. The washer, a circle, signified the group's emphasis on fellowship and good company: the circles they gathered in.

According to Amy, Jay was just as caring as he was tenacious, and she shared about what happened when Jay realized that she didn't have a way to listen to worship music in her car. One day he said, "Give me your keys." Figuring he needed to run an errand, Amy handed them over. When Jay came back hours later, she found he had personally installed a cassette player in her car so she could listen to worship music.

When Memorial Park's full-time youth pastor took a different position, Jay's internship turned into a full-time role. He was entrusted with not only the youth group, but also all the children down to the nursery. He was also responsible for hospital visits to the elderly. He had little preaching responsibility but assisted the head pastor in every other way. Jay was ordained in the United Presbyterian Church and ended up working in this position for seven years.

Up to this point, Jay and Carol had been able to witness great examples of ministry in California, had been able to serve in multiple churches, and had even been able to start ministries like the youth group at the Marines base. Now, for the first time, they were responsible for an established church ministry and had the opportunity to implement the ideals they had learned. On the top of their list of goals was to develop a youth staff.

Instead of Jay leading the youth group by doing all of the ministry himself, he and Carol wanted to cast a vision for reaching the students that could be carried out by college students and young adults in the church. Jay reached out to the congregation with a challenge to make a difference with their lives by serving the church's youth, and several people agreed to help. Jay and Carol invested a significant portion of their time into this newly formed group, fostering community with and amongst them. The youth staff formed a deep bond as they began to learn and serve together.

With the help of the youth staff, Jay established two weekly meetings for the youth group. The group that met on Sundays he named FUDD, which stood for Fisherman's Union of Devoted Disciples. The title was taken from Mark 1:19, which readers might remember is the very first passage Jay read with John White. "Follow me, and I will make you fishers of men." FUDD focused on building disciples and leaders, and each Sunday they broke into small groups led by members of the youth staff.

In the middle of the week the youth group had a second gathering that was focused more on outreach. The outreach component was called AGAPE, after the Greek word for unconditional love. This meeting gave the members of FUDD an opportunity to minister. With the youth staff being discipled by Jay and Carol, and FUDD being discipled by the youth staff, the natural response was for the high school students in FUDD to want to invest their time reaching the students in AGAPE.

At first, Jay led worship at FUDD and AGAPE but always wanted to find people who were more musically gifted to lead; one of his earliest recruits was Amy. Many wonderful musicians emerged from the youth group, and the depth and quality of worship quickly became a highlight that the students valued far beyond group games and activities. "We literally learned *how* to worship together," says Jay.

Jay did not confine his work to the church building, either. He went to North Allegheny High School at lunchtime to sit with the students, supporting them and raising up ministry right where they were. It worked both ways: inviting students to church and bringing the church to them. Seeing the students only at church, it was impossible to know anything more than how they were at church. Among them at school, Jay could learn about their lives and see them being touched and changed.

If Jay heard of a member or members of his youth staff being at a Pirates game he would say, "Did you bring someone with you?" If they hadn't brought somebody from FUDD or AGAPE, he would challenge them not to miss such an opportunity.

The members of FUDD grew in relationship with the Lord and learned what it meant to be in godly relationships with one another. The students gathered for fellowship at their schools for Bible studies. Wherever they lived, they felt they had a place to belong. However fun youth group might have been under Mr. Yuk, it had not made them seek extra fellowship. This sense of belonging was a new phenomenon.

Many of the members of FUDD were not from churched families, and their parents were seeing a change in their children. Parents began to attend Sunday services. FUDD went on missions trips together across the country, and upon their kids' return, parents would say, "Now when are you going to do this for us? We want go on one of these!"

Jay and Carol didn't have any idea at that time what was in their future, but they were uncovering and practicing North Way's defining principles of discipleship, fellowship, worship, and outreach. They did these things because they felt they were the right things to do. They also couldn't yet know that some of the youth staff they were investing in at Memorial Park would become essential leaders at North Way — their focus was on building ambassadors for *God's* kingdom, regardless of where those ambassadors would be sent.

With all that was on Jay's plate leading the youth group and other facets of ministry at Memorial Park, he was allowed to bring on an assistant. This opening led to a multi-generational connection with an essential North Way family.

Marcia McCabe had felt an inexplicable hunger for God from an early age. She attended Maxada private school with her sister, Sherry, which today is called the Ark and the Dove and became the birthplace of the Catholic charismatic movement. "I can't help but believe that there was prayer that had gone into that place and that the power of the Holy Spirit was heavily at work," Marcia says. Marcia and Sherry heard the gospel years later from "Rev. Ev" Evelyn Carter at a meeting in Homewood and came to know the Lord.

Part way through college, Marcia was living with her parents and found herself in a difficult place, looking for direction. Her mother could tell she was struggling and left her a small slip of paper that gave her two options: either to move out and find an apartment of her own or to go intern for Jay Passavant at Memorial Park. Marcia chose the latter and found that while being Jay's intern was incredibly demanding, she also was able to dig deeper into her faith along with the youth.

Marcia met a young man named Ray at Memorial Park. Ray had accepted Christ just months before at a Full Gospel Business Men's meeting he attended with his father at a restaurant in Wexford called "Mr. B's." Just as Ray was undergoing a transformation as a new follower of Jesus, the youth group at Memorial Park needed someone to play Jesus in their Easter Pageant.

Bobby Anderson, who was directing the play, heard that Ray had just gotten saved and that he had some acting experience. Bobby was hoping to find someone from outside the youth group, so the youth wouldn't recognize the person playing Jesus. Ray said, "I'm not worthy to tie His shoes, let alone play Him on stage." Bobby replied, "Who is?"

Since Marcia was working with the youth group, she met

Ray when he showed up at Memorial Park. "I pulled up in my VW bus — headband, new crazy ex-drug addict, you know — and she was the first person that greeted me," says Ray.

Three years later Ray and Marcia married, and the whole McCabe family had their first introduction to Jay Passavant. Marcia was the youngest of five siblings. Susie, who was married to Marcia's oldest brother, Kirk "Mac" McCabe, sang at the wedding.

Scott, the brother closest in age to Marcia, got to know Jay at Ray's bachelor party at the Steak and Ale on McKnight Road. At the time, Scott was in business with his father, and though there had been a prophetic word spoken over his life when he was young that he would be in ministry, he says that he had not recently been hearing (or listening for) God's voice. Scott says, "I wasn't a close follower of Christ at all, but I went home that night and I said to Missy, 'I'd swear God said to me that if that man (Jay) ever starts a church, we're supposed to be there.'"

Marcia says, "I think it's really interesting when I look back historically and I realize that what some people don't ever really think about is the brokenness of people in the process. Like, Jay's always been going somewhere. But for some of us it wasn't quite like that. And for me it was my mother handing me a piece of paper saying, 'I want you to go,' and then there was a whole lot that happened in a whole lot of lives in those connections after that."

Another important connection Jay and Carol made for the future of North Way during this time was an established couple at Memorial Park named Grant and Rosa Lee Smith. Grant was a respected adult Sunday School teacher and Rosa Lee was president of the women's ministry. They were also involved in small group ministry. They had three children, two of whom were teenagers in Jay's youth group.

Rosa Lee says, "Coming out of the difficult late '60s, we were concerned for our children and wanted them to be 'on fire' for the Lord. One of the things that attracted us to Memorial Park was their youth program. When Jay came as their youth group pastor, we were impressed with his energy, his heart for God, and his desire to see our young people grow in worship and commitment to the Lord. Jay's leadership seemed to inspire that."

At one point, Grant became concerned that the commitment piece was becoming a bit cultish. When I asked Grant about this he said, "Yes, there was a brief time when I became concerned about Jay's leadership. He was teaching the kids about the cost of discipleship, which the youth took to mean they should reject the word of their parents. I felt I needed to talk to him about it, and a result of that conversation was that he softened his approach with the teenagers. I appreciated his openness to my correction, and my concern went away."

This conversation could have been difficult but was instead handled with humility, and Grant and Rosa Lee's support for Jay's ministry was strengthened. Grant became someone on whom Jay knew he could rely for wisdom and prayer. The discerning quality that caused Grant's initial concern would prove invaluable.

Jay and Grant actually had a number of things in common when it came to their journeys as Christians, and they aligned on several ministry ideals as a result. Like Jay, Grant became a Christian as a teenager but found growth difficult and slow. Then Grant got drafted into the Army at the age of 19 during the Korean War and met a new friend who provided that same missing piece called *discipleship*. "His mentoring and encouragement were a radical new thing for me, and I began to grow in many significant ways," says Grant.

Similar to how Jay grew in his faith by tapping into ministry with John through the Fellowship of Christian Athletes, Grant grew alongside his friend through ministry and summers of training with the Navigators in Glen Erie. In both cases, acting upon personal growth by engaging in ministry was an important development for further personal growth.

After his time in the Army, Grant attended college at Wayne State University in Detroit, where he majored in industrial design. At Wayne State, he joined the InterVarsity chapter where he grew through small group style fellowship. "In that chapter, I also met a lovely young lady called Rosa Lee, and we got married soon after I graduated," says Grant.

Rosa Lee had become a Christian as a young girl when she was invited to a Baptist Sunday school class by her two neighborhood girl friends. "When I heard the Gospel, my heart responded," she says. "I was 11 years old, and my family was having problems. The church nurtured and cared for me through those difficult times."

Grant and Rosa Lee both grew in their faith through the active and vital InterVarsity chapter, and both became student leaders. They were married in 1960 and moved around for a time between Christian work and graphic design employment; from Indiana, to Detroit, to Illinois, where they worked for His Magazine through InterVarsity, and finally to Pittsburgh where Grant became Manager of the Graphic Design Department for the Westinghouse Corporate Design Center.

Here the stories of the Passavants and the Smiths diverge in a pivotal way. After going back and forth between Christian ministry and design work, Grant landed in design. While Jay was being called to pastoral ministry, Grant was establishing a successful career that would allow him to be a stable financial support for future ministry.

During their years in youth ministry at Memorial Park, Jay and Carol were always wanting to discover a deeper level and experience of true community, a process that could be quite experimental at times. On one occasion, they reconfigured the basement of their 1,100 square foot home to allow for the college-aged youth leaders to live with them. Four young men stayed in their one-room basement, and two young women slept in the living room. Carol had a baby at the time. This experiment in Christian community lasted over a week, but they realized that living together under the same roof was perhaps not exactly what the Lord was after, except by necessity. They all laugh looking back on that experiment but also remember it as a special time that shaped their ideals for future ministry and allowed them to grow closer.

A few of the college guys on staff did end up renting a house together, which they called the Hedwig Hotel. The house was on Hedwig Drive in Allison Park and was owned by the parents of a friend from the youth group. Two of the guys who lived at the Hedwig Hotel, Ray Speicher and Dave Van Gorder, built a table — eight feet in diameter and decorated with mosaic tiles — so they could host the youth staff for their weekly meeting and eat together regularly. They gathered there often for prayer, and the house would remain a common meeting place in the formational days of North Way.

The guys held an array of fun and spiritual events at the house and continually opened their home to members of the youth group. The house was split into two sides for football games between Penn State and Pitt. Blaine Workman, another member of the youth staff who lived at the Hedwig Hotel, was a graduate of Penn State. With 25 or so kids from FUDD over for games, two or three would join Blaine at the small black and white TV on the Penn State side while the Pitt fans enjoyed the color TV that did not look as much like a "blizzard." In Pittsburgh, it may be that fellowship must include football.

Bruce and Kathy continued to date, and when they went to college they stayed connected to and through the youth group over the weekends and summers. Bruce attended the University of Pittsburgh and Kathy attended Grove City College, so when Kathy came home each weekend to serve in the youth group, they were able to see each other. Bruce was deeply inspired by Jay's love of the Word and the importance of knowing and understanding it. After two years at Pitt, he transferred to Grove City and completed a degree in Religion and Philosophy while Kathy completed hers in Business Administration. Just after graduating, they were married: Mr. and Mrs. Bain.

"One of the things that was so valuable in all those years in youth group was worship. It was powerful, meaningful, life-changing. Just so sweet," says Kathy. While Bruce also valued Jay's emphasis on discipleship, studying the Word, and having a personal relationship with Jesus, he agrees that knowing God in worship was what made it all real. North Way's future *number one priority* was being established and proven.

Another member of the youth staff and lodger at the Hedwig Hotel was named Don Edinger, a gifted pianist and worship leader. "He could just follow the Spirit and float from one song to the next and to the next in a way that really led you into the presence of the Lord," says Kathy. The songs were mostly choruses, with words that were easy to remember. Don was flexible and led the group spontaneously through hits by Maranatha! Singers, Nancy Honeytree, The Imperials, and many more.

Don's gift left an indelible mark on members of the youth group and kept the future North Way members who were present hungering for similar expressions. Ray says that Don set the "gold standard" for worship leaders and that their time in worship was the stuff that glued the group together. "It was the intimacy of that worship — not the bigness of it — but the intimacy of it. The tears flowed and people were able to process, and there was a lot of time to go and encounter the Lord."

"Don was so instrumental. His music led us to the throne," says Marcia. In that place, Marcia says, God met needs and healed hearts. She believes that Jay valued worship as much as he did out of the humble knowledge that God's ability to heal in worship went far beyond his own ability to pastor.

The youth group at Memorial Park became so vibrant that they put on their own events and concerts, bigger than any events hosted by other local churches. They were responsible for bringing many Christian singers and rock bands to Pittsburgh just as contemporary Christian music was beginning to explode. They hosted Petra, Glad, Randy Stonehill, Larry Norman, and even Resurrection Band, which Kathy says was, "pretty hard rock for a Presbyterian church in the North Hills."

Ray remembers both Randy Stonehill and Larry Norman staying with the guys at the Hedwig House while they were in town. Marcia says, "We made a spaghetti dinner for them, but they cleaned up. They wouldn't let us clean up; they wanted to serve us. It was amazing."

Jay and the youth group attended a number of Jesus Festivals — Jesus '75 and Jesus '76 were both close by in Pennsylvania. These music festivals drew top Christian artists, which further inspired the youth group's passion for worship. Jay and the youth group put on some of their own events as well, including something they called Vision '77, held at Lt. J.C. Stone Field in North Park, in association with a movement called, "I've seen it." Printed on billboards and worn on pins,

"I've seen it" was a conversation starter about faith. "Well, what have you seen?" many would ask. All the members of FUDD and AGAPE were ready to answer with their personal testimonies and with more information about the event.

Vision '77 was a three-night event with exciting guest speakers, including Steelers offensive lineman, John Kolb, and Ben Kinchlow, evangelist and co-host of *The 700 Club*. Many young people came to faith in Christ, so they planned another similar event in 1978 featuring evangelist David Wilkerson, author of *The Cross and the Switchblade*. Rather than the church putting on events to draw and entertain its youth, the youth at Memorial Park were putting on events to draw and minister to hundreds upon hundreds of people in and outside their church. Jay seemed to have no interest in what was typical and expected of a youth pastor, a youth group, or even the local church.

Ray says, "I don't think a lot of us knew the joy of the Lord until we had it. Then once you did, you could recognize it in other people. That was a distinguishing characteristic: the joy of the Lord, and being surprised by it. When the joy came out of worship and when a real broken tenderness came out of worship, it was like, this is so real that I need other people to know that this is real."

Marcia says, "One thing that's been consistent for all of us, whether we stayed or whether we didn't, is that we didn't manufacture it and it can't be manufactured. There's never been anything quite like it. I mean, it's happened for other people in other places, but it was something that happened because the Holy Spirit brought us together. He was doing something, and the dynamics were just right. Seek as hard as we could to find it elsewhere, we couldn't find it elsewhere. Not in the same way."

In 2016, members of Jay's youth ministry at Memorial Park from the years 1974 to 1978 held a reunion in Pittsburgh. Close to 100 people attended. Several members had embraced a life in full-time ministry since high school, and many others were actively engaged in their local churches, supporting the work of the Lord. Testimonies were shared of how God had used the youth ministry in their lives and all the places they had served since then. Many shared previously unspoken stories of their home lives from the time they were involved with FUDD. Some had faced terrible persecution and abuse from their families for their choice to follow Christ.

Amy is now the executive director of a vital Pittsburgh non-profit and helped put the whole event together. "Dozens in our youth group were rescued from Satan's jaws and became lifelong disciples," she says. "The impact they've had on the Kingdom is evidence of Jay and Carol's faithfulness." Amy found that the washer necklaces were remembered, and many had been kept over the decades!

The testimonies shared at the reunion demonstrated how Jay and Carol were used by God to touch souls during their season of preparation. Even with their primary life's work still ahead, many lives had been changed through their ministry at Memorial Park. Jim and Diane Beck are another couple who met in the high school youth group at Memorial Park. Jim and Diane moved to California after being present for the start of North Way and went on to lead lives of disciple-making and service in their local church. Just before the reunion, Jim wrote to Jay:

> I can't say thank you enough. You, your wife, and the loving team around you poured out Jesus' love to me in a way that changed my life forever.
>
> Not only did you introduce me to Jesus, but you taught me how to love His Father and how to be filled with the Holy Spirit. It was such a sweet time, where seeds that would be the foundation of my faith were planted by you and your team.
>
> I wanted you to know that we are so thankful for the sacrifice that you and your family made and for the hard work that you did to help us during the early years. Your impact on our lives has been reflected outward to the lives of all the people that we have touched over the years.

CHAPTER TWO:
LAUNCH

When Jay came to the youth staff one day and said, "I need you to pray," they took him very seriously. Jay had been serving at Memorial Park for more than five years, and they all knew it was time for something new. They committed to meet every morning to pray about what God might have around the bend for Jay and for themselves as well.

Jay and Carol had a deep influence in the lives of the youth staff. Under Jay's leadership, the staff had grown to love ministry and to expect big things from God. The staff devoted significant time to helping with the youth group and wondered what the group would look like if Jay left town to pastor another church.

Every day, except Sundays, the youth staff met at 6 a.m. to pray for an hour. They met in a small house right next to Memorial Park church. The church had bought the house when the previous owners moved out, but it was not used for much. The house had low ceilings, with just enough space for taller folks to stand up inside, but at prayer meetings tall ceilings are not a requirement.

These meetings continued daily, six days a week, for two years — likely totaling over 500 hours of corporate prayer. Jay's youth staff were the core of the prayer group, but others joined over time. Some days there were 30 to 40 people squeezed into the house to pray, some of whom would eventually become members of North Way, but many who would not. All who came had a desire to see God do something great through Jay and something great in Pittsburgh. They could not have known that they were praying for the birth of North Way Christian Community, but they felt something was going to happen and wanted to be a part of it.

Bruce and Kathy, now married and in their early twenties, sensed God carrying them along in those days. They were dreaming about various possibilities for their own lives, but knew that they were connected to God's direction through prayer at the small house. "God was really birthing something incredible. I'm sure that that prayer was part of what began to break through the barriers," Kathy reflects.

With the possibility of Jay moving away, Bruce thought perhaps now was the right time to go back to school. He had been wanting to pursue a seminary degree, but it was difficult to imagine an end to this time under Jay's discipleship. Around this time, Bruce and Kathy became pregnant with their first child, which added another level of complication and emotion as they wondered what lay ahead.

Bruce began researching several schools, and he and Kathy fasted and prayed. They got together with Jay and Carol and prayed with them. Jay and Carol were good at helping them see beyond the possible immediate losses of any given decision to its possible future benefits. Bruce and Kathy remember wanting to ask for the answers but felt that Jay and Carol were teaching them to walk by faith and to seek God's will for themselves. Jay and Carol could lead by example in this way, since they were facing a bend in the road themselves.

Bruce and Kathy made a visit to Westminster Theological Seminary and a longer road trip to Trinity Evangelical Divinity School in Chicago. Neither seemed like the right fit, and they were surprised to feel a clear "No" impressed on their hearts regarding Westminster. They felt they were receiving the wait signal, and were not sure why, but they knew they should listen. Today they are thankful they were patient; they know that if they would have gone ahead to Westminster, they would have missed out on something God was about to do in Pittsburgh.

While the Bains were waiting in Pittsburgh, another important couple for North Way's future was arriving: Jay and Sue Dawson. Jay and Sue first met each other when Sue ventured off campus from Colgate University to attend a football game in Princeton, New Jersey. Jay was playing for Princeton University, where he was a pre-law student, and the two met at a party after the game. They got married and moved to Pittsburgh after graduating, and Jay started law school at the University of Pittsburgh.

Jay's parents were from Pittsburgh and attended church in Mt. Lebanon. Jay and Sue tried attending with them and appreciated the spirit-filled evening service, but it was a long drive to Mt. Lebanon from their apartment in the North Hills. They looked closer to home and found Memorial Park Presbyterian. After a service where Jay Passavant gave the message, Jay and Sue raised their hands in response to the altar call. They had both grown up familiar with church and Christianity, but they wanted to be able to say they knew they were born again. They went back to their apartment, knelt together, and gave their lives to the Lord.

When the senior pastor at Memorial Park stepped down, Jay Passavant and another associate pastor, Fred Steele (who would someday also be a staff member at North Way), shared the teaching responsibility while the church searched for a new leader. Together, Fred and Jay led vibrant ministry and saw exciting spiritual growth. They were both considered to be too young for that position (and perhaps too charismatic as well), and after several months, a new senior pastor was hired.

Under the new leadership, Jay felt a strong nudge to pray and search for what his next assignment should be. With his team of prayer warriors backing him, he submitted his resume to the Presbytery and waited to hear from churches that were looking for leadership. Churches from within the denomination started contacting him, sharing what they were about, and inviting his application.

For the next 18 months, Jay and Carol received "No" after "No." They applied all over the country and traveled to candidate at a number of churches in Ohio, Pennsylvania, and New York. Each application process took significant time and care, from the waiting involved in weeks of "snail mail" communication to the emotional investment of meeting congregants and writing candidate sermons. At one church in Philadelphia, Jay was one of the final two candidates for a head pastor position, and they chose the other candidate.

What was happening? Was God saying no? Or was it just the people? Or was the devil getting in the way? It was one thing to say, *God's saying "No" so He can give something better* for the first few, but it was a true exercise in trust to keep saying that. At some point, a rejection letter can simply feel like a sign of failure.

At last they received a "Yes." Almost. In the Fall of 1980, a church in New York seemed to be a go. The church had 200 members and was located 40 minutes from New York City in a small town called Suffern. Jay and Carol got along well with the search committee. The committee traveled to Pittsburgh once and had Jay and Carol to New York twice. The pastor stepping down was retiring after 40 years, so the committee knew it needed to find just the right fit.

On November 1st, Jay preached his candidating sermon and got enough votes to be approved. He and Carol had a bittersweet flight back to Pittsburgh, knowing they would be leaving deep roots behind but also being excited for this new opportunity. They stood up in front of Memorial Park and announced that they would be leaving to take a new job in New York. The church applauded and gave them a warm thank you for their time in ministry there.

One Sunday later, they had to stand up again and say,

"Forget that — we're not going there." Just a few days after their first announcement, they had received a call from the Executive Presbyter of New York City. He said, "I don't know that I've ever made a call like this, but ever since you were here, I've had people outside my office saying that there's been a mistake."

The Presbyter said he needed to investigate and said he would get back to them. Three days later he called and said the situation was a mess. People in the church were divided and upset. Some felt that the search committee had rushed the hiring process. "It would be a tragedy for your family and this church if you came," the Presbyter concluded.

Jay and Carol's long awaited "Yes" had turned into the most resounding "No." At first, they wondered if the dispute was spiritual warfare; they prayed and sought advice from friends. They quickly felt sure that such an unprecedented statement as, "This would be a tragedy," was not just people saying "No;" it was God saying "No," one last time, in order to give something greater.

Jay and Carol turned down the position in New York but felt it was too late to go back to Memorial Park. Even with a possible extension of their current role, Jay and Carol were sure it was time to move on. Carol says of that time, "We knew we had let go of one trapeze, but the other one wasn't just quite in sight yet, so we just had to wait in that gap to see. We had to move on what we were sure of (needing to let go), even though we didn't know what the future held."

Jay believes God wanted them to surrender all control of

the situation. Once they found themselves truly at a loss for what would happen next, God could lead them to something they would have never imagined otherwise. This was also a chance to leave Memorial Park on a good note. The elders at Memorial Park agreed that it seemed God had something special for them around the bend and sent them out with a blessing.

"Who knows what could've happened if we had taken that position," Jay says. The church in New York did find a pastor who was just right for them, and it is easier to understand looking back why Jay would not have been a good fit (it had mostly to do with them finding out he was more charismatic than they were comfortable with). At the time, however, Jay and Carol just knew that God had said "No" in a very dramatic way, and that they needed to obey.

"This story, like any story, isn't there to be duplicated by somebody; it's to help encourage people to obey the Lord, to do what the Lord's calling them to do. Because if you go back and highlight those times when we obeyed, that was the difference," Jay says. "That's the story: faithfully pursuing God and wanting His best, not just what was good enough."

One friend with whom Jay spoke about New York was Grant Smith. Grant had told Jay that he was praying for him during his pastoral search, and Jay remembered this. Grant and Rosa Lee had felt a change of direction under the new leadership at Memorial Park. Something had been happening at Memorial Park under Jay's leadership, and they took a keen interest in where he would go next. "He had taught the youth to be free in their expressions of worship, and we adults were yearning for that too," says Rosa Lee.

Jay asked Grant if he would be willing to gather for prayer with a number of other men who had also been praying for him during his pastoral search. Grant says, "We all welcomed the idea and began meeting on Saturday morning for several weeks. God seemed to take this group into a great level of unity and harmony."

The way the New York incident had unfolded had given Jay and Carol a sense of confidence that they weren't the ones making things happen. The fact that they had looked so many places and then had the door shut so dramatically on the one they accepted gave them freedom to ask if God wanted them to start something brand new. They had not engineered the situation that made them so available, but if God had, they knew they could trust Him to lead the way forward to unchartered territory.

Jay and Carol began to investigate if there was any viability of starting a new church. They thought that Cranberry looked to be the next fertile field of harvest, so they approached the Presbytery with the idea. Even that door closed. Jay was too radical for the Presbyterians: radically Spirit-filled when it came to worship and radically traditional when it came to theology. Multiple doctrinal issues were dividing the Presbytery at the time, and a new church headed up by someone from a fringe element did not sound like a good idea.

Now Jay and Carol truly had a blank slate. Jay saw this as a watershed moment — unbound by any limitations and open to God's leading, they had the ability to ask God what He wanted to do and respond directly to His leading. Becoming more confident that God might be leading them in a new direction, Jay had a difficult but important phone call to make to his parents.

He called and told his father and mother that the plans for New York had fallen through and that they were going to look into starting their own church. Jay's parents had been very supportive of his work at Memorial Park, an established, thriving church. Upon this news, however, Jay's father said he was coming over to talk in person, father to son.

Jay's father had expressed concerns before Jay left for seminary, but this was a bit different. Back then it was Jay and Carol on their own, but now they were taking an even bigger step into the unknown, with children to feed.

"You have three children! You don't have any income, you don't have any insurance, and you won't have any place to live for long..." Anyone reading this might imagine how the conversation might go with their own father in the same circumstances or what they might say to their own children for that matter.

Jay shared his reasons for believing this was his and Carol's next step and said, "Dad, I can't answer those questions because I don't know how it's going to work, but all I can tell you is that I believe this is what we are supposed to do. If God's in it, then God will supply. And if He isn't, then I'll be looking for work."

As soon as Jay explained where he was coming from, Jack

did not push back anymore. He needed to hear Jay say he was convinced and needed to make sure Jay hadn't gone crazy, but after that, he continued to support his son's efforts.

Next, Jay shared the idea for starting a new church with the men in his prayer group and asked if they and their families would be willing to gather and discuss this possibility. Grant and Rosa Lee Smith agreed, as did Ray and Marcia Speicher, Jay and Sue Dawson, and Bruce and Kathy Bain. Blaine Workman also agreed, even though his father was an elder at Memorial Park. Blaine had not yet met his wife Lynne. Jay also asked one other single young man named Doug Stone, who would meet his wife Pam after the start of North Way. Jay called Paul and Linda Gregg and Gene and Arlene Rink, two more couples from Memorial Park, and they agreed to meet.

If one thing is most widely known about the history of North Way Christian Community, it is that it all began with nine couples in a basement. Including Jay and Carol, with an allowance for the two young men who were not yet married, all the folks in the above paragraph would become the founding "nine couples."

Their first gathering was on January 2nd, 1981, in the finished basement of Jay and Sue Dawson's home in Cranberry. They talked for several hours since they all had the day off following the holiday. This was the start of a series of meetings where they would pray, study, and discuss what a new church in Pittsburgh might look like.

"Once we recognized that a new church was being formed,

the importance of prayer, worship, and Bible study became very important," says Grant.

They began to study the early New Testament church, analyze historical church structures, and discuss books together. From the start, they agreed that they needed to glean everything they could from the early church's example in the Bible. They fellowshipped together through prayer, worship, and sharing meals; not only going back to the drawing board in their study, but also putting the basic elements of godly community into practice day by day.

Starting a brand-new community gave them the chance to look at the Bible and take their ideas and ideals directly from what it says. It did not have to be about whether they felt more comfortable with the Evangelical Presbyterian Church or the Presbyterian Church (USA) or any other branch that was beginning to split off at the time. They could start fresh from the ideals of the 1st century church and ask God how these concepts could be realized in the 21st century.

Jay met with the men at 6 a.m. multiple times a week just for prayer and with the families in the evening for study and fellowship. From morning to night, the whole process was bathed in prayer. Jay says, "Before we ever held a public meeting, we had established a prayer discipline." Sue Dawson says, "We just prayed and prayed and prayed."

Sue and her husband Jay didn't know everyone in the group at the start since they were relatively new to Memorial Park, but they found themselves growing spiritually as they hosted many of the meetings. Sue saw it as a great opportunity to be a part of this group — not only learning from Jay Passavant, but also being with people who had been serving with him for years.

The nine men called themselves the Servants Council. Grant quickly noticed and was encouraged by the lack of hierarchy within the group. Even though everyone recognized Jay as the leader, there was even and open contribution from each member. This appealed to Grant's deep roots in the Plymouth Brethren.

Still without a formal role within this new church, Jay did, however, need an income to take care of his family during this time of preparation. At one of the earliest meetings in the basement at the Dawsons, Jay was upfront and said that he and his family would need support going forward.

The Council asked Jay how much Memorial Park had been paying him and what it would take for his family to feel stable during this time. Jay said that he had been making around $2,000 a month in his position at Memorial Park, and the Council said that they could match that. They said they would have to take it one month at a time, by faith, but they committed to do their best.

Jay and Carol remember looking around at the six couples and two single young men and wondering how they were going to come up with Jay's full monthly wages. Each family or Council member wrote down on a piece of paper what they were able to contribute. Bruce and Kathy remember feeling like they did not have very much, but they gave what they could and it balanced out with offerings of more established couples.

After working for Westinghouse for seven years and running his own graphic design business for three, Grant Smith had joined Reed Agnew and Don Moyer from Westinghouse to form Agnew Moyer Smith, a company which is still functioning today under the name ThoughtForm, Inc. Agnew Moyer Smith was up and running just around the right time in order for the Smiths to be of significant help to Jay and his family. Through starting this company, Grant also gained the business expertise to be able to offer many important insights in the founding of a new church.

The practice of tithing to the local church is well taught and familiar: to give 10 percent of one's income to the church to support the ministry and offer to God one's first fruits. Going above and beyond that for a church not yet officially in existence, however, shows an uncommon measure of faith. That each of these families and single men agreed on the spot to give of their resources demonstrates that they believed God was really doing something: something valuable.

Without any campus launch fund or large check to work from, Jay and Carol were supported so that they didn't miss paying one bill. Carol says she doesn't know what they did with health insurance and doesn't remember missing it or feeling the need to worry. "When you know God is in something, it just makes it kinda easy," Jay says.

When they had received the job offer in New York, Jay and Carol had put their house on the market, but they pulled it right back off and stayed there. Sharing this story now in the comfort of his home in Allison Park, Jay laughs and says, "See that rug there? That house was a little bigger than that, but not much."

They had bought the little house in Shaler for $27,000, and it included furniture from the elderly person who had lived there before them. The house totaled 900 square feet; 1,100 if you included the 200 square foot sunroom. Jay and Carol lived there with their daughter, Amy, and their two sons, David and Jonathan, from 1974 until 1983. Two bedrooms, one bathroom, three children.

"In those times, when you know you're in the will of God, as long as you feel like you're being fair to your spouse, you just don't even think or worry about things," says Jay. He credits the faithfulness and bounty of God for providing month by month through the Servants Council and beyond.

Many career paths may require temporary sacrifice in order to reap future rewards and financial payoff, but there were no assurances here. The Servants Council believed that with commitment growth would be the natural outcome, but Jay says it was never their goal to create or become a big church. "It was always our goal to become faithful, committed disciples."

The Council's first goal in imagining a new church was to agree on what its foundational principles should be in light of the New Testament church and the way the original church fathers pursued life. Jay recounts how they began with an in-depth study of the first six chapters of the book of Acts, and "landed squarely" in Acts 2:42-47 as a compelling summary of the essential components of the fellowship of believers. This passage says:

> They devoted themselves to the apostles' teaching and to fellowship, to the breaking of bread and to prayer. Everyone was filled with awe at the many wonders and signs performed by the apostles. All the believers were together and had everything in common. They sold property and possessions to give to anyone who had need. Every day they continued to meet together in the temple courts. They broke bread in their homes and ate together with glad and sincere hearts, praising God and enjoying the favor of all the people. And the Lord added to their number daily those who were being saved.

In this short passage, the Council found ten elements to be unavoidable. They also determined what each one should mean for this new church.

1.   They devoted themselves to the Apostles' teaching: strong Biblical teaching would be essential.

2.   And to fellowship: they should love one another and spend time together.

3.   To the breaking of bread: they should eat together. They took this to mean not only the sharing of the sacrament of Communion, but also the simple experience of sharing meals.

4. And to prayer: this already well-formed habit would need to remain essential.

5. Everyone was filled with awe at the many wonders and signs performed by the apostles: they should have an openness to the expression of the Holy Spirit.

6. They sold property and possessions to give to anyone who had need: though they would have to study and brainstorm further about the practical extent of this one, they should be willing to share their lives and resources openly with each other and with all those who shared their vision.

7. Every day they continued to meet together in the temple courts: here they found the call for regular meetings in a corporate environment for worship.

8. They broke bread in their homes and ate together with glad and sincere hearts: and here the equally important component of regular meetings at homes for horizontal relationship and meeting the needs of one another. Home based small group fellowship was to be central to how life was to be lived.

9. Praising God and enjoying the favor of all the people: following these principles faithfully, their lives would be an expression of praise to God, which would draw people to their fellowship and impress them with the beauty of what they would discover.

10. And the Lord added to their number daily those

who were being saved: as a byproduct of living life authentically, surrendered to Christ and committed to each other, they could trust that the Lord would add new believers to their number consistently.

With these elements in mind, the Council's second goal was to figure out how to put them into practice in a church body: how they should structure their church. For the next three weeks they met almost every night for two or three hours to discuss these things. The Council saw this as an identity-building process for their new church and a critical responsibility. Since it would not be easy to change the things they based the church's identity on, they knew they had to get it right from the start.

The Council agreed that there was no modern-day model for what they wanted to accomplish. Many churches had good ideas, but there wasn't any one existing church model that felt right to adopt. The ideas that were out there were not posted on the internet or searchable on Google. It was going to require some pioneering and some creativity for this new venture to reach the region and culture with the ideals of the 1st century church.

For about a week, the Council contemplated the idea of pooling their families' resources and purchasing a farm together. Though the idea may sound cultish, they saw grounds for considering it in the book of Acts, and they did not want to ignore any Biblical possibilities. The Council imagined buying a hundred-acre farm somewhere on the way to Grove City, raising crops, and spending time growing in Christ together. It sounded great to be unencumbered by outside influences, but this would also move their new community away from one of its primary purposes: to influence the world.

Jay explains that while the early church members spoken of in Acts had known each other for years, some of the people on the Servants Council had just met each other and were just becoming acquainted. While a more communal approach may have been a practical and perhaps even necessary step for the apostles and early church, the Council decided it was not the best way forward for their group. The discussion proved, however, that they were searching for a way of life, not just a new church to attend. They read about a couple of modern churches where all the members were moving into the same area or neighborhood to have more fellowship, but that also did not seem quite right. Bruce Bain says, "We were just dreaming: what does community look like?"

Discussions of possible fellowship structures led to discussions of possible leadership structures. The Council had great diversity of opinion on how a church could best be governed. As mentioned before, Grant came from a background in the Plymouth Brethren, a church where no one is a designated pastor and every member is considered ordained by God for some role in ministry. Other members of the Council were more comfortable tying specific offices and importance to specific giftings of the Holy Spirit, believing God calls a man with a vision and that the people are called to support it.

The Council went through a raw study of Scripture together. They found that each church body in the New Testament was typically founded by an apostle and then convened and established by the appointment of a board of elders (Acts 14:23). The Council agreed that theirs should be an elder-led community church, with the freedom to employ one or more elders to take significant responsibilities. At the start, the Servants Council held a similar role as a board of elders and would eventually be restructured and renamed to reflect this. The Servants Council called Jay to be the first pastor.

"Pastor" was defined by the Council as someone responsible to provide leadership, to spend time in prayer and fellowship with God to discern vision, and to be prepared to speak consistently, but not necessarily exclusively. If any other Council members felt they had something they would like to share, Jay would defer, and if he had any questions, he would submit them to the whole Council. They would not embrace the idea of a Senior Pastor until 1984, so Jay's first business cards had the title "Staff Pastor."

After coming to an agreement on church government, the Council still had a lot to decide about how to structure their ministry. Having studied the Bible and shared ideas from their personal backgrounds, they now looked for more ideas in books. Jay mentions that in 1981 there was no way to do online research to see what certain kinds of churches were up to: no search engines leading to helpful articles or blog posts, no church websites, sermon videos, or podcasts. Not a lot of people were writing about new ideas for church structures, but Jay remembered one recommendation he had received during his time at Fuller for an author named Howard Snyder.

Howard Snyder's book *The Problem of Wineskins: Church Structure in a Technological Age* was published through InterVarsity Press in 1975 after he spent six years as a missionary, pastor, and seminary teacher/administrator in Sao Paulo, Brazil. Snyder's time ministering in a big city outside the United States had allowed him to rethink prevalent American church models. In his book, he sought to offer some fresh, Biblical conclusions.

The Problem of Wineskins drew its title from Jesus' words in Luke 5:37-38: "No one puts new wine into old wineskins, for the new wine bursts the old skins, ruining the skins and spilling the wine. New wine must be put into new wineskins" (Living Bible). Snyder understood *new wine* as signifying the gospel — ever new, potent, and essential. The *wineskins* were any man-made structures that were formed to hold that wine and deliver it to the world. In looking at the institutional church of the time, Snyder believed that ineffective wineskins were being clung to at the expense of the wine.

Wineskins were just what the Servants Council was trying to decide on. By starting fresh with the book of Acts, they had defined some essential elements of their church, but now they wanted to find the best patterns for reaching their culture and generation. Snyder's book covered many topics that he believed should inform the church's choice of wineskins, from its identity as the *people of God*, to its mission of bringing *good news to the poor*. He asked questions like, "Are church buildings superfluous? Must a pastor be a superstar? What is the place of spiritual gifts?"

Perhaps the biggest thrust of the book was recommending small groups as the core unit of the church. In comparing modern urbanization to parallel elements of the 1st century, he argued that a return to the earliest church habits might be the most effective way to reach the world with the gospel. This focus on small groups was established by what the New Testament calls *koinonia*: the fellowship of the Holy Spirit.

Snyder published another book, *The Community of the King*, in 1977, digging deeper into the theology of how a church community should operate spiritually. The members of the Servants Council all bought copies of both books and began to read them in-depth, starting with *Wineskins*.

The Problem of Wineskins is out of print but can be found on eBay. Jay loaned me his copy of *The Community of the King*, which shows significant use. His copy has underlining (and/or brackets, asterisks, and notes) on 135 out of 170 pages; in orange colored pencil, red pen, blue/black pen, and green pen; with red and green tabs sticking out the side; and fourteen scraps of paper with notes on them, which are now yellowed where they have been sticking out the top of the book. It is quite special to imagine how this book affected the life of North Way.[1]

---

[1] Since Snyder's books were so important to the Council and the start of North Way, I have written an extended summary of key points from *Wineskins* and a couple thoughts from *Community of the King* as well. I have included the summary in Appendix Two at the back of this book. These are my thoughts as a younger member of North Way reading Snyder today. As I point out how Snyder's ideas tied to what the Servants

Perhaps of equal importance to the future personality of North Way as the books and the scripture that the Servants Council studied was the way that they and their families embodied the Biblical ideals they discovered. They were not just after a dictionary definition of *koinonia*; they were seeking to live this concept day by day. To be a fly on the wall at these early meetings would not just be to overhear some in-depth conversations; it would be to observe real life happening and seeing future leaders blossoming in an atmosphere of joyful fellowship.

"I do remember we ate a lot," says Sue. "Where Jay Passavant is concerned, there's gotta be food. We had meals together and just did a lot of fellowship together." They also worshipped together. Jay says, "Because we believed worship invited the presence of God, we always saw it as our job to be worshippers first." Comparing these formational meetings with all the records of key European church councils, one may wonder if the stern doctrinal debates of history ever opened with the singing of a few songs and if that might have resulted in greater unity.

At evening gatherings, there were typically 10 children present, from toddlers through teenagers. Jay and Carol had their three: Amy, 6, David, 4, and Jonathan, 2. The Greggs had Jeff, 7, and Jason, 5. The Smiths had Vicki, 20, Neil, 19, and

---

Council was studying and deciding, I will humbly suggest their relevance for today.

Nathan, 9. And the Rinks had Jimmy, 15, and Laurie, 10. The Bains were expecting, as were the Dawsons.

These children witnessed the spiritual dedication of their parents, and it stuck with them. Several of them have ended up in full-time ministry — at North Way, at other churches, and overseas. By bringing their families along for this ride and sacrificing their time and resources to pursue God's best, the Council was setting an example for their children of what they believed mattered most. The children would not soon forget it.

Some evening conversations took place with the men in the basement while the women fellowshipped upstairs and looked after the children. Other conversations took place around the dinner table. One conversation that took place with everyone in the dining room was deciding what to call this new church they were envisioning. Some ideas were funny, thanks especially to Ray. The families laughed together and had a great time. Blaine offered a serious suggestion of "New Haven," an idea he had gotten from their study of the book of Acts.

Of the four words in the name they finally landed on, each was significant and required discussion. The first word they agreed on was *North*, which made sense because they were located north of Pittsburgh. "North Star? Jesus is the Way, we're on the Way following Him...North *Way!*" There was a new shopping mall in Wexford called Northway Mall, but this was unrelated and didn't bother them.

No other word could express so well what they were after from the start as *Community.* After reading Snyder's second book, they knew this word was inseparable from what they wanted to be. Relationships were already key to everything they did, and every branch of ministry down the road would be born out of community and the needs of community: "North Way Community." What was missing?

They wrestled the longest with a word they ended up deciding not to use. It was not an oversight to leave *Church* out of the name. Jay looks back and says there have been times he wished they would've gone with "North Way Community Church" to save a lot of grief and explanation, but by leaving it off, they underscored North Way's uniqueness. Jay suggests that a name can cause people to lean in further to see what is going on or it can allow people to explain something away without even a second thought. But even without *Church*, "North Way Community" wouldn't do.

"North Way Christian Community" could do. The word *Christian* would denote that they were uniquely committed to Christ and His atoning work on the cross. They wanted to be known as Christians, not as Presbyterians or Catholics or Lutherans. They would be a community of people who had experienced true, bona fide salvation. The word *Christian* would show they weren't hiding their identity; they simply wanted people to imagine more than a "church" that you *go to*.

The decision was unanimous, and North Way Christian Community has kept its name from that day on. Jay started the discussion by saying, "There's no way we're going to decide this today," but they ended up coming to a confident decision much quicker than he expected.

After six weeks of continual meetings for prayer, study, and fellowship, Jay and the Council decided it was time for their next step: to hold an information meeting and gauge outside interest in this new community. They did not advertise, as they did not want to look as though they were trying to poach people from other churches. They just told a few people what they had been doing and said anyone with questions would be welcome to join them for a meeting in February.

The meeting was held in the community room at the Northway Mall, and to the Council's great surprise, 90 people showed up. The interest went deeper: of the 90 people who attended, 45 made commitments to join small groups. It seemed there was a hunger and a desire for this new community, and the Council was very encouraged. They wanted to know if God was really in this project, and with this step, it sure seemed He was.

The Council formed and led four new small groups with the people from the information meeting, with two Council families or members in each group along with 10 or so new people. These groups began meeting regularly over the next six weeks until North Way's first public worship service.

Jay says, "Before we ever met for public worship, the church was already meeting as small groups. Small groups are in the formational DNA of North Way. It's not a program we added on: it's who we were before we ever met as a church for public worship. And why was that important? Because it underscored one of our non-negotiable values, which was community. It was so central to our identity of what we valued, that's what it was: a core value."

After another six weeks, three months total since the first meeting of the Servants Council, the Council decided they were ready for North Way's first public worship service. They announced (word-of-mouth again) that services would launch on March 29th. They didn't have a space to meet in but had faith they would find one in time. Just eight days before the service, they were still knocking on doors and came to The Bradley House, a large catering facility that had until recently been a restaurant called Mr. B's.

Jay, along with a couple friends, managed to speak with the owner, George Bradley. "Mr. Bradley, we'd like to rent a room," they said.

Bradley said, "We don't rent rooms — we're a catering facility."

Jay had an idea, and said, "Well, how much food do we have to buy to use the space?"

Bradley thought and said, "The best I can do for you is I'll give you juice, coffee, and one danish pastry per person for $4.95 a head." The room would come with it.

Jay agreed and jokes that for the first time he did not know whether or not to pray for a big crowd. A big crowd did show up, but Jay and the Council felt peace and were greatly encouraged. The headcount was 250, and they gladly paid Bradley over $1,000, which was supplemented by a freewill offering at the service.

Jay figured that perhaps many of the attendees from the first week had just come to wish them well, and that it was realistic to expect the group to be cut in half the second week. The number dropped slightly down to 205, but going forward, attendance remained above 200.

Jay says that 200 people is a landmark for any church to cross, and that any church with more than 200 people will require more than just one staff pastor to minister. Starting at this number fit right into Jay's strategy to equip the saints for ministry instead of doing it all himself.

One couple that showed up the second week was Scott and Missy McCabe. Scott had been right to think that if Jay ever started a church, he and Missy were supposed to be there. There were big things in store for them and through them.

After North Way's second meeting, the Servants Council stopped taking up an offering and simply put donation boxes in the back of the room for anyone who felt led to support. Week after week they paid Bradley based on the attendance, and the Council continued to support Jay's family financially until the giving became consistent enough for the church to support him as the first staff pastor.

Sue Dawson shared enthusiastically about those first meetings, "We never called people together, you know; we never advertised. People just showed up! It was incredible! We had our first meeting at the Northway Mall — there were all these people there. We said, 'How'd they hear about this? Where did they come from?' And then we had our first worship service, and there were tons of people there! Like, what the heck?! And it just grew from there. And, you know, when the Holy Spirit leads — when God has a plan — it's out of our control. It was really amazing to all of us."

Jay Dawson did the legal work of incorporating the church, and North Way Christian Community was officially Pittsburgh's newest church fellowship.

CHAPTER THREE:
ESTABLISHMENT

North Way continued to meet week by week at the catering facility. Those interviewed for this book have referred to that space by a variety of names, from Mr. B's to The Bradley House, The Restaurant, and even The Chadwick, which is the name it operates under today. For continuity, we will call it The Bradley House.

The Servants Council families would arrive early on Sunday mornings to set up the space and clean up from whatever event was hosted there the night before. Weekends when there was a wedding, there were plastic drink cups to pick up and ashtrays to dump. They set up chairs in the banquet hall area to be the sanctuary and set up port-a-cribs around the bar to be the nursery. Kids ministry eventually began in the hallway behind the banquet hall.

Typically, they set up so that people would enter at the back of the room with the stage being furthest from the door. Sue shares a story of one time when this was reversed: "This always cracked me up. Jay got irked when people would show up late, and so one time he said, 'Alright, I want everyone to turn your chairs around. Today, I'm going to stand *here*.' Which was where everybody walked in. So, we all turned our chairs around. Fortunately, I was on time that day. So, when people walked in, we were all facing them — we were looking at them like, *oh you're late!* People weren't late for a while after that. Jay was creative."

Regardless of the meeting place, Jay took things seriously and saw it as his job to cultivate commitment. Jay recalls preaching very in-depth sermons during these first years, seeking to lay a Biblical foundation. Sue says, "He was an excellent teacher. I kept all the notes back then. Probably because I had a lot to learn. But he gave excellent sermons. They were well laid out. He had good notes. I always filled in the blanks. And I still have those notes, and I remember to look back at some of them because I remember what they were about. I really appreciated his teaching. I *learned* a lot from Jay."

Kathy became the first unofficial church secretary and was responsible for typing up the sermon outlines that Sue is referencing. Kathy remembers being pregnant at the time and having a typewriter delivered to her home so she could work from home. Jay would run things over to her on Fridays so she could type them out before Sunday.

It may sound silly today, says Bruce, but the decision of what brand of typewriter to buy was a big one. During a Servants Council weekend getaway to a cabin in the woods north of Pittsburgh, they discussed this. They planned to spend $700-$800, which gave them two choices: a used IBM Selectric, or a new off-brand Royal. *What would be better, something new or the brand reliability of IBM?*

Blaine says, "I just think: we went from the place where the leaders of the church were concerned about what kind of typewriter was going to be the best deal, to the place where now you look at the church, and how many thousands of people, and different campuses, and multi-million dollar campus buildings… it was just a blessing to see the growth go from there."

For their first four years, North Way did not own any property or have a well-established location. However, Jay refers to 1981-1985 as *the establishment years* because it was during these years that North Way developed its unique personality and solidified its core values and system of leadership. Regardless of the location of the Sunday service during this time, North Way's priorities were being strengthened and its culture was taking shape as members met in small groups and learned how to minister to the needs of their community. "This is when we became who we are," says Jay.

For the first year, the nine men on the Servants Council performed an overseeing role similar to a board of elders, but they found that the name *Servant* was helpful during this time. It was accurate to their flexible role of helping with all the needs and questions that arise from a new church body and signified that they were approachable and accessible to the members. It was announced and well known that this group of nine met consistently and that they were set apart to serve the congregation. They met to talk about the needs of the church at least every other week, and they also met at least twice a week at 6 a.m. just for prayer.

The Servants Council knew that they were charting new territory in Pittsburgh by starting North Way. Though they were working from an ancient foundation of Biblical ideals and had picked up a few ideas elsewhere, they did not have a blueprint or a guidebook for exactly how to pursue these in a modern context for the specific group of people they were serving. This called for more prayer. The Council's well-established prayer discipline was at the center of their leadership, and many of the key decisions that shaped North Way were made in the context of these prayer meetings.

Along with and supported by prayer, one of their top considerations was the importance of putting their beliefs on paper so that anybody could look at them and understand where the church stood in its doctrine and its priorities. Jay worked together with the Council to craft a bulleted Statement of Faith for North Way. As a non-denominational church, there was no easy copy/paste option for this confession, so they studied each essential belief of their community, laboring over how to represent it as clearly and meaningfully as possible. They landed on 10 concise points.

The statement the Council wrote can still be seen on North Way's website under a tab called *Our Beliefs and Values*. When written, there was no church website or even world wide web to upload them to, but they were kept ready on paper to share with visitors and members and were covered in membership classes. We will include the statement here in full and expound slightly on the importance of individual points.

North Way Christian Community is a non-denominational church, and as such, is home to members from a wide spectrum of church backgrounds — and some with no church background at all. We say that to say this: you are welcome here no matter where you came from. While we do not subscribe to any particular denomination, we practice an evangelical tradition which holds the following tenets of belief:

- We believe that the Bible is the Word of God and is inspired and inerrant as originally given.

- We believe that God is eternal, three persons in One: Father, Son, and Holy Spirit.

- We believe in the deity of the Lord Jesus Christ, His virgin birth, His sinless and perfect life, His vicarious and atoning death through His shed blood, His bodily resurrection, and His present dominion at the right hand of God the Father.

- We believe in the present ministry of the Holy Spirit, whose indwelling enables the Christian to lead a Godly life; and whose baptism provides power for service.

- We believe in the resurrection from the dead of both the saved and the lost; they that are saved into the resurrection of life and those that have not known God into the resurrection of judgment.

- We believe in the spiritual unity of believers in the Lord Jesus.

- We believe in the table of the Lord, commonly called Communion or the Lord's Supper, for believers.

- We believe in the personal return of the Lord Jesus Christ in power and glory to receive His church unto Himself.

- We believe that worship is our number one priority.

- We believe that prayer is the touchstone of our power.

Jay says it was no accident that the first statement was about the Bible. North Way needed an authority from which to operate, and they believed that if it was not going to be the written Word of God, it was going to be something much less reliable and less consistent. The words *inspired* and *inerrant* were both very important. The inerrancy of Scripture was a big doctrinal debate at the time, and many churches were taking different paths. By *inerrant*, Jay and the Council simply meant *without error*. Believing Scripture to be *inspired* included believing it to be alive and relevant today just as it was to its first audience. It was not meant to be interpreted legalistically but was meant to be, "Living and active, sharper than any two-edged sword, piercing to the division of soul and of spirit, of joints and of marrow, and discerning the thoughts and intentions of the heart" (Heb 4:12).

The next statement expressed the eternal and triune nature of God as Father, Son, and Holy Spirit, followed by a complete and strong statement about Jesus. "We did not want to leave any ambiguity about the nature of Christ," Jay says. This is the longest point of the 10 in North Way's statement of faith, and each part was seen as essential. There are many world religions and cults that claim to believe in Jesus but toss out certain parts of the Biblical narrative, if not the whole thing. The virgin birth, for example, has been contested as an impossibility amongst those who are skeptical of miracles. The Council didn't want to leave room for error.

It is important to realize that North Way's founders were able to craft their statement of faith with a modern audience and modern debates in mind. Each point was drawn from Scripture but could be stated in simple English in a way that would make sense to the congregation and would be distinguishable from society's most recent lies and confusions. Even here, they were putting the ever-new wine of the Gospel into new wineskins.

Next, the Council made a point to establish their view on the Holy Spirit, which was distinct from a number of Christian denominations. The statement mentions the *present* ministry of the Holy Spirit and seeks to express the belief that although every believer has the Holy Spirit, His baptism can further empower them to fulfill their spiritual calling. The Council wrestled with what to write on this topic because they knew it could cause a lot of uncertainty about whether or not North Way was a Pentecostal church.

The Pentecostal movement was proliferating in many parts of America at the time and was well-known in Christian circles due to popular radio personalities and shows such as Kenneth Copeland, Kenneth Hagin, Jimmy Swaggart, and the Full Gospel Business Men's Fellowship. Pentecostal churches typically made much more extreme statements about the filling of the Holy Spirit, claiming that His indwelling came with His baptism, separate from one's initial conversion. Some claimed that baptism in the Holy Spirit was an essential step in salvation, and most asserted that baptism in the Holy Spirit must be accompanied by a sign, such as speaking in tongues. The Council did not want to imply any of these ideas, but they did want to put special emphasis on the active work of the Holy Spirit.

Jay and the elders did not shy away from difficult doctrines and next wrote about the afterlife. The reality and justice of heaven and hell are essential doctrines for any church that preaches the Word of God as *inspired* and *inerrant*. Jay says that the older he gets, the more mysterious such truths become.

Next is a short statement about the unity of believers, which Jay recommends is very profound in its purpose. It is not talking only about fellowship between believers at North Way, but about all those who trust in Jesus for salvation. The Council was saying that though many believers hold different doctrines, if they are in Jesus, they have more in common with North Way than anything separating them. This was an important statement for a new, independent church. One common clue that any "church" body is actually a cult is when it says that membership in its congregation and full acceptance of its doctrines is essential to salvation. North Way's stance would allow the church to partner with believers from many backgrounds and denominations to impact Pittsburgh and to be blessed by the diversity of the body of Christ.

The statement of faith proceeds to include a nod to the traditional doctrine of celebrating the Lord's Supper. Keeping this statement simple said more than expounding, leaving off any of the extra significance tied to this tradition by other churches. North Way would celebrate Communion to remember Christ's work on the cross and to proclaim the faith.

Boiling down the dizzying possibilities of eschatology into one sentence was not easy, but the Council settled on one essential statement they all believed with certainty. Across a wide range of more specific thoughts on the end times, all agreed that they were looking for one more appearance of the Lord on earth, when He will call the church to Himself. The Council chose not to include beliefs about tribulation, rapture, millennium, etc., and yet their statement held radical and life-changing implications: this world is not the whole story, He's coming back, it's going to be glorious, and that's something to get excited about.

The last two statements are significant and personal, getting to the core of North Way's identity. Jay expected to hear a good amount of grief over such a strong statement as, "We believe that worship is our number one priority," but received very little. With such a statement, North Way was saying, "We are here for God, not God for us." Worship is the natural and essential response of believers whose posture was thankfulness to their Savior. Worship could not just be something to tack onto North Way's events; it would be the intention behind everything. Though it seems radical at first glance, the truth in this statement has been expressed long ago in another way: "Man's chief end is to glorify God and to enjoy Him forever" (Westminster Shorter Catechism).

Calling prayer the touchstone of North Way's power was a unique way to say what the Council learned of prayer in the Bible and what they had experienced at every step in establishing a new church. The very first thing Sue Dawson said about North Way when we met to talk about this book was, "North Way was born of prayer." Every story I have heard since confirms this. The founding members believed in the power of prayer with all their hearts. Closing the statement of faith with such a profoundly worded sentence about prayer will never cease to be appropriate, as prayer has accomplished all that North Way's thousands of members are and have.

Sue says, "After things got going, we continued this emphasis on prayer. I remember times when we'd stay up all night at church, praying around the clock for something. Or we'd take time slots, you know; we'd sign up for a certain time all night long praying about something. I mean, prayer was just all-important in our church. And I attribute the great growth we had in the beginning to that strong emphasis on prayer and reliance on the Holy Spirit."

Jay says, "Prayer is how we commune with God, and when we're in communion with God, we're accessing His presence and His power." Jay recommends that many churches fail on this point by simply talking about prayer without providing the opportunities to put prayer in action. He quotes one of his favorite books, *Destined for the Throne* by Paul Billheimer, saying, "Without the power of prayer, the church is basically running an ecclesiastical treadmill." Without prayer, North Way would simply be expending religious energy, without really going anywhere. "Prayer is what blasts open the gates, and releases the captives," says Jay.

Over the following years, North Way would develop three core values which can still be seen next to the statement of faith in the *Our Beliefs and Values* section on the website:

- *Following Jesus* | "And he said to them, 'Follow me, and I will make you fishers of men.'" Matthew 4:19

- *Doing Life Together* | "This is my commandment, that you love one another as I have loved you." John 15:12

- *Engaging and Influencing Culture* | "As you sent me into the world, so I have sent them into the world." John 17:18

These values were uniquely worded to capture North Way's heart and identity, and each included a key Bible verse.

In conversation for this chapter, Jay simplified these values even further: *Following Jesus* = discipleship, *Doing Life Together* = community, and *Engaging and Influencing Culture* = outreach. All three of these values have their origins in the earliest parts of this story, from Jay's mother first being invited to *Do Life Together* with her neighbors in a small group, to Jay being taught how to *Follow Jesus* by John White during college, to Jay's desire to *Engage and Influence* his campus, his Marine base, and beyond.

As covered in the statement of faith, worship was North Way's top priority, and prayer was the touchstone of power. Worship and prayer fueled each of the three core values, since knowing God for who He is was essential to all three. Jay says that North Way didn't just get lucky in its growth and its ability to impact Pittsburgh with the gospel; everything flowed out of the church's desire to know God intimately and in community.

North Way's first mission statement was:

Making disciples of the Lord Jesus Christ who would be loved, nurtured, and equipped to minister to God, one another, and the lost of the world in the power of the Holy Spirit.

Jay recalls this as an awkwardly long but comprehensive and accurate statement. Such a specific statement was fitting for a new church that was being careful to represent what it was. While other mission statements have and will accompany

North Way through various seasons of growth, this first statement offered a powerful summary of goals that were baked into the church's identity.

Jay and the Council found that there were a few key doctrinal issues that would benefit from a more in-depth treatment than was possible in the statement of faith. They wrote "white papers" on these topics to express the unified stance of the leadership, papers that could be shared with North Way members and with visitors who had questions.

Though the move for Jay and other members from Memorial Park was amicable, there had been a few doctrinal issues that had begun to cause tension during that time. These were some of the topics that needed to be addressed in particular, as they were not only the points where North Way was departing from the Presbyterian denomination, but were (and remain) controversial topics in the broader church in Pittsburgh, America, and the world.

These white papers further illustrate the devotion of North Way's founders both to faithful study and to unity and are well worth a read, even if North Way's wording and presentation of these beliefs changes in the future. A reader from any doctrinal background may recognize and learn from the faithfulness to clarity that was so important to the founding of this church. We have included drafts of three white papers in Appendix Three at the back of this book.

The Council's study of Baptism was one that brought about change, and the topic brings up some great North Way stories.

Jay had been baptized as an infant and had grown up with and had accepted the position that babies born to Christian parents were included in God's covenant — similar to children born to Jewish parents in the Old Testament. From this view, infant baptism replaces circumcision as a sign of the covenant.

When Jay began to study for himself, he says he found that the Bible had as much to say about infant baptism as a blank sheet of paper: "Not a word" (See Appendix Three for a more nuanced explanation). Jay came to believe that baptism was to be a sign of personal faith; that as a person's faith became their own, they should declare that publicly by being baptized. Memorial Park had practiced infant baptism, but with the start of North Way, Jay had the opportunity to pursue a personal stance, not a denominational one.

Jay was the pastor of a new church, but in order to teach baptism as a step of obedience for the believer, he knew he needed to lead by example. "Almost everything I struggled with, or sought to understand, I did so knowing that if I was going to teach with integrity, I had to act on my beliefs," says Jay. There was no baptistry at The Bradley House, and since they were renting, they were not allowed to fill up a hot tub. A new church called North Hills Christian Church on Thompson Run Road allowed them to use its baptistry, and Jay was baptized there by Grant Smith.

Jay and Sue Dawson asked to be baptized by Jay that first winter, and the church in the North Hills let them borrow its facility again. "That was pretty funny," Sue says. "There was a snowstorm, but some of these wonderful, die-hard early North

Way people showed up. Jay Passavant put on these long, high boots — it was freezing — and got in this baptismal, but my husband is this big football player and was heavy, so Jay went down and his boots filled up with water when he baptized my husband. Fun memories."

As the weather warmed up and the church continued to grow, North Way began holding larger baptisms, and the McCabe family offered their pool for outdoor baptisms. New believers were baptized for the first time, and other former Presbyterians were re-baptized. Ray Speicher had the privilege of baptizing his own father, as his father's elder. "Now that's out of the box, man," says Ray.

Many children and grandchildren of North Way's founders are following God and serving at North Way today because of the example they grew up under, but Ray says that the *parents* of many on the Servants Council also saw that something special was happening and became involved with North Way. He says that a change came in the parents because they saw the Holy Ghost changing the lives of their sons and daughters through worship.

Before North Way, Ray's dad had been a devoted Methodist and his mom a Catholic. They had faithfully prayed him through times he doesn't believe he would have survived otherwise. His parents became good friends with Jay's, and Ray marvels that these parents of the Greatest Generation humbled themselves to learn from their children. "I always thought that was one of the wonderful miracles. Fathers and sons, and daughters and mothers were all experiencing the newness and the joy together, and that was extraordinary," says Ray.

Since baptism at North Way was now for believers, babies were dedicated rather than baptized. Within North Way's first year, two new babies joined the young church: Julia Dawson and Jennifer Bain. With fewer members at the time, each baby could be dedicated individually. Sue Dawson remembers each member saying something for Julia, which was personal and special.

Sue says, "I'm so thankful: our three daughters are all happily married, two of them are married to pastors, and they're all solid Christians — you can't ask for more than that! No, we're blessed, and I attribute a lot of that to them growing up here at North Way surrounded by so many fellow good Christians and by families who were just supporting one another. All of our kids grew up well because of the support of the church."

Soon after starting, North Way needed more of an office than Kathy Bain's house. Though they did not have a permanent place to hold worship services, the Council was able to rent an office space in the upstairs of Open Door Christian Bookstore, which was owned by the Rinks. An office was one step, but they were also realizing they had a greater need for pastoral staff.

The Servants Council met one day in the summer of 1981 at Grant Smith's house and discussed how the ministry of North Way was exceeding the capacity of one staff pastor. One of the men turned to Blaine Workman and said, "Would you consider filling that need?"

The others affirmed that Blaine would be a good choice, but a full-time ministry position had not been on Blaine's radar before this moment. It was not difficult to imagine a life in ministry since it was already a passion for him, but he was also already on an ideal career trajectory as a CPA.

An alumnus of the Memorial Park youth staff and one of the single young men on the Servants Council, Blaine was leading the youth group at North Way while working for Coopers & Lybrand, a large international accounting firm. Blaine had met Jay at Memorial Park while he was in college and credits Jay with encouraging and helping him grow in his early years of faith.

After graduating, Blaine had taken a job with Coopers and continued over the next five years to help with the Memorial Park youth group and then the Servants Council in his free time. When the Council asked him about coming on staff full time, he had quite a decision to make. Being a pastor at a startup church wasn't exactly a normal step in the career path for CPA's in Pittsburgh — in fact, it would mean abandoning his successful career and cutting his income in half.

Blaine prayed for a month and came back to the Servants Council to say that he would leave the accounting firm and come on board as the first ministry staff person alongside Jay. God had put ministry on Blaine's heart, and despite having to leave behind an enviable career trajectory, he loved what God was doing more and was excited to be able to participate.

Like Jay, Blaine had to face the doubts of his family at first.

A WWII veteran and faithful Christian, Blaine's father worked for the same company, Western Electric, for 40 years and attended a small Presbyterian church in Warrendale with similar dedication. When Blaine's parents saw their son's faith growing at Memorial Park, they left their comfort zone and followed him to Memorial Park. Blaine's father became an elder there. Then Blaine left to start a new church. *And then* he told them he was leaving his accounting firm to become a youth pastor and church administrator at North Way.

"They thought I was certifiably crazy," Blaine says. "They thought North Way had to be a cult that would cause me to make that kind of decision. It just didn't make sense."

Blaine's parents weren't the only ones who questioned him, but he felt he had a good example in Jay. "I mean listen," Blaine says, "Jay needed to have the faith to step away from the security of the denomination and the pension and benefits and all of that and basically entrust his livelihood with a young family to nine families who pledged to support him. For Carol, raising these kids, that was an act of real faith. When they asked me to step away, it was like, 'Wait a minute, you spent five years in the best training environment you can get for a business career and now you're going to go be a youth pastor? Are you nuts?' Some of the people at work who knew me well understood that my faith in Christ was the most important thing about me, so at that level it wasn't surprising, but from a career standpoint it was shocking."

With Blaine's full attention, North Way's youth group began to grow in its commitment and outreach, much like the youth group at Memorial Park had under Jay, despite the fact that the youth had no place to meet. While The Bradley House worked just fine for Sunday worship services, they could not rent it out on a weekday as a space for youth recreation. They alternated between renting gymnasiums and school buildings for occasional events, but their normal weekly gatherings centered around ministry opportunities.

At the time, *The A-Team* was a popular TV show, starring Mr. T as part of a group of ex-military "tough guys" who helped people suffering injustice. The A-Team had a souped-up van — a popular icon in the '80s — and they would drive into dangerous situations to right wrongs. Without a permanent meeting space, the youth group called themselves The A-Team and went out in vans to do ministry in the community.

Four or five people from North Way agreed to let them borrow their vans on a weeknight. Parents would drop their children off in the parking lot of the shopping center below the church offices at the Christian bookstore, and the youth would load into the vans. Blaine designed opportunities in advance, so they always had places to visit and serve. Eventually, the A-Team found its headquarters in a small space that a church member owned in the Wexford flats.

Jay trusted Blaine with full control of the youth ministry, giving him the chance to design the programming and to come up with creative solutions for each problem. Jay could have micromanaged Blaine's leadership based on his own experience in youth ministry, but he had already invested in Blaine as a leader and saw that Blaine was up against different challenges.

The youth ministry at Memorial Park had been focused on just two main school districts, so Jay had had the ability to plant himself in one of the schools and support many of the students from FUDD/AGAPE. At North Way, however, Blaine could count over 40 schools represented in the youth group. As North Way's vision was drawing people from a wide range of communities, Blaine needed freedom to come up with different ways to reach the students.

Blaine was put in charge of organizing some retreats and ministry activities that included Memorial Park, North Park Church, and Allison Park Church of the Assemblies of God. While the start of North Way was in no way a church split from Memorial Park, Blaine felt these events were very special as they quickly helped to heal any personal feelings of division that had resulted.

The leaps of faith by North Way leaders to leave traditional career paths for the ministry did not stop with Jay and Blaine. North Way's unique leadership structure and administrative demands over the next decades would bring pastors out of many different career backgrounds.

At the start of North Way, Scott McCabe was vice president of a fire safety company he operated with his father, but Jay quickly saw his potential as a spiritual leader. Within the first year of North Way, Jay put his hand on Scott's shoulder and said, "You're going to be our next small group leader." Scott says that was just the beginning.

The Servants Council continued to meet for prayer, and Jay

remembers these regularly scheduled times always being dynamic and passionate. The Council understood prayer to be a conversation with God, so when they prayed, they also listened. Jay says that while they did not receive prophetic words all the time, on occasion they did. Jay explains, "Just to demystify it, it would usually be something like, 'I have this strong impression on my heart, I can't shake it, that the Lord is calling us to do this…' Or, 'I think the Lord keeps saying in my mind that…' Not, 'Thus saith the Lord, go four miles north and turn left and you'll find the building.'"

A *word from the Lord* could, however, come with a very specific wording impressed on the heart of one of the Council members. One of the most unique and memorable *words* shared in these meetings came from Gene Rink. Gene was not exactly sure what it meant, but he felt very strongly that God was saying, "I will send you all that you will care for." At the end of that meeting the Council asked what God was saying through Gene and what it would mean for North Way.

"I will send you all that you will care for…"

"Maybe it means we should not concern ourselves with how we are going to draw people, but concern ourselves with how we are caring for the people God is sending."

While many churches labor over how to get more people to attend, the Council considered what it would mean to leave that concern up to God, instead focusing on ministering, discipling, and meeting the needs of each person who came through the door. If God did the sending, they would not have to create special church programs to reach outside. Instead of asking, "How do we get them to come?" they could ask, "How are they being received?" They could focus on return rate, seeing if those who were sent by God once came back again.

This had great implications for the focus of North Way and its leadership, and it came in the form of a promise. The Council agreed: "If we are faithful to care, He is going to send more." Over the following years, this proved to be the case. Every time North Way started to see a dip or even a plateau in attendance, the leadership examined their care process.

"The first thing we would do is say, 'Alright, let's examine the ministry,'" says Jay. For example, they might realize they needed more small group leaders or more kids ministry volunteers. Each time, as soon as they fixed the problem, within a matter of a couple months the attendance would start to grow again.

Leaving the sending up to God required trust, but it made sense on a practical level and from a Biblical worldview. Jay suggests that when people are cared for, they come back, and they bring others with them to receive the same care. They also share the gospel with those around them and bring new people to the faith. "Healthy beings, healthy believers for sure, naturally multiply," says Jay. "Anything in God's created order that's healthy has a component of multiplying."

Though the promise was new, North Way had seen God's act of sending right from the start. To quote Sue Dawson once more, concerning North Way's first information meeting and first worship service, "God just sent people to us." From day one, "People just showed up." As long as people kept coming, the leadership knew it was their job and the church's job to care for them. North Way has seen steady growth ever since, growing not by focusing on how to grow, but by demonstrating faithful stewardship of everything and everyone the church is entrusted with.

Sometime between the first and second year at The Bradley House, the men on the Servants Council came to the agreement that it was time to move to a Board of Elders. Though the Servants Council was a critical part of initiating North Way's launch process, some of the men had recognized that they were not called to continue as elders at the time. They asked the congregation to nominate candidates for eldership. Many people said, "Well, the nine guys that started it are doing great — keep 'em on!" but the Servants Council wanted to open up the leadership to others God had brought to them as well.

The Servants Council met, and each member talked about whether or not he felt called to continue on as an elder and what his commitment might look like going forward. Bruce Bain was one who believed it was not time for him to serve as an elder, so he was given the task of taking nominations and tallying votes from the congregation.

The votes were helpful in determining the top three candidates, but they wanted to choose five elders, so the Servants Council met again and discussed further. Bruce remembers this discussion taking place in the Hedwig House.

The Council looked to 1 Timothy 3:1-7 for the qualifications of an elder:

Here is a trustworthy saying: Whoever aspires to be an overseer desires a noble task. Now the overseer is to be above reproach, faithful to his wife, temperate, self-controlled, respectable, hospitable, able to teach, not given to drunkenness, not violent but gentle, not quarrelsome, not a lover of money. He must manage his own family well and see that his children obey him, and he must do so in a manner worthy of full respect. (If anyone does not know how to manage his own family, how can he take care of God's church?) He must not be a recent convert, or he may become conceited and fall under the same judgment as the devil. He must also have a good reputation with outsiders, so that he will not fall into disgrace and into the devil's trap.

Informed by this list of qualifications, the Council put forward three main responsibilities of elders at North Way: 1. They were to live Christ-centered lives, 2. They were to love others as Christ loved them, and 3. They were to serve wherever and in whatever capacity or giftedness God called them. As they made their decisions on North Way's first five elders, the Servants Council presented the elder position as being a position of real gravity, something to be highly respected.

Part of the value of accepting nominations from the congregation was that it showed who was already seen to be serving the congregation like an elder, whether in the Servants Council role or without any title. Of the first five elders, three were from the Servants Council, but two were from the congregation. The three from the Servants Council were Grant Smith, Ray Speicher, and Jay Passavant. Since the Council had determined from their study that the office of pastor was not a separate office from an elder but rather a possible added duty of one, they saw it as important that Jay was called to eldership. The remaining two elders from the congregation were Roy Guenther and Jack Irwin.

Ever since his time at college, people seemed to be drawn to Jay's leadership and personality, but he and the Council knew that they never wanted North Way to be a pastor-driven church. Jay was submitted to the authority of the elders, and they had the power to vote against him on any decision where they thought he was not being reasonable or felt he was going in the wrong direction.

It was common for Jay to hear, "Well, I know you have elders, but you're the one who makes the big decisions."

"No," Jay would answer, "I take the big decisions and share with my elders and they vote. If they ask for my opinion, I give it to them, but that may or may not influence the outcome."

Jay says that while there is no perfect way and while there are other possible ways, an elder-overseen church seemed to be the most Biblical option. It was actually a more difficult way to operate than some other models they considered, but Jay found that the safety and stability it provided were well worth the effort.

Jay took primary teaching responsibilities as staff pastor, but other elders shared with the whole congregation on occasion. This *ability to teach* was a requirement for eldership found in 1 Timothy. In the first years, Grant Smith gave several teachings based primarily on the New Testament epistles. Looking back on that time, Grant says, "My memories of those early years are mainly marked by a sense of encouragement, feeling very invigorated, and simply pressing on in the journey with Jesus."

With considerable prayer, by 1984 the elders embraced the idea of calling Jay from the position of Staff Pastor to that of Senior Pastor. They found that it was too easy for things to be missed when responsibility was shared so widely among the elders, and appointing Jay as senior leader created a better organizational chart.

Though the church started with just five elders, North Way added to this number as the church grew. Chuck Conway was an early addition, as was Scott McCabe.

In 1983, Kathy took some time off from working in the church office as she and Bruce welcomed their second child, Daniel. Soon after, they moved their family to California where Bruce enrolled at Fuller Theological Seminary to earn his PhD in Philosophy. Bruce and Kathy were thankful they were able to be a part of the beginning years of North Way, and they would be back with their children for future seasons of growth.

Jay and the elders knew that someone would need to fill Kathy's shoes in the office, and they also knew, with all that was happening at North Way, that this need would only grow. Over the next decades, they would come to appreciate just how essential a dedicated and gifted support team would be in seeking to expand the Kingdom of God through dynamic, Spirit-led ministry.

Many of the most indispensable people to North Way's ministry would labor entirely behind the scenes, making it difficult to demonstrate just how vital their service was every step of the way. Jay says that many served for years with passionate hearts, seeming called to do so by their very personality, temperament, and spiritual giftedness. One such person was Arlene Rink.

Gene and Arlene were the managers of The Open Door Bookstore where North Way had its office in the early years. As one of the founding couples represented on the Servants Council, they were *all in* from the first day that the idea for a new church was open for discussion and prayer. Jay says that Gene was blessed with an exuberant and expressive love for Jesus and was willing to serve wherever and whenever needed, while Arlene was gifted with a warm and caring personality and some strong gifts in administration and organization.

Located on Route 19, just three miles south of The Bradley House, the Rink's bookstore housed early morning prayer meetings even before the upstairs was used as North Way's office. In 1983, it became clear that in order for Jay to invest in relationships and provide consistent teaching and discipling of leaders, as well as partner with the elders in defining church vision, he needed to have a capable professional assistant to release him from the details that were associated with all that was going on in the early growing season of North Way.

It was determined by Jay and the elders that Arlene Rink had both the qualifications and the spiritual giftedness to fill this role with passion and excellence. She would go on to serve in this position for the next 25 years and would have a truly incalculable impact on North Way's ministry. Kathy, who preceded and succeeded Arlene as Jay's professional assistant, says that it would be a huge oversight for this book not to celebrate Arlene's years of devotion to the Lord.

Jay says it cannot be overstated how many times Arlene took on not only the responsibilities defined in her position, but also made herself available whenever a need arose that affected him or another important opportunity or resource that the Lord provided for North Way. Arlene's devotion to her call was evident to all who had regular contact with Jay or who had special responsibilities or associations with North Way as a church. In the same way that those responsibilities, relationships, and opportunities grew through the years, Jay watched Arlene also grow in her ability to manage these diverse and demanding responsibilities while constantly maintaining a pleasant and professional demeanor with everyone with whom she interacted.

Jay recalls that one of the most important qualities that Arlene brought to this position was one of helping him to be sensitive to needs in the congregation as they were brought to her attention, while shielding him from things that others could easily handle without him getting involved. This provided the freedom for Jay to give his primary energies where they were most needed while not missing the personal touch that a member of the congregation might greatly appreciate in a time of need. So much of what the Lord did as North Way grew in the grace and blessing of God, Jay says, was to help provide the energy and attention to detail needed to execute everything from a simple personal visit to a major leadership conference.

"Together, Gene and Arlene served North Way with warm and generous hearts and helped to shape the spirit and personality of our church family for 25+ years," Jay says. "These two were very special, cherished, and beloved friends, as well as co-laborers in our ministry in these fruitful years."

~~~

Right from the start, North Way demonstrated a unique devotion to the art of worship. Jan Sherman was the first worship director and established a team that led the congregation to new levels of intimacy with God. Jay was involved on a weekly basis choosing the songs that best fit the week's message, supporting Jan's ideas and her search for God's heart.

Within a year of North Way's launch, Jan and her worship team released a CD called *Lord, Make Me an Instrument* so that the congregation could listen throughout the week. Before the release of their second CD a year later, a new volunteer showed up to help.

Susie McCabe and her husband Kirk (Mac) showed up to North Way late compared to Mac's younger sister Marcia, who was half of one of the Servants Council couples, and his younger brother Scott, who had attended since the second week. After meeting at Northern Arizona University and getting married in Yuma, Mac and Susie had moved back to Pittsburgh in 1971 and attended Crossroads Presbyterian Church in Gibsonia, where Mac became an elder.

Susie, who had majored in voice, minored in piano, and received her degree in music education at NAU, took a position teaching music in the Fox Chapel Area School District while Mac worked as a geologist for the Mine Safety and Health Administration. In the years when the Memorial Park youth staff were growing and being prepared for their future ministry, Mac and Susie were gaining different experiences, including being part of two small groups led by future Christian leaders: Lee Kricher (founder of Amplify Church) and Wayne Alderson (founder of Value of the Person).

In 1980, God moved Mac and Susie from Pleasant Hills back to the North Hills, albeit in unpleasant circumstances. After having to leave his stable government job, a door opened for Mac in management at Bayer Corporation. At the time, they had three children: Shannon, Bryan, and Cameron.

Attending Bakerstown Alliance Church for a time, Mac and Susie quickly tired of hearing from multiple close family members about a new church that was just starting up and swore they would never attend. It wasn't long before they gave in, however, as Mac says that by 1982 they felt called to attend

North Way, "Basically, join the rest of my family."

Soon after Mac and Susie began attending North Way, Susie heard that the worship team was putting together a second CD, *With My Whole Heart*. Susie knew she could use her musical training and teaching experience here and offered to help however she was needed. She ended up directing the choir.

Susie went on to volunteer in the music ministry for five years before joining the staff as assistant worship director to Jan. We will follow Susie's contributions in the next chapters, but she credits Jan with laying a foundation for North Way's pursuit of excellence and depth in worship as well as in the use of various arts in worship. "She was fearless in stepping into what God was doing, finding it and birthing it," Susie says. Under Jan's leadership, there were structured and spontaneous times within the worship service. She and her team taught worship and nurtured it.

Jan took her volunteers (Susie included) to a Worship Symposium held at Duquesne University that used drama, dance, banners, flags, and instruments to enhance the worship experience and to minister in the spirit of God's glory. "It was eye-opening and exciting to realize the magnitude of God's creative nature that could be expressed through so many venues," says Susie. "We learned the scriptural basis behind them all, and volunteer leaders like Mimi Wlodek and Gloria Karn were inspired in so many wonderful ways. This foundation carried through the many years impacting the Eternal, breaking through strongholds, and declaring the glory of God."

~~~

At the start of North Way, Carol had her hands full with her three young children and with helping Jay, but when Eden Christian Academy started in 1983 and was looking for a volunteer PE instructor, she said yes and started with one class. Jay and Carol's son David was the first child to enroll at Eden, and North Way was the first church to endorse and sponsor the school. Once the school got rolling, it grew quickly and North Way stayed committed to its vision.

During the early years of the school, North Way had a full column of praises and prayer requests about Eden in the *North Way News* for people to stay up to date on its growth. No wonder, prayer was all important here as well. The first praise report listed in January 1985 was that, "Additional people have become involved in our Monday night prayer times." They went on to list more praises and to ask for prayer regarding searches for facilities, personnel, board members, and financial support.

Carol started Eden's PE program and built it over the next eight years until it needed a full-time director. In the early years, she got Eden parents to volunteer their time and help her build equipment that the school could not afford. "It was really a fun time to develop that program," she said. Since then, Eden has grown to three locations and added grades from preschool all the way through high school. It has grown from that single PE class and now has a reputable Athletics department.

Jay and Carol's children attended Eden through middle

school. Since Eden's high school program did not start until years later, they went on to attend public high school at Pine Richland. Jay says that was a good chance for them to live out their faith in a public context. He says they all did well there and are all following God today.

Even at the very start, when North Way was busy developing its own community, no one wanted it to be a church that stuck to itself. Along with supporting Eden, North Way members also sought other ways to love their city.

Ray had a heart for people in prison in Pittsburgh. He called Chuck Colson, founder and head of Prison Fellowship, and said, "I want to go into prisons." Colson directed him to a man named Jack Sullivan, a manufacturer's rep who was self-funded as the state director for Prison Fellowship. Jack told Ray to meet him at Western Penitentiary that Sunday. Jack quickly became involved with North Way, and he and Ray ended up not only serving together in prisons and as elders at North Way, but they started a for-profit company together, called TLC International (The Lord's Company), that funded their non-profit ministry to the prisons.

Ray persuaded more North Way people to get involved in the prison ministry and would go with a couple of the elders to hold a Sunday morning service down at the jail. Afterward, they would come back while the service was still going on at The Bradley House, and Jay would say, "Brothers! How was it today at the jail?"

North Way's members certainly didn't wait long before seeking to impact the city of Pittsburgh. Even before they owned their own building, they were asking how they could help others. Ray feels that North Way attracted many who brought an entrepreneurial spirit and says that they tested and tried many ideas. "I think there was a fearlessness in some ways to push envelopes and see what God wanted to do. I think it was characteristic that when people would come with a ministry they cared about, they'd have a good shot that they might get a hearing and support."

North Way also established a heart for reaching the poor in Pittsburgh during these early years. The banquet described in the following *North Way News* report from 1985 was just a small start compared to some of the events and ministries North Way would establish in the coming years.

CHRISTMAS BANQUET FOOD DISTRIBUTION

As you read this in February, the Christmas Banquet on December 19, 1984 probably seems far away. However, as I write this in late December the memories of it are still so vivid in my mind. I want to take this opportunity to express my great thanks to all those who helped in any way with food distribution. So many people helped in so many ways that I couldn't possibly begin to personally say thank you.

Through the combined efforts of many, 450 bags of food were given away. Each bag contained a 5 lb. canned ham or a 6 lb. roasting chicken, 5 lb. each of potatoes, cheese, flour, and cornmeal, 1 lb. of butter, 2 lb. of rice, 4 lb. of powdered milk, and 2 cans of baked beans and soup. All bags but those for senior citizens received a large loaf of bread and all bags except those for our North Way families contained a New Testament.

All of this food was donated, and I thank those who helped to get it. We had made a purchase agreement for the hams and chickens, which was over $3,000.00, but Operation Blessing, through the 700 Club, said they would pay for the meat.

We had over 16,000 pounds of food and about 40 people that helped get that food into the give-away bags. Will anyone who helped pack, move, sort, or work in any way on distribution ever forget the fun we had packing that food? I cannot thank enough of you who spent the entire day getting food ready for distribution. The packed bags weighed 35 lbs. each, and many picked up, stacked, packed, and carried those 450 bags many times that day. A special blessing from our Lord to you.

Thanks also to the Hobbs and Stone home groups who worked at the tables distributing food and to Bev and Phil Lapic and Bob and Vicki Darkey who were my troubleshooters. Also, thanks to the men and teenagers who helped after distribution by carrying bags, sometimes as far as a bus stop.

Thanks would not be complete if I didn't mention the

girls in the North Way office with Carl Adler and Ron Myers. I spoke with them many times each day as we made plans, and they were always so patient and lovingly had time for me.

The greatest joy to me personally was to see God open doors and make a way where there should have been no way. I took on this job only 17 days before the banquet, and I didn't know where we would get the food at that time, but all I had to do was obey and be available, and everyone just gave and gave. To Him be all glory and praise!

-Lois Woloszyk

The "Missions" section of the same *North Way News* issue shows further how North Way donated and distributed hundreds of toys and other items to poor families through Open Door Gospel Mission. Though we have not met "Brother Barry" in this book, the comments about his influence are particularly relevant to the development of North Way's ideals.

AN OPEN DOOR THANK YOU

Praise God for what He did through you to make the 1984 Christmas Outreach at the Open Door Gospel Mission a success.

We at the Open Door want to thank each of you who brought toys, children's clothing, and much needed food. Also, special thanks to everyone who came down to the Center on Friday night and/or Saturday to help organize and distribute these items to the families. Each one of you was a precious addition to the "crew." We particularly appreciated the young people who gave up their Friday night and Saturday to come, work, minister to the children, run errands, carry heavy bags, help pack chickens, etc. Your enthusiasm and willingness was a real blessing.

Thanks also to our brother in Texas who sent 150 handmade cars and trucks for the children. This was truly a labor of love.

God provided so abundantly for us that an overflow of toys and clothing went to Washington Christian Outreach (a mission similar to Open Door) for their Christmas program.

To give you some understanding of some of the people we serve, one woman who came had been taken unexpectedly ill and spent two months in the hospital. During the time that she was ill, her landlord sublet her apartment. When she finally returned home, she found most of her possessions stolen and her checking account "clean". Had it not been for the Christmas Outreach, she and her child would have had a bleak Christmas!

In regard to the work of the Open Door Gospel Mission,

it is with a real sense of loss that I have to tell you that Brother Barry will be leaving Pittsburgh at the end of February to accept a call to Atlanta. He has been called to the pastorate of a Baptist Church in one of Atlanta's suburbs. Brother Barry has been a true and faithful servant of the Lord. His ministry has provided North Way with the opportunity to become involved in the inner city. We have had the privilege of ministering to abused children and their families, of participating in the Christmas Outreach to some of the County's neediest people. Some of us have attended Brother Barry's course in Urban Evangelism to learn to be effective in witnessing. All of these contacts with the Open Door have brought the opportunity to be "doers of the Word." We are most grateful for these opportunities.

I am sure that you will all join me in wishing Dr. Barry and his family all the best that God has to offer. He truly epitomizes the servant described by Jesus in Matthew 26:34-36. He has fed the hungry, given a cup of water to the thirsty, clothed the naked, visited the sick, and ministered to those in prison. We pray that he will be blessed abundantly.

-Nancy Goettman

Along with all of the doctrines, values, and systems of leadership that were established during North Way's first four years, the church remained focused on relationships. Jay says, "Life change happens best not in rows, but in circles," hearkening back to the washer necklaces of years before. Members met in circles all throughout the week and formed circles in each Sunday service to pray for each other.

Blaine says of these years, "The emphasis was really on building the church through relationships and small groups; identifying growth group leaders and putting together groups that met in homes. That was really key and foundational as we started. As the church began to grow, we really encouraged people to find their home in growth groups because you weren't going to find your home in the identity of a building. People weren't going to point to Mr. B's and say, 'Oh, that's our church.' In fact, we were still renting there years later, and so every Sunday morning we had to come in and had to clean up the cigarette butts and the drinks that were left everywhere around the room and convert that place from a party room to a place for worship. So the identity was not in the place. Our identity was found in the groups of people that met in home groups all over the North Hills."

CHAPTER FOUR:
GROWTH

After four years of meeting, North Way had not yet found a home base. Then, the church even lost its ability to rent at The Bradley House when it changed ownership. Attendance had now tripled from the first week, making the weekend crowd more difficult to mobilize. North Way managed to rent the recently vacated facility of a Catholic church in Ross Township. Jay trusted that God had a plan and wrote to the church in the following article for the front page of the February 1985 edition of *North Way News*.

WHEN THE SPIRIT REALLY "MOVES"!

Although the engraving in the rock says St. Teresa's, the sign in front of the doors says North Way Christian Community! Thus we have formally completed our transition into the temporary facility that the Lord has provided for us in the closing days of December.

As most of you know, the decision to leave The Bradley House was made only after considerable effort had been expended in reaching a negotiated agreement with the owners of the building. Although our discussions had seemed to be moving in the right direction, significant reversal in the middle of December necessitated our relocation to another facility. I simply have to say that the way that the Holy Spirit "moved" to bring about our "move" had the undeniable mark of His handiwork. For example, administrative "red tape" and other similar obstacles that would normally take two to three months to negotiate simply melted away under the combined efforts of the staff of St. Teresa's and our North Way brethren led by Scott McCabe. From the very start, it was obvious that the Lord had opened the doors of the hearts of the people at St. Teresa's to receive us, and for that we have nothing but the deepest appreciation.

Further confirmation of God's hand in the relocation process was made evident as so many of you contributed so freely of your time and energies to transform the empty facility into a very workable and accommodating meeting place for us. In our four years together, I don't recall ever having seen more "flexibility" and "creativity" exercised by our Body! That's not to say that I was surprised; I was refreshed to see that that same quality of softheartedness and adaptability still burns brightly in our hearts.

I don't suppose that we need to be reminded very often that this facility isn't the new North Way Christian

Community. In fact, North Way Christian Community continues to thrive throughout the North Hills and surrounding areas, regardless of where we assemble for worship and teaching. However, the mentioning of that truth may serve to remind us that these present facilities are only temporary and have been given by the Lord to supply our need while He prepares us for the next step in adequately accommodating the growing ministry that He's entrusted to us. Believe with me that God will clearly unfold the specifics of His provision for us in the coming months, while at the same time allowing us complete liberty and fulfillment as we minister in the new facility.

Beloved, God is on the move by His Spirit, and as long as there is breath within us we are committed to moving with Him. In the fullest dimension of its meaning, let's commit ourselves to "moving on" together!

-Jay

Jay was not the only leader who sought to make the most of being literally "moved" by the Spirit. Jan Sherman, North Way's first worship director, wrote the following article about celebratory worship for the same newsletter.

CELEBRATE!

The people of Israel loved to celebrate. At every event, for each season, in response to all the Lord's miracles - they called a feast, held a worship service, built a memorial, or had an impromptu celebration. Check it out in the Word: after the parting of the Red Sea, the people danced and sang; after his family was spared from the flood, Noah built an altar and worshipped; when the foundation of the temple was rebuilt, Ezra held a public worship service which was beyond compare!

As the leaders of Music Ministry met recently and studied Nehemiah 12, we began to crave a celebration like that one at North Way. After all we have much to praise God for. . .His miracles of healing performed in our people, His provision of a facility, His bounty in the Christmas banquet, and so on. Soon the Lord opened our hearts and minds as one opened a treasure chest; we were spinning from the bounty of the treasures within! As the Lord began defining how these times would be ordered, the idea of a Concert of Prayer began taking shape, or should I say "shapes," for His creative hand will be sure to make each one different.

The focus or shape of this month's Concert of Prayer is one of celebration. As you prepare your heart for our evening together, let the anticipation of great rejoicing fill your soul; let the Holy Spirit refresh you with the childlike expectation. We in Music Ministry can't wait to see what will happen when God shows up on Friday the 15th. Won't you be there to meet Him? "And they offered great sacrifices that day and rejoiced, for God had made them rejoice with great joy; the women and children also rejoiced. And the joy of Jerusalem was heard afar off." (Neh 12:43) So be it for us, also!

-Jan

Through the uncertain times, North Way's leaders were not only rejoicing and calling for celebration, but they were also continuing to teach members how to grow in spiritual disciplines. Another article by Jan for this same February issue was about how to sing praises together in the home, as a family, around the dinner table. Jan closed this article of admonition saying:

If you've never tried singing together, step out in faith and try it. Watch the Lord do a work as He prepares your hearts for your communion together. Your only risk is allowing God to have room to work! In the meantime, the Lord will receive your praise and honor!

Anticipating a multitude of cheerful feasts,

Jan

Fred Steele, Jay's former fellow associate pastor from

Memorial Park, wrote the short article below in the same newsletter, reinforcing North Way's emphasis on small groups and challenging the groups to broaden their focus beyond fellowship of the body to evangelism and the inclusion of outsiders. This is something Howard Snyder recommends in *The Problem of Wineskins*, arguing that small groups should be an expanding unit. It is likely due to this focus that North Way stayed strong and continued to grow even while its weekly place for worship services was not ideal.

HOME GROUP MINISTRY-EXPANDING ITS VISION

The vision of small bands of Christians meeting together in homes is as old as the church itself. In fact, the church was shaped as new believers gathered together devoting themselves to the foundations of scripture, prayer, fellowship (deep relationships) and community (breaking bread together) (Acts 2:41-47, Acts 4:32-35).

In the past we have viewed Home Group participation as the significant basis of identity with the Body at North Way. In other words, Home Group participation became the means of care, oversight, and accountability.

The nurturing of one another in Home Groups will continue to be foundational, but God has been working in us a vision which broadens our responsibility as members of Home Groups.

We believe that everyone is to share in this vision and pray fervently toward its fulfillment. Our goal is simply to allow the Holy Spirit to make us a bridge for new life to enter into our midst. Our hearts are to open to the searching, the lost, the forsaken.

Allow your focus to extend beyond the comfortableness you have known in your group to enfold the broken, hurting, upset, and angry. We will be stretched in the process and richly blessed!

-Fred Steele

Rosa Lee Smith was Editor for *North Way News* and worked with a small team to publish articles from staff and members of the congregation. By sharing a few of these articles we gain an idea of the atmosphere and energy of young North Way. There are reports on prayer groups and ministry efforts, admonitions toward unity, birth announcements, and even ads for cars and houses for sale.

One noteworthy article focused on how several members of North Way had worked with passion and dedication on a banner to raise up at the new temporary location. They assigned special significance to each color they employed in its making, a tradition that has its roots in the Old Testament, but that is rarely, if ever, seen today. This article, below, is another illustration of the joyful trust North Way was placing in God during this season of moving, leading to literal jumping, clapping, and shouting for joy.

OUR SHINING BANNER

(Vine's Bible Dictionary defines banner as "that which shines" or "that which is lifted up.")

On Monday, December 31st, North Way moved from Bradley's to the vacated St. Teresa's Church in Perrysville. The church was now our Chapel and we wanted to put our mark on it; we wanted something up at the front and rich in color, something that would make a statement for us as a Body of believers even when we were not in the building.

What would it be? It would be a banner of red and gold, purple, blue, and green, declaring the words of Psalm 34:3 - "Let us exalt his name together."

On Wednesday, Gloria Karn sketched the design in about 45 minutes and then began to make the pattern of pieces. On Thursday we selected the fabric. Friday she prepared the banner background which measured 5'x24'.

Before we began the work on Saturday, we prayed that God would give us the desire of our hearts, that we would complete the project and have it hung for our first Sunday in the Chapel.

The work began! Carol Conley, Jean Santoro, Dodie

Wills, Mable Glunt, Ellen Gozian, Gloria, and I cut and glued until late afternoon. At six in the evening, Paul Woloszyk, Gene Rink, and Wes Dawson raised the banner while we shouted and jumped and clapped for joy. It had been accomplished! Alleluia!

We even discovered that our prayer before our work began and the celebration at the banner's lifting was of the Lord, for Psalm 20:4 reads: "May the Lord give you the desire of your heart and make all your plans succeed. We will shout for joy when you are victorious and will lift up our banners in the name of our God."

-Mimi Wlodek

In spite of these praises, Jay looks back on the time at St. Teresa's as an awkward and difficult experience. While he encouraged the church and tried to keep spirits up, he had to admit to himself that this location could not work for long. Jay describes the building as stark and made of stone — just the opposite of the atmosphere North Way was trying to achieve. Jay preached that life change happens best in circles rather than in rows, and yet here they found themselves in wooden pews.

St. Teresa's was a much longer drive for many members than The Bradley House had been, making it difficult for members from Cranberry to attend, let alone invite people from their community. It was also very cold in the building during the winter, and people sat in the pews with their coats on. Jay felt that if they didn't find a solution soon, things would start to unravel. *This could be the beginning of the end,* he thought. *Are we going to make it?*

Jay recalls the history of North Way both in terms of broad seasons and of key significant moments. We have already seen personal crossroads for Jay like the one where he decided to go to seminary or where he had to tell his father that he was leaving the denomination to start a new church. Here North Way was facing a watershed moment of its own, perhaps its most significant challenge since its start five years before. While this book seeks to celebrate years and seasons of ministry that ran smoothly, it is perhaps some of these moments of uncertainty that offer the greatest inspiration for today.

After leaving his accounting career and putting everything on the line to serve at North Way, Blaine could have easily been worried during this time. What we see from Pastor Blaine in North Way's newsletter, however, is only excitement about an upcoming opportunity for the youth group to go on a two-week mission trip to Mexico City. In Mexico City, they would serve with Lisa Anderson, a missionary in Christian Camping. Lisa had been an energetic teenager in Jay's youth group at Memorial Park and was sent out by Memorial Park and supported by North Way as well.

Even during a time where the way forward for North Way looked dim, its leaders stayed faithful to God's calling and continued to put faith in His blessing. Years earlier, when looking for a church to pastor, Jay had said to Carol, "Once I know what God is going to call us to do, I'll give 110%. Whatever obstacles come, we'll be confident that God has called us to it, so we'll get through those obstacles. We'll go over or around them or through them." They had found what God had called them to, and now they were facing an obstacle.

Jay and the elders had actually tried to buy The Bradley House the preceding Fall, offering the owner $1.4 million. This sum took no small measure of faith for such a new church body, but they were turned down flat. Jay and the elders sensed that it was not just a man who was saying no and trusted that it was God, but they had to wonder why. The Bradley House was a perfect location for North Way, and they could easily imagine renovating it for better use.

With 750 people attending, they could not find any place big enough to rent until they found the less-than-central St. Teresa's. They wondered and prayed for four months at St. Teresa's, and then something happened the day after Easter Sunday, 1985. Jay got a call from his dad, who told him to check the newspaper. There Jay saw a listing for The Bradley House that said, "For sale by auction." The auction was set for April 30th — just nine days away.

It turned out that the most recent owner of the building — a real estate investor from LA who had no personal connection to Pittsburgh — had gone bankrupt, and now North Way had another chance at the place. Jay and the elders had no notice until this moment that the auction was coming, but they met and talked about how much they could offer for the building.

After a cold winter at St. Teresa's, Jay attended the auction on a beautiful Spring day: 70s and sunny. Jay went with one other elder named Bill James, a banker from Mellon Bank.

Riding there together, Bill said to Jay, "This will probably go better if you let me do the bidding." Having never been to a real estate auction, Jay couldn't argue with that.

There were about 20 people at the auction, including several wealthy and well-known real estate figures who Bill recognized. Jay watched as one man pulled up in a Rolls-Royce convertible — a man who owned 15 McDonald's franchises in Pittsburgh. Word was, he was there to buy The Bradley House to be an administrative hub for his franchises.

"It was just like your auction you'd see on TV," says Jay. "Who'll give me..."

The auctioneer opened the bid at $600,000. The elders had decided that the most they could spend was $800,000. Nobody spoke.

Jay turned and whispered to Bill, "Nobody's bidding, why don't we just grab it for $600,000?"

"Let me handle it," said Bill.

Someone bid at $200,000, and then it started to go up. Finally, the bid reached $600,000 again. There was a long wait and Bill said, "Okay, let's do 6." That was the final bid; North Way won. They had a quick negotiation for all the chairs, tables, desks, etc., and got all of them for another $25,000.

Bill went to the man with the Rolls-Royce and said, "We're thrilled that we got the building, but we're curious: you had the resources..."

"Well, you're right," he said, "But something in me wouldn't let me bid against the church."

Having obtained the building for less than half of what they had offered the previous owner, Jay could see that God did have a purpose and a future for North Way. Thinking back on that auction he says, "God still moves the hearts of kings."

The auction marked a turning point back to renewed hope and ignited new growth. Jay suggests that just like the children of Israel, the times of wandering make the provision of a *promised land* that much sweeter.

North Way renovated the building over the summer and moved back in in August. The nursery would no longer be around the bar, and the job of cleaning up cigarettes and drinks was a thing of the past. For the first time, North Way had a place to call its own. With a well-established identity and set of ideals from the preceding season, the church was poised to put the building to its best use.

The next years for North Way were filled with answers to prayer. Jay calls them the "Years of Rapid Growth." Growth happened as the members lived out their faith in their communities. Jay feels that Acts 2:47 sums up this time in North Way's history well when it says, "And the Lord added to their number daily those who were being saved."

Jay says, "This was not because we were out there trying to draw big crowds, but it was just healthy — people were bringing people. Honestly, there were days I'd step out there, when you do it every week, you start to see, right in front of your eyes, there are 50 more people than last week. That was the kind of interest that was being shown. We had won the credibility war."

North Way continued to be driven by the core values it had named at the start. Having spent the first months together trying to hear from God and searching the Scriptures for what He would want them to be about, members now found themselves in what Jay calls the "enviable, but somewhat scary position" of getting to explore the best ways to live out those values. Most churches around were still denominational, each tied to a set of beliefs and structured ways of expressing them, but North Way was free to search and try things.

North Way's leadership really believed that worship was to be the number one priority, but that meant they needed to work at it and ask how to truly prioritize it. They knew that prayer was the touchstone of their power, but what were the best ways to connect the congregation to that touchstone? They wanted *relationship* to be more than a buzzword, but what were the best ways for people to actually share their lives, their needs, their dreams, and God's Word? North Way's goals went beyond filling pews: members of the church should learn how to truly care for one another and love one another.

Jay remembers doing a teaching series during these early years on 33 "one anothers" from the New Testament — love one another, serve one another, encourage one another, accept one another, speak truth to one another, bear one another's burdens — to name a few. These commands and many more were given directly to the church in Scripture, and they don't all come naturally. As he worked through the "one anothers," Jay pointed out to his congregation that there was no way to practice these commands if they weren't in close fellowship with one another, let alone any way to receive feedback and improve at them.

One of the "one anothers" was, "Greet one another." Both Paul and Peter admonished the early church to greet one another with a holy kiss, or a kiss of love (1 Peter 5:14, 2 Cor 13:12). While North Way stopped short of kissing, the message was clear that greetings were important. The practice of greeting had a good start with the years-long requirement at The Bradley House for each attendee to be supplied with a danish and a juice. From the start, it was not a culture where you would slip into an aisle after the bell tolled. Fellowship before service was essential.

Everyone wore name tags, not just the staff and volunteers. Each Sunday when a family showed up, they would take down their name tags from a large board or fill out a new one if they were visiting. Setting up the name tag station always took some work, especially before owning a permanent building, but it helped accomplish one of the "one anothers," and that made it worth it.

This focus on "greeting one another" lives on at North Way today with the hospitality teams and Connect Centers at each location. Free, quality coffee is a high priority. *Author's note: I met my wife Angela at North Way when she was leading the hospitality team at North Way Oakland in 2015.*

The concept of a circle, which Jay had applied in FUDD back at Memorial Park, continued as an important and powerful image for North Way. Most people who visited in the early years were accustomed to experiencing church in rows and finding a quiet place to face forward as a member of the congregation. The pastor's place was at the front, where he would face his audience and preach. North Way had started as a circle of the original couples and had multiplied via circles as more and more small groups were added, but Jay wanted this concept of circles to be present even in the Sunday service.

Face to face "prayer circles" soon became a standard part of every service. Jay remembers standing up hundreds of times after worship and saying, "These next few minutes might be uncomfortable for some of you, but for many of us, this is the most important part of the service. We're going to turn and form little groups of four or five people, and all we're going to ask you to do is to listen to one another, whoever has a need, and we just want you to pray for each other."

Jay says he would always qualify and say, "Look… you don't have to do it at all; you can just be seated. But, I encourage you to at least stand up, and if you're new just say, 'Hey, I'm new, I'd like to listen.' That's all you have to say, and that's great."

"So many things happened in those prayer circles; *so* many things," says Jay. "Because that's where folks got connected to each other. 'Oh, you live over in Brookway Farms? I didn't know that — that's where I live!' *Boom*, now you have a relationship going. Or, 'You have a child who's on the autism spectrum?' Whatever the situation might have been, prayer happened! How in the world would you pray if you had a thousand people? You don't have time to pray for a thousand people. But if you turn in circles, and you have 200 circles of four or five people, everybody gets prayed for! Well, that became a distinguishing mark."

The prayer circles continued as a staple of North Way's Sunday service for over 20 years. Eventually, through feedback from a growing diversity of backgrounds that were drawn to North Way, the church did move away from this practice, but over the years countless thousands of personal prayers were offered up by and for the people of North Way. This was just one way North Way accomplished the Biblical directive to, "Pray for one another" (James 5:16).

The experience of genuine community at North Way had a natural outworking: the desire to spread the gospel. For people to enjoy God's love and the fellowship of the Holy Spirit in such a tangible way and not want to share it was unthinkable. The leadership believed it was inescapable that healthy churches should have a passion to win the lost. In Acts Chapter 8, they saw an example of how God could accomplish His purpose, even if His people were dragging their feet. In this passage, it seemed that God allowed circumstances of persecution to scatter the church, ultimately using those circumstances to accomplish the spread of the gospel. Christians were forced out of Jerusalem to the surrounding regions, and they preached as they went, starting a movement that would reach around the world.

As North Way grew and grew, the leadership knew that they needed to reach beyond Pittsburgh. Even with the overwhelming concerns of being a relatively new church and caring for their own people, they couldn't simply put off the needs of the world until they felt ready. It was tempting to say, "We'll get to that," or, "Let us grow up a little bit and get an education, and then we'll start fulfilling our purpose later," but the leadership believed they shouldn't have that luxury. The early New Testament church certainly hadn't.

One way North Way showed its heart for the spread of the gospel right from the start was to tithe its income to missions. These missions could be local, national, or international, but had to be outside of North Way's control. The church gave to organizations and ministries that it felt shared its values and demonstrated fruitfulness and a very high degree of financial efficiency, but this surrender required faith that God's kingdom and plan was much bigger than North Way. For a new church starting out, taking 10% right off the top took no small measure of faith, as is the case for any individual when first tithing, but it set an important precedent that still stands today.

The missions effort grew at North Way, and by 1985 warranted the addition of a missions director to the church staff. This pastor's sole responsibility would be to lead North Way's charge to empower and equip members to go out and make disciples. The Great Commission in Matthew 28 specified the need to *go* — and gave the command to reach not only local area codes, but *all* nations. "We took that seriously — how could we not?" says Jay.

Mark Geppert became North Way's first missions pastor. Jay had met Mark outside of North Way, but says Mark fit right in and was perfect for the position. At first, North Way didn't need a full-time person for this role, but Mark already had his own ministry called SEAPC (Southeast Asian Prayer Center), and he was able to divide his time between North Way and SEAPC. Mark's passion to take the gospel to remote parts of the world allowed him to lead North Way into many new opportunities.

Mark and Jay agreed that there was no better way to develop a heart and passion for missions than to actually go on a missions trip. Mark excelled at organizing trips for North Way — real bona fide missions trips that allowed people to experience life in other places and to see what it's like to do the hard work of a missionary. The church knew that Jay had a passion for missions, but Jay believed that he needed to demonstrate that passion and lead by example. He went on several overseas missions trips during this season and wrote home to share what he learned.

North Way continued to expand its focus on training and sending missionaries around the world and would eventually become its own sending agency with full-time staff. This will be covered more in the next chapter, but it is important to note how early North Way showed devotion to global missions. The decision right from the beginning to tithe to missions and the hiring of Mark to lead this initiative gave the church a strong start.

Biblical teaching remained a key emphasis at North Way and offered a significant draw for new members. Jay was a different kind of voice in Pittsburgh, bringing both a heavy emphasis on doctrine and an openness to the Holy Spirit. Jay credits this balanced approach to the unique background God brought him through.

As we saw in the first chapters of this book, Jay grew up Catholic and was then Presbyterian for 25 years. His in-depth Biblical training at Fuller gave him the "theological chops" to be credible to people from similarly formal backgrounds. It was also during his time at seminary that his deeper experience of the Holy Spirit began. He gained a healthy understanding of the work of the Holy Spirit while diligently studying the Word, and he entered his first pastoral job at Memorial Park with the ability to calm the apprehensions of his fellow Presbyterians.

Jay's teaching was greatly affected by Spirit-filled teachers like Jack Hayford. Jay listened to Hayford as much as he could and was shaped by his writings and teachings. Hayford emphasized the work of the Holy Spirit but said that no emphasis should become central above the reality and uniqueness of who Jesus is. He inspired Jay to seek a healthy balance between strong doctrine and spirit-filled experiences.

Though Jay was open-minded and sought the truth expressed in many different approaches, he never could buy into the Word of Faith or the Prosperity Gospel movements. In both, Jay observed that one particular emphasis had become central and thrown off the balance.

Informed by his background, training, and continued reading, Jay's approach to teaching attracted many to North Way. People seemed hungry for such a balanced approach. Jay admits that his sermons were quite long in the early years, but this was a vital time to lay a Biblical groundwork. This depth of teaching also helped accomplish one of Jay's ideals that we have mentioned: equipping the saints to do the work of the ministry.

Jay did eventually begin to trim the length of his sermons as he received some comments that they could be too long. "The people watching the kids were dying — and that's not a little thing!" says Jay.

Of utmost importance to Jay was that he lived the things he preached. While many were drawn to North Way by his unique teaching style, Jay believes that people only stayed if they saw his teaching to be consistent with who he was. "Discerning people sense the difference," he says. It was not enough to preach good doctrine or to encourage heartfelt worship — he had to live these things.

North Way added elders consistently as the body they were called to oversee grew. By 1985, there were about a dozen elders compared to the original five, but they realized this was too many to be involved in the regular operational decisions and duties of the church. The group was meeting on a weekly basis, but they found it to be unsustainable to be responsible not only for the functional and operational affairs of the church, but also for spiritual, directional, and Biblical issues.

It was at this point that the elders decided to create a spinoff called the Elder's Council. The elders would remain the ruling body with ultimate authority for spiritual leadership, but the Elder's Council could pick up responsibility for fiduciary duties; legal, financial, human resources, etc. Half of the elders continued as elders, while the other half — with a couple additions — made up the Elder's Council (EC).

To be on the EC, men had to be identified as having all the qualities of an elder, but they also had to have a unique giftedness or expertise to help with the church's more practical operations. Jay says that they never rushed the process, even while in need of elders or EC members. Even if someone owned a business or came with other helpful experience or skills, it was essential for his spiritual fruit to be demonstrated within the body.

Whenever North Way's elders recognized the need to expand their number, they would give the congregation a couple months notice so they could pray and recommend names of those they believed had the qualities of spiritual leadership. Once the elders had a list of people who had been put forward, the existing elders would determine if there was any reason to disqualify anyone before the interview. Except in very difficult and unusual cases, they ended up interviewing all the names who were submitted.

Then, in the initial interview with the candidate, they would start by asking, "Are you interested in being considered?" They figured there was no point in going through the process and asking tough questions if the candidate didn't actually want to be an elder. Though there was never a case where someone flat out didn't want to be an elder, there were a few times where the candidate would say that the timing wasn't right considering his job, children, etc.

The congregation seemed to appreciate the ability to recommend people for eldership, and it wasn't unusual for their recommendations to be approved. Oftentimes, the existing elders were aware of and watching the very same people who the church would put forward, and it brought great confidence to know that the congregation felt the same way the elders did. Each new elder was ordained in the Biblical sense, but not in the legal sense.

The elders were not required to rotate out after a certain number of years, as seen in many denominations. The elders didn't see anything in the Bible about a term and felt that if a person was deemed to be of elder quality, there was no reason to ask him to step down from this important role, provided he kept up the qualifications. The position of an elder would be renewed every three years, provided each examined his life and had a conversation with Pastor Jay or a couple of other long-standing elders. This conversation was to ensure that nothing important was missing in the elder's commitment or responsibilities.

Those who served as elders enjoyed it, but sometimes it would take a toll on an individual, and he would be granted a year off. This was rare, and when the elder came back he was not required to re-qualify or be re-nominated. "You'll be an elder a year from now," each would be encouraged. Typically, elders remained in their positions for many years, which brought a healthy continuity to the board and to the congregation.

The renewable terms were slightly different for the Elder's Council, since those on EC had more practical roles than visionary. The EC also renewed three years at a time, but could only be renewed twice, so the longest one would be on the Elder's Council was nine years. Even this was a significant term, allowing for great continuity. There was not a set amount of allowed elders or EC members, so more could be added organically as the church grew and there were more things to be overseen and accomplished.

Another important decision for the elders in this season was to bring Scott McCabe on staff. As mentioned in previous chapters, Scott had seemed destined to be a pastor from the time he was a teenager but was in business with his father when North Way started. He had attended Grove City College years before as a religion major, and his wife Missy says that when they were married she thought he was going to be a pastor. By the time he had met Jay in 1980, Scott was established in business and had mostly given up on the idea of ministry, but he heard a unique call that he and Missy should be at any church Jay might start.

Even while he got fully involved at North Way as a small group leader and an elder, Scott imagined he'd stay in business forever. Then he went through a job transition and had a chance for his early calling to come full circle. While he was figuring out his next move, he worked part-time for Jack Sullivan, who ran the Western Pennsylvania Prison Ministry and The Lord's Company. He also worked part-time as administrative staff at North Way. He felt like he was in a tug-of-war between two extremely strong leaders, Jack and Jay, but says, "It didn't last very long — Jay won." Scott was ordained in

March of 1985 and has been on staff at North Way for the past 35 years.

Jay and Scott's leadership strengths were different and complementary. Scott describes Jay as an, "unusually high-level visionary leader," while Jay describes Scott as, "the ultimate utility player." When Scott pursued a second degree, it was not a seminary degree, but rather a Masters in Organizational Leadership.

Scott says, "I'm not a theologian. I wasn't trained as a pastor. Most of my experience had been business-oriented. The leadership I provided for decades alongside Jay's was organizational leadership. It was always behind the scenes, just working the processes."

Scott and Missy raised their young family at North Way, as North Way itself matured. Missy says that being involved with North Way from the first weeks was very much like raising their children. "Everything was so new because there was no model. So there were times that we went through that infant stage, and then we went into that toddler stage, and eventually into the teenage stage... it was just amazing to watch this growth thing that happened."

Ray and Marcia moved to Ligonier and joined an Episcopalian church, but they are proud of how their brother has stayed and served at North Way. Ray says, "Scott, in our family, he's why things happen. Quietly, never lording it over or anything — he's open-handed about it and we assent. We appreciate his leadership. I think North Way's been really lucky to have Scott because he's the ultimate connector of talent.

Scott's been responsible for making sure hundreds of guys have felt they're in and they're a part of it."

One of North Way's first ever weddings happened shortly after they bought The Bradley House. Blaine Workman — though he had been single while he was on the Servants Council — met a young lady while serving as North Way's first youth pastor. Lynne Santom had started attending North Way because her younger brothers were in Blaine's youth group.

The wedding was held in January of 1986 and brought Memorial Park and North Way back together in a beautiful way. The ceremony was held at Memorial Park, with Jay officiating alongside one of the pastors from Memorial Park. The reception was held at The Bradley House — now officially North Way.

Since Blaine knew everyone at North Way so well from being on staff and still had family ties at Memorial Park, it felt funny to try to narrow down the guest list for the reception. Instead, they approached the reception as a community event. North Way members cooked the food, and the members of Blaine's youth group served it. "Oh goodness, it was crazy," says Blaine, "There were 600 people at our wedding."

One of the remarkable things about the story of North Way is that there are many founding members who are still involved at North Way. North Way has never had a church split, and there are many families now represented by three generations. Another valuable perspective to the broad picture of what God has done through North Way, however, comes from the stories of founding members who have moved on. Not all members have stayed, and those who have pursued God's calling elsewhere enrich churches around the city, country, and world with lessons learned at North Way. Blaine is a perfect example of this.

After being on the Servant's Council and serving as North Way's first youth pastor, Blaine felt compelled to pursue a seminary degree for further ministry. After five years on staff, he stepped down to pursue his studies full time at Trinity School for Ministry in Ambridge, PA. Blaine and Lynne moved to the North Side to be closer to Trinity and started learning about the culture and people around them.

They soon realized that none of their neighbors were going to drive out to Wexford to church with them. Lynne was surprised one day when Blaine said that he thought it was time to look for a new church home in their community. She knew he had been so deeply involved in the start of North Way that it would be hard to leave. Jay encouraged them in this decision, knowing it was best for them to bloom where they were planted. They began attending Allegheny Center Alliance Church in the North Side. Blaine ended up on staff as a pastor there and still serves there today.

Blaine says that his five years at North Way offered key preparation for his ministry at ACAC. Not only did he receive his call to ministry at North Way, but he also got to be involved in all the planning and navigating necessary for a church to grow from 200 to over 700 attendees without the luxury of consistent buildings and facilities.

Welcoming 700 people for worship was one thing, Blaine says, but organizing and supporting small groups for all those people was another. And then there was the question of youth ministry, including junior and senior high. Making all this happen in a startup church in the absence of physical resources was just the challenge Blaine needed in order to navigate in his ministry at ACAC.

Serving and managing ministry at ACAC, a church with over 2,000 people who meet on a property of just two acres, Blaine says he is often reminded of the early days of North Way. Pastoring at North Way in the season before it had a church home, he developed the mindset that he would use any facilities to the fullest for ministry rather than protecting them.

Reflecting back, Blaine realizes that though he could only follow God one step at a time without the whole picture, everything makes sense now in how God was weaving things together, from his business background, to his five years of ministry experience at North Way, to his move to the North Side, and his search to understand the community there. "I would never have seen how the Lord would have put all these eclectic things together and use them in a way for His glory," he says.

Though Blaine's active role at North Way ended years ago, he is one of many who were a part of North Way for a particular time or season and have continued to this day to serve God and impact the city of Pittsburgh and beyond.

Another young man who made North Way his home

during his formational years was Michael Geer. Michael came to Pittsburgh in November of 1980 — just months before the start of North Way — to work for WPXI-TV Channel 11 News as a Senior News Producer. Michael had already been working for ABC News in Washington D.C. for two years — partially during college and for six months after graduating. Michael's degree from the University of Maryland was in American History, but he much preferred working to school and was eager to take the full-time position in Pittsburgh.

Michael didn't know a soul in Pittsburgh, but he found an apartment in a complex called Hickory Hills, above the Showcase Cinema in Wexford. Michael had an active faith and wanted to find a good church to attend. At the bottom of the hill from his apartment happened to be a Christian bookstore, so Michael decided to stop in one December day to ask for advice. The bookstore owners were Gene and Arlene Rink, and Michael told them that he was new to the area and looking for a church.

When Michael described the kind of church he was looking for, Gene and Arlene said, "We don't know of anything specifically like that right now... but there's a group of us that have been praying that God would start one." Gene and Arlene spent the next few months meeting with the Servants Council to start that church they were praying for, and in March, Michael heard about North Way on WPIT, the Christian radio station.

Michael had been part of a Christian Musicians Fellowship in D.C. and had met some members of the musical group Glad.

The advertisement on the radio said that Glad was going to be doing a concert in Wexford, and Michael figured he should go see it. The host was North Way — already bringing in guests for concerts just months into its existence.

After the concert, Michael began attending North Way and quickly got involved playing on the worship team. His main instrument was piano, but since the worship director Jan Sherman usually led from the keyboard, Michael played mostly guitar or bass. Michael was a part of North Way's first album, *Make Me an Instrument* and remembers playing on one song, "Unto Him Who Made Us" with Amy Scheuring singing.

As a member of the worship team and the worship team small group Bible study, Michael started to get to know Pastor Jay, who was integral and involved with all things worship. Jay was interested to hear about Michael's work with the news station, and Michael soon became involved in a men's Bible study with Jay. Michael says that his relationship with Jay was instrumental in guiding him as a young man and young professional. Michael says, "Jay was focused on building spiritual growth in different members of the church and especially people who might have roles in society to take the Christian message and make it impact society more broadly."

Michael met his wife Susan at North Way, and Jay officiated their wedding in January of 1982. Susan became pregnant with their first child just a few months later, and while she was pregnant, she and Michael both read a book that had recently been published called *Abortion: The Silent Holocost,* by Jesuit priest and author John Powell. That book was the Geers' first significant introduction to the issue of abortion from a Biblical perspective. The topic hit on a more personal level as they went through their own pregnancy and got to see their first ultrasound.

As they awakened to the gravity of this national issue, they began connecting with other people in their small group at North Way and discussing the importance of the church's role and response to it. Susan spoke with other young mothers and pregnant women in the church about their thoughts and started organizing prayer gatherings on the topic of the sanctity of life.

Michael says, "Whenever Jay would sense that God was putting a call or direction in someone's life, he would seek to foster and encourage it, to pray for them and, whenever possible, to engage the church and its resources toward seeing that person take leadership in that particular realm." When an opportunity came up for Susan to attend a conference on the topic of pro-life ministry, North Way, under Jay's leadership, provided a scholarship for her to go. Michael decided to pay his way and go along for the conference, so he and Susan took a few days and flew down to Florida. On the flight, they overheard two college students talking in the row in front of them, and one said that if she ever got married and found out that the baby was not the gender she wanted, she would get an abortion.

The conference was held at Coral Ridge Presbyterian Church in Fort Lauderdale, led by Dr. D. James Kennedy. Coral Ridge was the hub of Dr. Kennedy's prominent television and radio ministry, and the conference brought in many notable speakers to focus on how the church could make a difference for the unborn and their mothers. One speaker was Curt Young, who was executive director of the Christian Action Council (CAC), which later became Care Net. Young presented a vision for pregnancy centers: places where women could go for counseling and resources when facing an unplanned pregnancy.

Along with exploring how churches could support and partner with such pregnancy centers, the conference presented other methods of ministry for the church to engage in. There were presentations about doing sidewalk counseling outside abortion clinics and even opportunities for attendees of the conference to go to local clinics and experience that scene firsthand.

Since North Way had sponsored Susan to attend the conference, she reported back to Jay and the elders on what she had learned and wrote a newsletter article about her experience. She shared about the college students they had heard talking on their flight to the conference and how on the way back they found themselves wishing they had another such opportunity, where they might have known better how to engage in a meaningful conversation on the topic.

North Way developed a prayerful presence outside Pittsburgh's abortion clinics. Sue Dawson remembers going to Wholey's for fish sandwiches after one of their first tries and sitting together, affected by what they had witnessed. They found that many women who walked into the clinics had an arm behind them, perhaps a boyfriend or a father directing them to the door. Though Roe v. Wade had supposedly been about a woman's choice, it didn't seem that many of these women wanted to be there. Michael says he still remembers some of the young women's faces as they looked for help.

North Way led a team of advocates, including people from other churches who would offer personal outreach and counseling to people right on the sidewalks. The team showed up every weekend to an abortion clinic that had recently opened in the Boggs building on the North Side, right on the corner where PNC Park stands today. Within a year, the clinic closed for lack of business. The lead abortion counselor had come to faith in Christ and renounced her work in the abortion industry. She started attending Covenant Church of Wilkinsburg and said specifically that it was a result of the witnessing and the love that she encountered from the people outside the abortion clinic. (The same building is currently owned by Smith Brothers Advertising, a company that is aware of the building's history and allows Christian ministries to use their rooftop facility for ministry.)

With North Way's support, Michael and Susan started meeting with some other couples from the church, including the Dawsons and the Speichers, to pray and talk about starting Pittsburgh's first pregnancy center. At first, they simply took out an ad in the yellow pages and ran a pregnancy hotline for women who didn't know where to turn for help. The team met with pastors from a number of other churches in Pittsburgh to raise support and formed a board of directors. Michael, still in his mid-twenties, served as the first board president.

Michael credits Susan for truly spearheading the effort and says, "It was clear that the spirit of the Lord was on Susan during that whole time period. There were a number of times on Sunday mornings there at Bradley's when Jay would want her to get up and give an update. She would start talking about the sanctity of life or unborn children. She would get choked up. It was evident that she was sensing God's heart related to the issue of abortion, and when you understand God's heart in it — rather than thinking of it solely as a political issue or a moral issue — that's the fuel that drives true gospel ministry."

The board received an anonymous gift of $5,000, which gave them the confidence to start searching for a building in which to do ministry. They brought on Amy Scheuring as executive director and opened the North Pittsburgh Crisis Pregnancy Center on Mother's Day of 1985. Since her time on the youth staff at Memorial Park, Amy had earned her Bachelor's in Psychology from West Virginia University and her Masters of Education and Counseling from the University of Pittsburgh. Michael says that Amy was a "true visionary" when it came to pro-life ministry.

In their first year, the pregnancy center saved four lives from abortion by coming alongside young pregnant women. One of these very first clients has stayed in touch until today with an ever-grateful heart. The same organization exists today in four locations as the Women's Choice Network (WCN) and now saves close to 400 lives a year. It has a full medical staff who offer pregnancy testing, sonograms, and STD testing and treatment free of charge, and a staff of trained advocates who counsel both women and men on their sexual health and their pregnancy options. WCN provides extended support through classes on relationships, pregnancy, and parenting, and connects clients with other resources that make a choice for parenting or adoption possible. It organizes and leads post abortion care groups and employs a team of speakers that gives hundreds of presentations a year to high school health classes in Pittsburgh area schools, helping students plan for healthy relationships as they begin dating. In 2020, WCN opened a consignment quality children's clothing store for its clients and the community of North Side. The store, called The Nest, is run by Lynne Workman.

Amy continues to lead the Women's Choice Network today, and what started as Jay's investment in Amy as a youth staff leader continues as a close friendship. WCN operates today with the support of dozens of churches, but North Way was key in getting it started and in equipping its leaders for ministry. WCN remains one of North Way's local missions partners, and each Mother's Day North Way members support WCN through a baby bottle fundraiser.

During the start of the pregnancy center, Michael was still working for the news station. While he was being prepared in multiple ways for a life calling he couldn't yet imagine, he also began to face a serious trial. He was noticing some pain in his wrists, and the pain gradually spread through all of his joints. Things worsened until he had difficulty just turning a doorknob or getting up off the floor. He was diagnosed with an advanced and fast-progressing case of rheumatoid arthritis.

In June of 1985, just a month after the pregnancy center opened, Michael went to St. Margaret's Hospital in Aspinwall to start chemotherapy treatments to try to arrest the course of the disease. His case was very severe and was likely to commit him to a wheelchair. The treatments might mitigate the disease for a time but held the risk for serious side effects and the possibility for the disease to return worse than before. Jay committed, along with his and Michael's small group, to fast and pray for two weeks for Michael's healing.

Though Michael couldn't work for weeks leading up to the treatments, Channel 11 never stopped his paychecks. At the hospital, Michael met many people with the same chronic disease. Many were in wheelchairs and described with honesty what Michael's future would most likely hold. The evening before the treatments were to begin, Michael was alone in his hospital room, waiting and praying.

As he prayed, Michael felt a significant warmth go through his body. Then he felt his symptoms relieve. The next morning, when the physician came into the room, he examined Michael. The swelling in Michael's joints had reduced and the redness was gone. His pain was alleviated. The doctor looked at Michael and said, "I don't know what happened here, you've improved so significantly I see no reason to start this treatment."

Michael continued to progress without any treatment to complete healing and the disease has never returned. This story of miraculous healing through the prayer of his North Way small group has followed Michael through his whole life.

From his first reading of John Powell's book to the conference in Ft. Lauderdale to the sidewalk ministry and the starting of the pregnancy center, Michael felt a clear and evident calling to make a difference in pro-life issues. In the Fall of '85, he was listening to a sermon tape from a national ministry and the preacher was talking about how many Christians just live from one weekend to the next, one paycheck to the next, without a vision or calling on their life. The tape suggested that many Christians haven't ever taken the time to ask, "God, what would you have me do?" Or, "How do you want to use my life?"

Michael realized he didn't want to be that kind of Christian and prayed, "God, use me however you want." As he prayed, Michael felt he was being pointed in a new direction and believed God was saying, "I want you to get involved in politics." Michael knew that this leading was different from his existing work in pro-life ministry and different from his work at the news station. He assumed it meant he should run for political office.

Michael shared this with Jay, and Jay and the rest of their men's group committed to pray for God's further direction. They also offered advice and guidance. Several months later, a man named Bob Slosser came to Pittsburgh on business. Slosser was the president of CBN University (now Regent University) and the author of several books, including *Miracle in Darien*. Since Jay was always eager to have people share who might bless or challenge North Way, he invited Slosser to speak at a

Thursday night event at North Way.

Susan happened to be busy that evening, but Michael decided to check out the event. When he arrived, Michael ran into Jay in the hallway, and Jay said, "Hey Michael, after the meeting's over I want you to stop by my office… I need to talk to you." Michael responded, "Okay."

Slosser spoke on the topic of the Presence of the Lord, focusing on Exodus 33. In this passage, God has tired of the stubbornness of His people and tells them to go on their way without Him. Moses humbly reminds God that the nation of Israel is His people and petitions God not to send them unless His presence goes with them. God not only relents, but also promises His goodness, mercy, and compassion. As Slosser brought the message to a close, he asked everyone to pray right where they were and ask God to provide His presence and guidance.

Slosser opened up the room for people to share what God was telling them and called on a number of people and shared a word of knowledge of what he believed God might be guiding them to do. Michael found himself hoping that Slosser didn't call on him to share because he was hearing a very clear direction and didn't know how he felt about it. Michael kept hearing strongly in his head, "Go to CBN University. Go to CBN University." Michael had never thought of going to graduate school. He hadn't enjoyed his time as an undergraduate, and he wasn't about to give a commercial for this man's school without knowing anything about it.

The meeting ended without Michael being called on, and

he said, "Oh, whatever," about the impression he had felt so strongly in the moment. He stopped by Jay's office as requested and said, "What's up, you wanted to talk to me?"

Jay said, "Yeah, you know, I spent the last couple days at a number of different events with Bob Slosser, and throughout the entire time I could not get your name out of my head that you should go to CBN University."

"Wow, well okay…" said Michael, and shared his own impression with Jay. "Maybe next year then?"

Jay said, "This seems like confirmation from God. If God's in this, and God's speaking to you, and I had this distinct impression… why not this Fall?"

Michael went for it, and though he did not have the best undergraduate record, CBN admitted him on probation. Michael took a graduate test to gain full admission and ended up with an academic scholarship. He quit his job at Channel 11 and enrolled in CBN's School of Public Policy. CBN was in Virginia Beach, Virginia, so Michael stepped down from the board of the pregnancy center and moved with Susan and their two children.

Many people in Michael's life felt this was an outrageous move, but Jay only encouraged him. Others would say, "That's really courageous to move away with two kids and no job." Being confident that this was God's leading, however, Michael felt it would take more guts to disobey than to obey. North Way provided some funding to help Michael in his training, seeing him as somewhat of a missionary to the political realm.

Michael graduated as the top student in his class, having

gained a Biblical foundation and premise for engagement in public policy and politics. When he started his degree, he imagined his goal would be to run for congress in Washington, D.C., but during his studies he came to appreciate the importance and significance of policy at the state level. When he graduated, he decided to move back to Pittsburgh to focus on the state of Pennsylvania.

Michael had worked in TV news in Norfolk, VA while he completed his degree and got hired back at Channel 11 when he moved back to Pittsburgh. Though he was determined to pursue his calling in politics, he ended up being offered another fulltime TV position in Ft. Lauderdale at the church where he had attended the conference with Susan. While he was considering accepting this position, Jay told a friend, Reid Carpenter, about Michael. Carpenter headed an organization called the Pittsburgh Leadership Foundation.

Carpenter passed Michael's name to someone in Lancaster County who had connections with the national organization Focus on the Family. Just as Michael was about to reluctantly accept the media position in Florida, he got a call from the guy in Lancaster saying, "Hey we're looking to start an organization in Pennsylvania focused on pro-life and pro-family issues and would love to talk to you about it."

Michael wasn't immediately offered a position since the idea was just in the works, but he liked the vision of an organization that would stand for Biblically based policies to strengthen families — an organization that could advocate for the sanctity of life and religious liberty in Pennsylvania.

Michael turned down the position in Florida and worked one more year at Channel 11 while the board was put together and money was being raised. When the Pennsylvania Family Institute was founded in Harrisburg a year later in 1989, the board offered Michael the position of founding president and CEO.

With the encouragement of Focus on the Family, the Pennsylvania Family Institute gave the church and Christians a voice in public policy related to issues that impact families, including the sanctity of life, education, marriage, and religious liberty. The Institute continues to operate today under Michael's leadership as a public policy organization that works with citizens and churches across the Commonwealth to encourage engagement, to build stronger families, and to develop an environment where the gospel can continue to be shared. Its vision statement is, "A Pennsylvania where God is honored, religious freedom flourishes, families thrive, and life is cherished."

Though it has been many years since Michael and Susan have attended North Way in person, the work they are doing in the state capitol upholds the liberty that North Way continues to enjoy. Michael and Susan's work is indeed consistent with that of missionaries who were raised and sent by North Way. While he continues to work in the political realm to which he has been called, Michael is proud to affirm the core values of North Way. When interviewed for this book, he graciously shared the following:

Over the years, I've had people ask me about the work that I did in the TV business, about how I got into the Pennsylvania Family Institute, how I've done pro-life work, or even about my healing. The thing that I have consistently expressed back to them is the critical importance of Biblical fellowship: to be part of a local church where people know the calling on your life, that you are reading and studying the Bible with other people, and getting the input and guidance of the pastor and others for your life, and to know that you are in a place where people will pray for you.

I've been away from North Way since 1989, so that's 31 years, and yet I would still point to Jay Passavant and North Way Christian Community as sort of my home church: as the place where God provided the guidance, leadership, foundation, fellowship, healing, and passion that I still cherish to this day — impacting not only me, but my own family and grandchildren, all because of the investment I made in finding a church and planting in that church.

In spite of flaws and the imperfect nature of every human being and every institution, planting in a quality local church that preaches the Bible and believes the gospel is — in terms of spiritual growth and your life — the most important thing you can do in your life; putting faith in God and trusting in others to help; being part of a body; and being transparent and

161

open about your flaws, your needs, and your pursuits.

~~~

North Way continued to grow in its use of the arts in worship, building on what the worship leaders had learned from the symposium mentioned in the previous chapter. Jan had met worship leaders from other churches at that symposium, including those from Amplify Church, Covenant Church of Pittsburgh, and Cornerstone Ministries. She began building relationships with them. Jan spearheaded yearly symposia to bring them all back together and allow the opportunity to learn and equip volunteers together. Each year, they brought in speakers and bands to share on countless topics to build worship for their region through fresh insight.

North Way and these other churches started doing large scale worship productions together. After putting together a program, they would perform it at each church so all the congregations could benefit. Steve Fry was a popular songwriter at the time and created an album called *We Are Called* and another called *Thy Kingdom Come*. North Way and the other churches put together a production of *Thy Kingdom Come* and rented Heinz Hall downtown, much to the delight of the musicians.

"Think about that — we just rented it!" says Jay. "It was the only place that was large enough. There was no confusing us with the symphony, but it was worshipful; it was good worship."

Jay was in the habit of meeting with the pastors of these and other churches. Combined worship nights and productions strengthened the partnerships and allowed for mutual influence as each church sought how best to experience community and how to reach the city of Pittsburgh. Beyond just having good worship for Sunday services, North Way was helping spread a fresh emphasis on the importance of worship generally.

North Way hosted many Christian bands, and other churches were invited attend these shows. North Way was one of the first stops for bands like Love Song as they worked their way East from California. These concerts continued to fuel North Way's love for worship and gave the worship leaders access to new ideas and styles.

Jan, with support from Susie and other volunteer leaders, cultivated gifts in the youth of the church. They put on a series of musicals with the elementary children at North Way. The musicals were written by a talented writer named Dian Layton. One was called *Seeker*, about a boy named Seeker and his allegorical adventures in the "Kingdom." These productions involved a large cast of students and called for extensive volunteer engagement to build sets and sew costumes. The musicals were well-received at North Way, and other churches began to attend as word spread.

Many North Way children got to experience acting, singing, teamwork, and working with adults, not to mention the opportunity of seeing God use them. Susie often said,

"Worship starts young." She believed that if you built the practice of worship — and leading worship — into young hearts, it would go with them into adulthood. Few things, she says, would build young people's faith more than seeing their gifts be used by God.

By 1987, Susie was on staff as Assistant Worship Director to Jan. Together they pursued worship: what it was, what it meant, and what God was doing across the nation in and through it. Ray Speicher remembers this collaboration between Jan and Susie and says, "They had a work ethic that couldn't be beat — they were a heck of a good pair!"

Jay was closely involved in this process of discovery and made it a priority to take the worship staff to conferences and churches across the country in search of new ideas and God's heart. As they saw worship music exploding in the '80s, Jay asked, "Why wouldn't God give *us* songs birthed out of what He's doing in *our* midst?"

To start, Jan brought in a songwriter or two, but Susie began taking time alone every Thursday afternoon to try her own hand. She quickly discovered one of her greatest gifts. Jan saw the songs Susie was writing and said, "Let's use them in worship!" Most songs came to Susie as she spent time in prayer and scripture at a piano. Many were based on Bible passages, and each was a testimony of Susie's own walk with God. More than 50 of Susie's original songs ended up being used in worship at North Way.

As a mother of three young children, it wasn't always easy for Susie to get her alone time to write, but Jay and Carol would let Susie use their piano to get away sometimes. One Thursday afternoon, she was at Jay and Carol's while the Passavants were out, but after a couple hours she hadn't seemed to get anything from God. She stopped by Kmart on the way home, and a song finally hit her all at once.

"Jesus is my Rock, Jesus is my Shield, Jesus is my Righteousness to Him alone I yield…"

"No, Lord!" Susie cried, in the middle of the aisle. "Not now! I won't remember it!"

"No evil can befall, when on Jesus' name I call. No power of hell will get me down… Jesus my joy and crown. Jesus is my Rock."

Susie managed to get the song down, and it was a hit at North Way. The team called it Susie's "Kmart special."

'Jesus is My Rock' and thirteen more of Susie's originals ended up becoming part of North Way's third recording project called, *Journey Through the Veil. Journey* was a praise and worship experience based on the Old Testament tabernacle, using all of the art forms they had developed. This work included songs by Jan and Jay.

The theme song for *Journey* was called 'Enter Through the Veil.' Susie says that when God gave her that song one day, she wept for two hours. "It was HIS heart: for people to just want to come and commune with Him." The song went:

Won't you enter through the veil and see

  The splendor of My majesty

Won't you linger at the throne of grace
    And savor My embrace
Won't you come and place your hand in Mine,
    Know me as Your love divine
Look into my Holy face, become My dwelling place.

Won't you hurry to Me and worship at My feet
I long to just be with you and make your joy complete
Search the narrow pathway, rise now from your rest
Set aside the manna, you'll find me in Me My best.

Once you have been with Me and know Me as 'I AM'
You'll be prepared more fully to represent the Lamb
Your eyes will see more clearly than they ever have before
Enlightened by My glory, you'll shine for me once more.

Susie says, "I just felt God's incredible heart for his people and his sadness that they weren't coming to commune with Him. It was just that unction for people to enter, enter, enter through the veil; don't stay in these outer courts just kinda playing around with me, ya know, *come*, and let's be hand in hand, heart to heart."

Susie says that this was the place that Jay wanted people to journey to. Jay loved *Journey* and still today speaks of it as one of the most creative and heart-moving works he's ever heard. Jay says that Susie was far ahead of her time. "She was doing things and introducing people to worship in a way that you now see with Hillsong, or Bethel, or Gateway — huge music ministries! We were none of those and had limited resources."

In 1990, Jan stepped down from the head worship director position to be part of a new church North Way was planting. For the next few years, Susie learned great flexibility under multiple other worship directors. For a year and a half, David Ed held the position. Susie describes him as "crazy gifted" and says he brought a different style.

David led large scale classical music events at the big hall at St. Teresa's new building. He rented out the Manchester Craftsmen's Guild downtown and the Chatham University auditorium for the church youth to do musicals. In December of 1991, David conducted the North Way Chamber Choir in a performance of J. S. Bach's 'Magnificat in D Major,' a monumental task for a church choir. The following December, they performed Ralph Vaughan Williams's 'Mass in G Minor.' Susie learned from David's approach, but he didn't stay in the position very long due to having such a different philosophy than the church had built regarding worship.

After David, Lee Kricher came in part time to fill in until they could hire someone else. Susie supported him until they hired David Fleming, who led worship for the next two years. Dave was a good fit but soon felt the call to do more preaching and pastoring. He ended up being one of North Way's main teaching pastors in the following season, and when it came time to search once again for a new worship director, he went to Jay and said, "Why in the world are you hiring somebody else when Susie is here and she can do all this?"

Susie's appointment was one that would last and one that reflected North Way's overall strategy during this time of raising people up into staff positions rather than searching for the biggest name outside the church.

By the late '80s, North Way was widely recognized as a place where big ideas were welcome. Since the average unchurched person wouldn't suddenly decide to go to church any given week, North Way was open to ideas and events that would bridge a gap and allow the church to build relationships with the broader community. Instead of expecting the community to always come to the church, North Way would bring unique opportunities to the community.

In 1991, they hosted a Christian bodybuilding team from Texas called Strike Force. The group reached out to North Way, and North Way was enthusiastic to have them. The group started with a Sunday evening performance at the church for a full house of adults and children. Then North Way helped facilitate getting the team into the local middle schools and high schools every week day. The team would perform their feats of strength and talk about good values, but then they would invite the students to see an evening show at North Way where they would share the full gospel. Scores of unchurched youth came to the evening shows and came to know Christ.

Keith Craft, the founder of Strike Force, was six-foot six-inches tall and 260 pounds, a former Dallas Cowboy, and also a pastor. An article in the *North Hills News Record* showed dramatic photos of Craft and his team splitting stacks of bricks with their arms, some of which were on fire. One photo caption indicates that Craft curled 420 pounds five times after smashing blocks of ice. The article shared about the team and their performances at North Way and quoted Craft saying, "Everything we do is symbolic. When I break a brick wall, it's breaking that wall of sin and fear."

These kinds of events communicated the gospel to young people in an exciting way and got them fired up about being Christians. 20 years earlier, Jay ran his first big ministry event at his college, and it was a strong man doing similar feats. He likely never imagined that he would end up pastoring a non-denominational church that would be able to host events like this for thousands of local students and their families, but God used even that early experience to prepare Jay, opening his mind to the many ways He can work.

North Way was open to big ideas from its own members as well, and Jay and the elders focused on equipping the members of the church to accomplish what God laid on their hearts. When people came to the staff with an idea, instead of the staff saying, "Okay, we'll get that going," they'd say, "What do you need to make it happen? If God put it on your heart, He'll guide you and we'll help."

Jay says he could never take credit for how North Way has

grown and reached people in so many different ways. "I couldn't come up with so many things."

North Way's Christmas banquet doubled in attendance the second year they held it, from 200 to 400 people. We read some in Chapter Three about how much food was supplied the first year and all of the special gifts that were made and distributed to the city's homeless and needy, but that was only the beginning. North Way wanted to be known as a suburban church that truly cared for the inner city. The banquets allowed the church to partner with dozens of inner-city ministries and show support for those ministries by caring for their people. At first, word of the banquet spread only by mouth, but Jay had a friend at the Christian radio station.

Dick Hatch had WORD-FM's 3 to 6 p.m. slot every day, and he appreciated the vision for the banquet. Dick had Jay on a number of times to share about it, which got the word out to other churches. Many churches were intrigued and began sending volunteers and asking if they could partner. The Christmas banquets already allowed North Way to bless the ministries they supported and all the homeless and needy people they fed — Michael Geer played in the band at the banquets and remembers reaching many families of Pittsburgh's incarcerated. Now North Way found an unforeseen benefit in inspiring other churches to reach the city as well. Each person who came sat at a table with a ministry they were invited by, and the ministries grew as a result.

The third year the banquet hit 1,000 attendees, and the

fourth it doubled yet again to 2,000. In the fifth year, the crowd doubled one more time and they fed 4,000 people at the old David L. Lawrence Convention Center. People came from all over the city, some connected with North Way's local mission partners, some not. The banquet was the first thing on the eleven o'clock news that night.

500 volunteers helped, not only from North Way, but also from many other Pittsburgh churches. Many of the volunteers had never met, but they all showed up in black pants and a white top and served together. The union workers who cooked the meal suspended their regular rate of $19 a head and did it for $7, and then North Way and the other churches served the meal themselves.

After sharing the Christmas meal, they had some moments of worship and thanksgiving with a full band. Then Jay stepped up to speak. Though North Way was growing steadily, they were nowhere near as large as that sea of 4,000 people. Jay felt a nudge in his heart from God, "One day you'll be speaking to this many people every week."

Jay shared the gospel and invited people to receive Christ. Since there were people from the local ministries and churches at each table, the attendees were encouraged to let someone at their table know if they had received Christ. People got connected with ministries who weren't connected yet, and each person, whether there to serve or be served, seemed to come away loving it.

They gave out some awards and celebrated leaders from the local ministries. The whole event not only fed and loved thousands of needy people from Pittsburgh, but also encouraged the ministries that did this day by day throughout the year. North Way wanted to show these faithful workers that the church wasn't just supportive from a distance, but that it actually cared for the people they cared for. The event wasn't about building North Way — it was about fueling what the ministries were doing. When the banquet was over, the people who attended returned to the ministries they came with.

Each person who attended was not only fed, but was also sent home with a 15 to 18 pound turkey. *4,000 turkeys!* Each person also went home with a sizable bag of thoughtful gifts. When North Way realized that 4,000 people would be attending that year, they knew that would cost about $65,000. Jay went on the radio station to ask for donations, and they were able to gather what they needed from individuals and local businesses. Any excess donations were given to the ministries, not to North Way.

The whole event was an expression to the city that the church cared for the most vulnerable. The fact that the event was covered on the two biggest nightly news stations was no small thing in Pittsburgh, says Jay, a city which leads the country in local news viewership. The city was watching, and it saw the church serving — literally — just like the Jesus they preached. "Almost everything you do gets criticized," says Jay, "But that didn't get criticized."

The following year, 1989, the attendance was similar, but down just a bit to 3,500 due to some bitter winter weather. This was the last year North Way hosted the banquet as the union could no longer offer a discount on the food, but over those five years North Way had strengthened important relationships with its ministry partners and with other churches. Together, they had fed thousands upon thousands of folks who could not afford a warm Christmas meal and sent them home with turkeys and presents.

An article appeared in *The Pittsburgh Press* on Wednesday, December 20th, 1989 talking about the banquet. "County Commissioner Larry Dunn and Steelers defensive lineman Tim Johnson spoke to the crowd," the article by Matthew P. Smith says. "After the dinner and some hearty Christmas caroling, the church gave away 2,000 toys and 1,650 food certificates. 'It puts together scores and scores of different people who come together to say we care about each other,' Passavant said."

The Christmas Banquet was actually the secondary topic of the article quoted above — its headline and main topic was "McCandless church to build a multimillion-dollar complex." Events like the Christmas Banquets put North Way in public view, and multiple newspapers were now keeping a close eye on what would come out of North Way next. Another article, below, appeared in the *North Journal* on March 5th, 1992, along with a photo of Jay preaching. It offered an overview of North Way's story, one that's well worth including here before we move onto North Way's next chapter:

IN SEARCH OF GOD'S HEART:

North Way Christian Community offers love and
acceptance
By Janet Jelinek, Staff writer

The same spirit that drew nine men together a decade ago to establish a church after God's own heart in the North Hills is alive and kicking at North Way Christian Community in Wexford.

From its humble beginnings in a meeting room at Northway Mall to its present location in the former Bradley House North off Route 19, the 11-year-old church continues to provide healing to a hurting world in an atmosphere of love and acceptance.

"Most people say that when they come they are drawn to the ministry because of the love of God they feel and the sense that God's presence is truly here," says the Rev. Scott McCabe, associate pastor of the 2,500-member, non-denominational church. "Many people come because they are truly finding their needs are being met."

North Way member Bonnie Marsh of McCandless has found not only a place to grow in the Christian faith she discovered as a high school student, but also the courage to go on despite the obstacles of raising two daughters alone.

A college friend of McCabe, the unemployed single mother began attending the church last October, bringing with her the pain of a rocky marriage that ended six years ago in divorce and the self-defeating patterns affecting her life as the daughter of an alcoholic father.

"I was looking for a church where I could feel comfortable, where I would fit in as a single-parent family," Ms. Marsh says.

The tools she's found through a support group at North Way known as Generations, which ministers to persons from alcoholic and dysfunctional families, has renewed her faith as she confronts the issues that stifled it for so long.

"I'm being challenged to see God as a loving God. Coming from a dysfunctional family and a broken marriage, I've tended to see God as my father or my former husband treated me. Now, I'm seeing God in a whole different light. I'm able to release myself to trust him more."

Dedicated to meeting the needs of people within the church, the community, and the world, North Way supports a host of ministries — from a children's program that brings the Word of God to life for several hundred children every week to the 18 full-time missionaries who serve communities from New York

City to India.

Last year, the church launched its first sister church in Moon Township and is currently planning to construct a larger facility in Pine Township.

Opportunities for individuals of all ages to live out their faith have evolved over the years since that first meeting in January of 1981, when the Rev. Dr. Jay Passavant, senior pastor at North Way, was joined by eight others to pray about and discuss the call of God on his life.

An ordained Presbyterian minister, Passavant realized then — and continues to realize — that he was not alone in his desire to have an "authentic spiritual experience" in a region dominated by traditional religious institutions.

"North Way began as a church for a community of believers committed to authentic relationships in Jesus Christ, along with a sense of care and concern for the people around us," says Passavant.

"To see that grow and develop in so many people's lives over the past 10 years has reconfirmed that this search is in the heart of many people."

For Bonnie Marsh, a search for a church is ended but the continual search for God's will in her life, as well as the joy of sharing her faith with others, has just begun.

"I'm being challenged to really grow, but North Way is enabling me to do that," she says. "As I'm being ministered to, it helps me to minister to other people."

CHAPTER FIVE:
EXPANSION

BUILDING

Though flourishing in creative expressions of its values and calling, the church began to face a major challenge in trying to accommodate the number of people who were coming to call North Way their home. From preaching the gospel and teaching the Word, to ministering to one another through community groups and worship, North Way was caring effectively for the *hearts* of all those God was sending. They did, however, need enough space for their *bodies* as well.

In the summer of 1991, North Way was pursuing the purchase of land contiguous with the facility at The Bradley House. While the leadership was going through the labor-intensive process of getting approval from 50 or so residential neighbors to build a new non-profit space on the additional land, they remained open to other options. They were not overly enthusiastic about the possibilities this land afforded, but they couldn't seem to find anything better.

One view suggested that North Way shouldn't worry about its particular location or property, but Jay and the elders began to value the concept of God's people being visible in the center of culture. North Way's first decade had been all about rediscovering the Biblical elements of fellowship and outreach that had seemingly been forgotten by many of the steepled cathedrals that rose high above the housetops. But now that the church was well established in the North Hills community, the leadership recognized the witness it might be for the community to associate a credible ministry with a building.

One North Way member felt she had a specific word from the Lord that North Way would become "a vision on a hill." The land adjoining The Bradley House was somewhat hidden and made this sentiment hard to imagine. Though the church had looked for two years and found nothing better, Jay continued to drive up and down Route 19 all summer, looking for alternatives.

One property Jay had looked at previously was a recently closed drive-in theater on Route 19. The screen was still up, but by nature, the theater was basically an empty field. The area was undeveloped, with a swamp below and hills above, but it had plenty of potential. The location in Wexford was ideal, right between Cranberry and McCandless. McCandless was already a stable area, and since Interstate 279 had been built recently, Cranberry was starting to explode with growth.

Unfortunately, when Jay had talked with the owner, Bucky McAfee, he found that the land was already under right of first refusal with Oxford Properties, which intended to build a large shopping mall there. McAfee was the owner of McAfee Automotive, the garage adjacent to the drive-in property, and was being paid a significant fee by Oxford just to hold the property. Since a year or so had passed since that initial conversation and the property remained empty, Jay decided to give it one more try.

He and one of the elders stopped by to see McAfee again on a bright, sunny day. McAfee was working under a car and pushed himself out from under it and wiped his hands on a red rag. Jay expressed their continued interest in the property behind the garage, and McAfee said, "Hey, I like you guys. And I'm so tired of waiting for Oxford to do anything, and they didn't pay me my fee to keep this right of first refusal. The price is 1.3 million for the 13 acres, and I'll sell it to you right away."

To this day, Jay doesn't believe that Mr. McAfee expected them to have the money; however, North Way had already raised about $750,000 through a campaign called "Prelude to a Promise." It wasn't a problem to get a loan from the bank for the rest. The elders all approved, and they only had to get permission from the town. It wasn't easy to ask a rapidly growing township to approve a church building on a valuable commercial lot, but Mr. McAfee was on the board for the approval process and that hurdle was soon behind them. North Way closed on the property within 30 days. Jay says it became the "real estate bombshell that hit the North Hills" because Oxford was pretty upset.

Though it was just an empty lot at the time, it was on a hill and it was visible from the road. It was surrounded by nothing but hills and trees — nothing to the North, nothing to the South, nothing across the street, and nothing behind. With a bit of imagination, however, the location seemed like the perfect place. The elders felt it was obvious that God had put this opportunity in front of them and accepted it as a gift from the Lord.

Jay says that countless people have since said, "Boy, you guys were really lucky to get this piece of ground!"

"Well," he says in return, "Let me tell you how that 'luck' started out!"

The next steps for Jay and the elders were to select a building committee and raise money for the building project. Jay describes church building projects as "fertile soil for discontentment and disagreement," but the elders had recently been through some significant testing and had established and signed a "leadership covenant" to keep them open, honest, and faithful to each other and the unity of the church. Jay wrote a full article about this covenant strategy in 2002, which was published in *Ministries Today* magazine under the title, 'Stop Strife Before It Starts.'

In the introduction to the article, Jay said, "The single most destructive force affecting a congregation is usually unleashed from within. And it usually has to do with one simple thing: the tongue." He shared the story of how some personnel changes 10 years into the North Way's history threatened to derail the ministry and talked about how the elders came back to a place of unity and together wrote the following seven points:

1. We will pursue honesty, openness, and grace in our relationships.

2. We will see that hurts, offenses, and differences are reconciled quickly.

3. We will honor and cover one another in word and action.

4. We will not entertain accusations against one another.

5. We will hear one another's opinions, honor one another's differences, hold love supreme, and wholeheartedly embrace our collective decisions.

6. We will meet together monthly to pray, share, worship, support, and pursue accountability.

7. We will remain faithful to intentional, personal evangelism.

Jay says in the article:

When we originally agreed to our covenant, we took a week to prayerfully confirm each of the points and then met together once again to sign a copy of the covenant, which was later framed and hung in our boardroom. We then had copies of it reduced and laminated so that it could be carried around in our Bibles, purses, and wallets as a reminder of our commitments to one another.

Few moments in my ministry have been more powerful than the time when every single pastor, elder, and spouse put their signature on this document. Something was broken in the heavenlies that has released our ministry to a deeper degree of love and fruitfulness.

North Way has never had a church split, but there were some close calls, including the near exodus of a third of the congregation when one pastor convinced many he was a prophet worthy to be followed. Mac McCabe says that it is worth noting that the church withstood significant challenges like these with the help of the Holy Spirit. His wife Susie wrote the following about Jay's leadership in this area of unity:

There were several challenging seasons where Jay's gift of "win-win" was so evident. I believe it was because he has a mercy gift and a lot of ability to listen and seek to understand. In watching him navigate the challenges of leadership over the years, he always took the high road and would meet with people, unveil vision, and when there was push-back, respect the other party but stay committed to what he believed was God's direction, yet submitting to his Elders Council. He averted these potential splits by his heart to have unity. Yes, we lost some people at these intersections, but unity was preserved to God's glory, and we were able to move ahead. I believe this is one of the things that allowed God's favor to be upon us for the long haul. Jay would sacrificially lean into difficulties, take the hits that are often given, and ask for wisdom for resolution. This held North Way well over the years and created a steadfastness that people could feel as they became part of the body of Christ at North Way.

In December of 1991, just months after finalizing the purchase of the land, North Way began publishing a seasonal newspaper as a way to carry information about its many ministries to the people of North Way. The paper was called *The North Way Observer*, and its inaugural issue announced the first steps for the upcoming building project, along with a report on the first Sunday services of a new church they had planted in Coraopolis, West Ridge Christian Community. *The Observer* included letters and updates from the missionaries and ministries North Way supported and also an announcement about the "new and improved" children's ministry, including the introduction of a "KiDZ in Worship" service.

Jay's welcome letter in the inaugural issue of *The Observer* was called, 'The Season of Mega.' He expressed his desire for North Way to see all that God was doing in its midst, saying:

As you'll read in the numerous articles contained in this first *Observer*, we serve a great God who has changed a great number of lives through a host of ministries, services, and many giving hearts. I think it's time that the word be spread even a bit more effectively concerning all that our great God is doing!

By the way, the profusion of the term 'great' in this article is no accident (nor evidence of a limited vocabulary!). Rather, it is to reinforce the fact that the New Testament frequently uses the word in Greek, *mega*, to describe the workings of God in His people. The exact translation of that word in English is the word '*great!*' In that sense, I am thrilled to be part of a *mega* church that is serving a *mega* God who is capable of meeting a *mega* number of needs among His people! Read on and enjoy the evidence of the fruit of God's blessing and presence among us!

The front-page article from that first issue of *The Observer* provides us with a good introduction to many aspects of the building project that North Way was undertaking, including the mention of one of its most integral characters, Roy Thompson.

PRELUDE OVER. PROMISE HERE.

After three years of waiting on the Lord, North Way Christian Community is now on the threshold of realizing the promise of being used as a light in North Pittsburgh. A Starlight to be exact.

On September 21, Church leaders closed the real estate deal whereby North Way became the owner of what used to be the Starlight Drive-In.

Located on Route 19 between Wexford and Cranberry, this property in recent years was owned by Dolores and William McAfee and was used to house her residence and an auto body repair shop. The property (map at right) is 13.5 acres of basically level ground right on the highway. Topographic and environmental studies indicate that this piece of property will be relatively easy to develop.

A crowd of 200 or more people gathered on October 13th to consecrate this property for God's use. After singing, sharing the vision together, and corporate prayer, small groups of believers walked around the property praying. Some groups prayed for other property issues to be resolved, others prayed for the highway barrier to be opened, and yet others prayed for wisdom in designing the actual building itself. Pastor John Syes had a powerful word from God, whereby he proclaimed, "I have said in times past that I will send you all you will care for, and you have been faithful. I now give you this land so you can expand your ability to care. Concern yourself with caring, and I will build your building."

Early in November, Pastor Jay Passavant initiated the final phase of "Prelude to a Promise" capital fund drive.

He challenged the North Way community to finalize the year by either completing their "Prelude pledge gifts" or giving to the new building fund. In order to finish the year with resounding victory, Pastor Jay believes the Lord for $300,000 in Building Fund and Prelude Gifts. As of this publication, $16,834.47 has been given toward this goal. Fund drive coordinator David Van Gorder indicates that meeting this goal will "keep North Way right on track as its building program heads into 1992."

A new Development Committee under the leadership of Roy Thompson is just now beginning to look into what kind of building will ultimately end up being constructed. According to Thompson, "We are just now beginning to explore various options that we will be submitting to the elders." However, he says that the committee is hoping to select an architect by the end of the year. He says, "It's a little early to be speculating about types of buildings." Thompson has asked the entire North Way Christian Community to be in prayer regarding this project. As Pastor Jay wrote in the *North Way Notes* on October 19th, those that attended the dedication prayer gathering, "left the property site with a satisfying sense that we were experiencing at least the first phase of God's fulfilled promise to us."

Roy Thompson had come to North Way from St. Stephen's

Episcopalian Church. St. Stephens is a historic church in the traditional and affluent community of Sewickley and had been growing in new ways under the leadership of evangelical priest John Guest. Though Roy was devoted to membership there for years and helped run the youth group, he heard about North Way and decided to give it a try.

"First time I heard Jay speak, I said, 'This is where I want to be.'" says Roy. "I just really loved his teaching. And we became pretty good friends." Roy's process of coming to faith had been a gradual one, and he said that sometimes he felt left out that he didn't get a flash of lightning. He had grown at St. Stephens, but there was something about Jay's approach to Scripture that caused him to start thinking and studying more on his own. Instead of following whatever the most recent fads were in Christianity, Roy pressed into a mature commitment to his faith in a way that impacted his whole life.

Along with growing his faith, God was preparing Roy through his professional life. By the time North Way was ready for its building project, Roy was president of a family company that did roofing and siding and had accumulated 30 years of experience as a subcontractor. He was accustomed to running things and managing construction projects around the country and even overseas. When Jay was looking for someone to head up the building project, Roy was the first person he thought of.

When it came to forming a building committee, Jay took a different approach than most churches and nonprofits. "Jay is one of the smart people," Roy says. "One of the things that happens a lot in nonprofits is they end up going to the biggest donors — the bankers and lawyers — and say, 'You're on the committee to build the building.' Well, they don't know the first thing about building. That's why contractors love bidding on schools and churches and all this sort of stuff because they know whoever's going to be on the committee has no clue what they're doing. And they can get all the extras in the world — they'll make tons of money! And Jay didn't go that way — he went to two of us. Jack Lightbody and myself. And we were the ones who he put in charge of building it."

Jack Lightbody was a commercial developer and contractor who built office buildings for Prudential Financial. He had built a number of high rises around the country and had come to Pittsburgh to build a multimillion-dollar, 50 story high-rise downtown. Originally from Southern California, Jack and his wife Katie checked out North Way after learning that Jay was a graduate of Fuller Theological Seminary. Jack and Katie became members and dear friends of North Way and remained involved through small groups and more for the next decade.

When North Way was hitting a myriad of obstacles in the planning process for the building, Jay approached Jack and said, "Jack, I can't begin to pay you what you might make from Prudential, but is there any way you'd consider becoming our project manager for this building as part of our team?"

Jack agreed, bringing invaluable connections, knowledge, and leadership to the project. Jack and Roy hadn't met before this project, but Roy was so glad they brought Jack on. Roy says, "I can tell you, we could not have done this, not survived without Jack Lightbody. As far as I'm concerned, he was the real hero of the whole thing. I just came along to do what I did. Jack was the guy who really helped put it on the map."

While Roy focused on contracting as the owner's representative, Jack ran more of the financial side of things as project manager. Roy says that Jack wasn't afraid to ruffle feathers when it came to the budget. "People wanted to spend a lot of money we didn't have, and he wouldn't let them. So they'd try bringing it to Jay, and Jay was notorious for saying 'Yes,' and Jack would say, 'No, we don't have the money for it.'"

Roy and Jack built a lifelong friendship through the building project, though Jack has since moved to North Carolina. "I just can't say enough about what Jack did for us. He's my hero. I just, he's a wonderful guy, a great friend. The two of us, we complimented each other."

Jay says, "Jack was also a friend to me and would often be on the lookout for needs that I might have with my growing family where he was able to access some of his connections and resources to help us when we faced some speed bumps. Jack had an awareness of the amount of stress that a project like this could potentially put on a Senior Pastor and went out of his way to absorb as much of that pressure, decision making, and resourcing as he possibly could."

Jay says that Jack was not afraid in any circumstance to put on his "work clothes" and get out and pick up a shovel or a rake, a pair of gloves or boots to demonstrate *volunteerism* right alongside many who wanted to make some sort of contribution to the construction of North Way's facility. "Jack was always available to help people with personal needs and was able to marshal an 'army of volunteers' to do everything from the initial cleaning and raking of the construction site all the way through to the final bits of landscaping and beautifying the campus and the building itself whenever professional help was not in the budget and could be accomplished by dedicated volunteers."

Jay comments further, "I was indebted to both Jack and Roy in the way that they championed the development of North Way's physical location and did so with an extremely tight budget and under pretty difficult conditions in a relatively short period of time."

The project North Way had in mind would involve a significant amount of debt and require no small dose of faith. Roy told Jay right from the start, "The only way I will do this is if you, Jack Lightbody, and me sit down once a week and just talk about and pray about what's happening." With regular prayer and communication, they proceeded.

They hired Williams-Treblecock-Whitehead as the architect firm, with Paul Whitehead doing the design. Roy says that Whitehead wanted to create the Taj Mahal and that he had to knock him down a couple times and remind him they just needed a place to worship. Whitehead's vision ended up balancing out well with Roy's practicality. Jay is glad to this day that they went with a proper architect, even though it was more expensive. He says that while most churches would pay less and let the builder build in his own style, working with a reputable architect allowed them to design the church to function for many future generations without growing outdated.

They originally hired Figgins Construction to be the builder. Roy and Jack both knew Dave Figgins well and knew him to be an honest contractor. Roy says Figgins was a great place to start, which during the project was bought by Trafalgar House Construction. "It was just a good fit," says Roy. "I was able to use the architect in conjunction with the contractor. We had a budget, we were able to control Paul — I mean, he had some beautiful designs — we were able to control Paul and bring him down to what we have today."

By Fall of 1992, the building committee was ready to share the design with the congregation in another issue of *The Observer.* The front-page article came with a number of computerized architectural renderings of a building that would be immediately recognizable to today's North Way members, though the lot at this point was still an empty field. Here is the article:

THE PROMISE UNFOLDS
Building Committee Hard at Work

Imagine, if you will, what you experienced when you either bought or built your own home. Now, take that times 50 and you will perhaps get a sense for what our brothers on the Building Committee are going through.

Since the last edition of the *Observer* came out, Roy Thompson, Frank Madia, Rich Beck, Jack Lightbody,

Dan Flora, Pastor Jay, and a covey of consultants have circumnavigated the design, approval, and contract planning process. There have been many meetings with architects, planning commissions, Township officials, traffic officials, and potential subcontractors. The result has been an opening of the final chapter in the planning process.

North Way is now poised to see the "Promise" unfold. In the next few months the Building Committee expects to see a number of key elements in this process begin to converge. Obtaining the necessary permits is well under way. The traffic issues are soon to be resolved. The final architectural plans are being drawn. And the financial program is about to come to fruition.

Committee Chairman Roy Thompson commented recently that, "Our challenge in fulfilling this promise is to be the best possible stewards of the resources that God has and will provide. In that capacity our team is continually searching for the best quality and price in our negotiations for products and services to be incorporated into our new facility." Jack Lightbody added that, "It would amaze most people just how much work is involved in a project like this. Beyond that, I have to say that I've never worked with a greater bunch of guys on this kind of project, and I've worked on a few. Our prayer is that God would confirm to everyone at North Way that this is the building He wants, and now is the time He wants it to happen."

In that light, the Building Committee forges ahead every week with bidding, negotiating, and preparing so that this very important project for the Kingdom of God can come to the North Hills with maximum impact and efficiency.

Pastor Jay summed up his thoughts at a recent breakfast meeting at Denny's by commenting that, "God has impressed upon my heart that we are truly on the threshold of seeing the promise of a generational church unfold. This vision will lay the foundation that ensures a strong and healthy spiritual future for our children and their children for generations to come."

The Building Committee urges the entire community here at North Way to be in serious intercessory prayer for the following:

1. That all the parties addressing traffic issues will come to consensus.

2. That the Township will approach the permit process openly and with the best interests of the community at heart.

3. That all the contractors and designers would communicate efficiently and would work well together.

4. That our Building Committee would have God's

wisdom as it begins the implementation phase of this very important project.

By the holiday edition of *The Observer* just a few months later, the Building Committee was able to report significant breakthroughs on all the prayer requests above. One article titled "Barrier Broken!" detailed how North Way and the township had come together on the issue of traffic patterns. Steven Victor of Steven Victor Associates, Landscape Architects had been hired as a consultant to obtain the building approvals.

To provide access to the eventual building, Wallace Road needed to be moved 400 feet north. This would allow for easy access from north and south off of Route 19. North Way also agreed with the township on the eventual need for a traffic signal at the new "plus" intersection. Pine Township and PennDOT agreed with the plans that Victor designed, providing North Way would construct and pay for the new intersection.

Another article in this same issue of *The Observer* titled 'Financial Victory Just Around the Corner' shared the progress of North Way's financial campaign for the building project called "Opening Our Doors." After the initial weekend of the campaign, over $2,550,000 had been pledged over the next three years, and more pledges were coming in daily. A chart and table showed an encouraging picture of the goals and actual commitments of the campaign, along with the promise that,

"The finance group is currently investigating all possible avenues for financing the new building, with an eye to keeping interest and long-term debt to a minimum."

While all kinds of work were going into the building plans, North Way continued to care for its people and serve the community. The building project was one that would involve years of planning and work, but many other things were happening. Later in this chapter, we will explore North Way's heart and work in the areas of worship and missions, which were alive and well in the early '90s, but I'd like to take a moment from the building progress to mention one special event.

The same issue of *The Observer* that held the two articles mentioned above had an advertisement on the back with a photo of a familiar face. The ad said, "Come and hear Billy Graham at Three Rivers Stadium, Pittsburgh, PA, June 2-6, 1993. 7:30 nightly, Wednesday through Saturday. 4:00 Sunday." Special guests would include Babbie Mason, Steven Curtis Chapman, Bill Butters, Johnny Ray Watson, Chiz Rider, The Gaither Vocal Band, Gary Anderson, Steve Green, and Chuck Colson.

Beyond being a week that many North Way members wouldn't want to miss, North Way had a special part in making it happen: Jay served on the executive committee for the event. This would be Graham's last crusade to Pittsburgh. *Author's note: my father, Jim, had just moved my family to Ohio around this time and taken a sales territory that included Pittsburgh.*

We attended the crusade when I was just two years old.

When Billy Graham passed away in 2018, Jay wrote the following:

ONE FAITHFUL SERVANT

By the time most of you read this post, you will have heard the news that Rev. Billy Graham passed away this morning at his North Carolina home at the age of 99.

There will be a multitude of these reports that will describe in detail the amazing accomplishments of this incredibly devoted servant of Jesus who preached in most nations of the world and held scores of crusades over the decades here in America.

However, it was his strong and passionate voice over the radio and then ultimately the emergence of TeleVision as the primary medium which Dr. Graham found his way into millions of households in our nation and around the world.

One personal story that I would like to share with you is about Dr. Graham's influence on my family and me at a very significant time in my life.

In the late 1950's our family relocated from the city of Pittsburgh to the little town of Beaver, which in those days was nearly a one-hour drive. My parents were very committed to visiting their parents on a weekly basis. Every Sunday afternoon we would drive into the city right after church and visit relatives in the Hazelwood and Bellevue communities. It's just what we did... No questions asked.

However, I have a vivid memory of the long ride home every Sunday evening. My parents seemed to plan our exit from the city around the time that Dr. Graham's national radio broadcast came on the air. For nearly an hour every Sunday evening, we would listen to George Beverly Shea, the crusade orchestra and choir, and most important, Dr. Graham's gospel message. Even as an adolescent I found his messages easy to understand and somehow very relevant to my life. I had the experience that many people share with me from time to time using words like "I felt he was speaking just to me."

There's absolutely no doubt in my mind that those messages prepared my heart to receive Jesus as an early teenager when we attended a small outdoor crusade somewhere around 1960-61. It wasn't with Billy Graham, but it was the same gospel message and I remember very clearly responding, confessing my sins and going forward to begin my relationship with Christ.

If I remember the story correctly, my mom had received Christ just before that experience and my father later at another Billy Graham Crusade in Pittsburgh in 1968. I wonder how many countless thousands of others could share similar kinds of stories about the influence of one faithful servant of the Lord who somehow managed to avoid the snares of the ministry to faithfully preach the word "in season and out of season" leading millions to know Jesus.

As a result of Dr. Graham's influence on my family and me, I counted it as one of the great honors of my ministry to serve on the executive committee of Dr. Graham's last crusade in Pittsburgh in 1993. Even in his later years, he was still able to draw the largest crowds of any evangelist or minister before or since his visit here.

The attached photo of Carol and me with Billy Graham in 1993 reminded me of the unmistakable sense that I had when we met – that this man was indeed humbled to be so powerfully used by God, and very authentically encouraging to those of us who were so greatly affected by his life and ministry.

And though our nation and our world will not be the same without him, they have been greatly changed because of the ministry of the gospel of Jesus through him, one faithful servant. For that, we should all give thanks and praise to God!

Blessings,
Pastor Jay

~~~

Since institutional building codes were more strict than residential ones, priority had to be given to sprinklers, fire alarms, and handicap accessibility. As they worked out what they could accomplish within their budget, Jack and Roy came to the conclusion that there would not be enough money for the planned gymnasium. They took that extension off of the building plans and were up front with the church that they just didn't have the money for it. Though no one seemed to hear them when they first announced this scale-back, people eventually noticed there wasn't any footage for the gym and started asking what had happened. "We told you...!" said Roy and Jack. Suddenly, the money came rolling in. The gym made its way back into the building plans, and Roy says that his faith in God's provision grew in the process.

The official work on the building began in November of 1993 but was quickly halted by the coldest winter on record in Pittsburgh. In January, the temperature reached a record low of -22 degrees Fahrenheit. The building had to stop for a month because the concrete couldn't be poured. The building committee had budgeted for an unexpected cost and spent that money quickly trying to continue work in the winter time.

The project gained time back as the weather warmed up and ended up being finished on schedule and within budget. With 30 years of experience as a subcontractor, Roy was thrilled to have the opportunity as contractor not only to use all the subcontractors in an efficient manner, but also to make the process go as well for them as he possibly could. Though he kept a close eye to make sure the subs didn't put in extras, he treated them with respect and many of them came to Roy after the project to say it was one of the best jobs they had ever worked on.

Roy made sure things went into the building in an order that made the most sense for everyone and for the project. He explains, "One of the things that happens in any building when you start putting pipes through walls is everybody — the plumbing or HVAC or whoever is putting the pipes in — wants to get there first so they don't have to play with the wall, which is understandable because it makes it easier. And the drywall guy wants to come through and put his bit up first before the plumber comes because it's easier for him to do it. I just made sure it worked the way it *should* go. There are cases where it makes sense to put the plumbing in first, and there are times when it makes sense to put the drywall up first. We did it that way."

Roy was able to hire a number of subcontractors who attended North Way, but they had to meet the specifications and they needed to come in low on the price. He'd say to each one, "If you're not low… just because you go to North Way doesn't mean I'm going to use you." Some people who worked on the building from outside North Way actually came along to church because of the witness they saw on the job. Roy says that everyone he used was top quality, both as people and as subcontractors.

Roy also planned with a possible future addition in mind. In the case that North Way might outgrow this building, Roy made sure the structural design would allow for the back walls to be knocked out to expand the sanctuary to be able to accommodate another 1,000 people.

One big part of building the sanctuary was planning for acoustics. "Most people don't realize," Roy says, "the walls aren't straight — they're sunk in, and we have what we call 'clouds' in the ceiling. We had a couple guys on staff that gave me, 'Oh we can do that, we can do the acoustics in here.' One gave me, 'I can do it for $15,000,' the other guy said, 'I can do it for about $4,000.' We got a professional bid for about $30,000. That's the one I took! Smartest thing I ever did. Because acoustics are huge. People say, 'It's not a big deal, we can save some money there'... you shouldn't. You couldn't. If you try to save money there, you're going to have problems. So I spent that money. Acoustics were done as we built it. From day one they were right."

The metal roof and steeple were made by Roy himself through his family's company. They brought the machine to the job site and rolled the 90-foot long slopes on the spot.

Jay says that the whole project was a unifier rather than a divider, and that it was a joy to be a part of from start to finish. Jay was always welcome to stop in and see what was going on and was able to keep the church updated on the progress. "Looking back through 20-20 hindsight, if I had to pick a piece of property to own in the North Hills, I would still pick that piece," says Jay. "I'm always just blessed when I think about it."

Roy has similarly fond memories looking back on the building project. He says, "It was a labor of love. It was the greatest building I ever put up... and I did buildings all over the world. I really enjoyed it. It was the most satisfying one I ever did. It wasn't the biggest I ever did, but just the way it went, you know, watching God be in the middle of it.

"It was run well. It was fun! We had a lot of fun doing it together. We didn't look at it as a job — it was a real pleasure to do it. And I knew I was doing it for the Lord and was happy to be able to do that, but it was just fun to do."

Jay says that while most churches build too small or too big, North Way was ready for this step. The church had spent many years in a somewhat nomadic state and had gone through the "nitty gritty" to grow to where it was. In fact, North Way managed to sell The Bradley House property nine months before the new building was ready and had the opportunity for one more pilgrimage in the form of several months of meeting at Marshall Middle School in the North Allegheny School District.

The consummation of the building project was that North Way ended up with the largest church building anywhere in the North Hills. With the reputation and respect the church had already gained, it was poised to use the building to its full potential, opening doors to all kinds of ministry opportunities.

Roy says that the project came out just $7,000 dollars over budget and that it would be common to come out hundreds of thousands of dollars over on a project like this. In addition to Roy's careful management of the budget, all of the deals he and Jack negotiated made the building's value much greater. They found great deals from their connections but never compromised on quality and always sought the top of the line.

Jack knew the owner of Otis Worldwide and got the best elevator on the market at a good price. They worked out a good deal with Don's Glass, which Roy describes as an extremely good glass company with a great reputation.

When it came to things like painting and landscaping, volunteers from the congregation came to help and saved the church a significant amount of money. Roy calls those who came along to take care of the building and grounds after they were complete "the true heroes." The ongoing care of many has kept the building looking new to this day.

North Way had the opportunity to choose whatever street number it wanted for the new building and chose 12121, or "one to one to one," encapsulating North Way's foundational emphasis on personal discipleship. In the early parts of this book we saw God's preparations for North Way happen from 1 person 2 another 1 person: from John White to Jay. Then, Jay helped bring Carol along in her faith, and he and Carol invested in future leaders through the youth group at Memorial Park. The Servants Council invested in the four original small groups and beyond through all North Way. Jay's effort to disciple individuals multiplied God's work at North Way and beyond as those individuals sought to invest in personal relationships with others.

The building was completed in time to launch when expected on October 16th, 1994. That Sunday when it was dedicated, the official headcount was 1,700 adults. A front-page article appeared three days later in the local newspaper, *PG*

North. Though it stretched the numbers a little and got North Way's name wrong, there are some memorable quotes.

CHURCH OPENS JOYFULLY
By Deborah Galle

The first worship service in the new $5 million North Way Christian Church was more like a joyous celebration Sunday with laughter and standing ovations mixed in with song and prayer.

About 2,500 people from throughout Allegheny County attended the service in the congregation's new facility on Route 19 in Pine.

The membership of about 2,000 had been using Marshall Middle School on Wexford Run Road as temporary quarters since March.

The audience included County Commissioner Larry Dunn, State Rep. Elaine Farmer, and State Sen. Melissa Hart.

Part of the 10 a.m. service was devoted to paying tribute to those who helped make the church rise from the remnants of the old Starlight Drive-In Theatre.

The Rev. Jay Passavant, senior pastor, thanked the membership, which pledged $1.5 million toward the project, and especially the 685 members who landscaped, painted, and removed more than 500 tons of debris from the property on 74 consecutive working weekends.

He recognized the union and non-union workers who worked side by side, as well as contractors and the 15 companies throughout the county that donated $1.3 million in materials and labor to the project.

Passavant recounted the church's history, which began in 1981 with nine couples. The church now has seven pastors and operates or participates in more than 60 ministries.

"And whatever this property may have been used for in the past... God has ordained a higher purpose for it now," he concluded amid laughter, while members of the drama team mimicked a young couple at the drive-in movies.

"Now that we're here, the next step is a team effort to ask how we can most effectively open up this facility to the community," the Rev. Scott McCabe, executive pastor, said later.

The *PG North* article went on to briefly list some of North Way's existing ministries along with a couple new ideas for the space. Neither the writer of the article nor anyone at North Way could have imagined many of the things that would come out of the following years.

As exciting as the dedication had been, North Way's leadership was surprised at first that the church didn't explode with growth. The Bradley House had seated 600 and North Way had been holding four services every Sunday. During its short stay at Marshall Middle School, the church had just done two services since it seated more. At the new building, the leadership decided to start with two services even though they knew neither service would be full at first, but it seemed they lost some of the urgency.

Jay says, "Even though we were getting wonderful feedback on the building, our attendance flattened out, and maybe even dipped. And we couldn't figure out what was happening, and finally realized: the facility was so big they felt they were going to get lost."

For a year, North Way focused on care and prayer. The doors were opened for a prayer gathering every morning at 6 a.m., and a group anywhere between 15 to 200 people would show up, many coming before work. This daily practice had its roots in the years before North Way started, when people prayed every morning and asked God what He wanted to do in Pittsburgh. The practice had continued for the first decade of North Way but had relaxed back to a couple times a week by the time of the new building. Now, North Way again had the chance to ask what God wanted to do and to put in the hours to seek His heart.

By the Fall of 1995, the church started to grow again and the growth didn't stop.

PURPOSE

Up until this point, North Way had been through several seasons. The chapters of this book are based around these seasons, and though some are much longer than others, each one is a vital piece of North Way's development.

First, in the *preparatory years*, founding members of North Way learned what community was all about, both from their own unique journeys and through a common search as members of Memorial Park and its youth group. The *launch process* provided a short but critical season of prayer and Bible study where many of the same folks were able to flesh out values and governance principles for a new church.

The *establishment years* allowed for the things these leaders had been unearthing together in their studies and prayer times to be put into practice with a growing congregation. Small groups multiplied and more hearts were touched through Spirit-filled worship and teaching. After the awkward experience of having to leave the rental space at The Bradley House to weather a stay at St. Teresa's, the church found itself settling back in The Bradley House as owners.

The next season was one of *rapid growth*, particularly in numbers. During these years, the church consistently followed the principles laid down for Biblical fellowship, worship, and teaching. People who joined were quickly made aware that there was much more to this church than the Sunday service. Members served at the Christmas banquets and some started ministries like the pregnancy center. The primary focus of Jay and the elders was developing a congregation of devoted disciples.

After finding a permanent location and constructing ample space for ministry, North Way was prepared to reach the community in new ways. One thing that had come out of years of focus on the needs of the local church was the desire for a more comprehensive ministry structure. The next season, discussed in this chapter, can be described as the *years of expansive ministry*. A key resource for this season was Rick Warren's *The Purpose Driven Church*.

Rick Warren was the founding pastor of Saddleback Church, a Baptist megachurch in Lake Forest, California, which he founded with his wife just one year before North Way held its first service. Warren, like Jay, had received his doctorate from Fuller Seminary, and Saddleback had started as a home Bible study before holding a public service of 200. When Warren published his book on "Growth without compromising your message and mission," he shared lessons and strategies from Saddleback's journey of growing to become one of the largest churches in the country.

Jay let me borrow his copy of this book, which showed tabs, highlighting, and brackets from multiple reads. Any quotes shared here will be ones he marked heavily. Early on in the book, Warren covers a number of myths about large churches. We will quote several lines underlined by Jay which show a strong similarity to the ideals North Way was already practicing.

Myth #1: The Only Thing That Large Churches Care About Is Attendance. The truth is, you *won't* grow large if that is all you care about. In the entire history of Saddleback's growth we've only set two attendance goals — and both were in our first year. We do not focus on attendance; we focus on assimilating all the people God brings us. (48)

Myth #3: You Must Choose Between *Quality* and *Quantity* in Your Church. The fact that many pastors wish to ignore is this: *Quality produces quantity.* A church full of genuinely changed people attracts others. If you study healthy churches you'll discover that when God finds a church that is doing a quality job of winning, nurturing, equipping, and sending out believers, he sends that church plenty of raw material. On the other hand, why would God send a lot of prospects to a church that doesn't know what to do with them? (51)

In the church's case, as long as there are lost people in the world we *must* care about quantity as well as quality. At Saddleback, we count people because people count. Those numbers represent people Jesus died for. Anytime someone says, "You can't measure success by numbers," my response is, "It all depends on what you're counting!" If you're counting marriages saved, lives transformed, broken people healed, unbelievers becoming worshippers of Jesus, and members being mobilized for ministry and missions, numbers are extremely important. They have eternal significance." (52-53)

Jay has said on numerous occasions that North Way never set out to become a large church, but rather to make disciples. Becoming successful at discipleship, however, naturally brought multiplication. While North Way already held several values in common with Saddleback, Warren had a way of illustrating and diagramming complex concepts that helped Jay better communicate them to the congregation of North Way, so they could be owned and pursued by everyone. Jay says that the larger you become, the simpler you have to be, and calls Warren a genius at organizational leadership. "It just made big things understandable," says Jay.

Jay went to Saddleback's annual conference in California and went back three more years with elders, pastors, and volunteer leaders from North Way. They found it to be a worthy investment, and it opened their eyes to ways they could embrace the purpose-driven strategy. From the start, the leadership at North Way viewed that strategy as a tool to better accomplish the ideals God had given them.

From around 1998 until 2006, North Way was recognized

as a purpose-driven church. This didn't mean it was theologically the same as Saddleback, nor did it imply any denominational affiliation. Jay says that what Warren offered was a model to help facilitate growth in a clear and understandable way.

One of the things Jay most appreciated about Warren's approach was the way he described the spiritual journey of involvement for church-goers. In one target-shaped diagram, Warren categorizes different levels of involvement with several "C" words. The outer ring is the Unchurched, which he calls the Community. One ring inward, the Regular Attenders equal the Crowd. The Members are the Congregation, the Maturing Members are the Committed, and the Lay Ministers are the Core (153).

With all five of these categories of people identified, the issue is how to bring people from each category to the next, eventually into the core. Jay's favorite diagram from the book is one of a simple baseball diamond, which shows "The Life Development Process" as one that brings people around the bases to deeper commitment, rather than keeping them in their category. Warren says, "You don't get credit for runners left on base" (144-145).

In Warren's baseball diamond, people who are led to Christ are encouraged toward a Commitment to Membership. Growing in Christ leads to a Commitment to Maturity, and then Serving Christ and discovering one's ministry leads to a Commitment to Ministry. Finally, as members share Christ they come to a Commitment to Missions. Saddleback had a series of classes, levels 101, 201, 301, and 401 that covered each of these steps and helped bring people around the diamond.

North Way came up with a similar process, but illustrated growth as a tree and included five instead of four steps, with worship being the final outcome. The *North Way Connections* newsletter from the year 2000 included a two-page diagram which showed the stages of growth and introduced a series of classes, building from roots upward. If you've ever wondered why a suburban church like North Way has a tree for its logo, it comes from this way of framing a believer's growth.

Below is North Way's framework for a believer's growth, as outlined during the purpose-driven era. The order was reversed in the illustration, with 101 at the roots of the tree logo, building its way to the top.

101 Connecting - Roots

We are adopted into God's family when we connect with Jesus. We then become connected with our brothers and sisters in God's family. The many family benefits we can enjoy include receiving loving support, encouragement, and friendships, gaining a healthy environment to grow spiritually, and having a place to discover and use our gifts.

201 Growing - Trunk

Once connected, we can begin to commit to an

intentional process of growth. Learning healthy spiritual habits improves our knowledge of and relationship with God and with others. Learning about God is a lifetime endeavor that brings us to ever-greater maturity, balance, and joy in our lives.

301 Serving - Fruit

God gave us each special and unique gifts intended to be used to help others. Discovering our unique design (or SHAPE) for serving is the first step in understanding how we're built to serve. When we operate in God's Will by understanding and serving in our giftedness and in our passion, we will be most fruitful in our service and joyful in our lives.

401 Reaching - Outreaching Fruit

A healthy, loving family will always share its blessings with others. The good news of God's unconditional love is best demonstrated through sharing authentic love for others in all parts of our lives. When we reach out and share this love with others, we invite them into the knowledge of God's great love for them.

501 Worshipping - Whole, Abundant Life

Worshipping God in every part of our lives gives us joy, health, and balance. An Abundant Life is one that is balanced and fulfilled through Connecting, Growing, Serving, Reaching out, and Worshipping God by placing Him in His rightful place in our lives. This worshipful, abundant Life is filled with love for God as we respond to His profound love for us.

North Way put out a new purpose statement that focused on the same five concepts:

To become a vibrant community

Connecting with Jesus and His family,

Growing with Jesus and His family,

Serving others,

Reaching people with His good news, and

Worshipping together in the joy of His grace.

One major theme of Warren's book is "Bringing in a Crowd." This is the focus of Part 4 of his book, a section that in Jay's copy has many red tabs sticking out the sides and much orange highlighting within. Becoming more "seeker-friendly" was a process that involved some changes to the Sunday service, but Warren's primary focus is on developing a genuine love for new people and for the lost. He gives advice on many ways to help visitors feel welcome, from how pastors can best be accessible to the crowd before and after services, to things like receiving "First Impression Cards," or as North Way calls them, "Communicator Cards."

One key aspect of this focus on welcoming new people, both at Saddleback and at North Way, was to remember the whole process of life growth outlined above that these visitors were being invited to. If mature members were involved and growing in small groups and were serving in the community as well, a more general accessibility for the weekend audience could be well received and even celebrated. In churches where small groups and discipleship are not high priorities, it would be much easier for a popularization of the Sunday service to be taken as watering down the church's primary spiritual food.

Warren saw the danger here and argued that it was important not to confuse expectations between the crowd and the committed, writing, "At Saddleback Church we do not expect unbelievers to act like believers until they are. On the other hand, we require a major commitment from those who want to *join* our church" (54).

Jay's welcome letter in *North Way Connections* serves as a good example of how new people were welcomed.

Dear Neighbor —

Welcome to our inaugural issue of *North Way Connections*! Whether you're new to the area or have been a long-time resident, I'd like to share some exciting things that are happening here at North Way! Maybe you have felt a bit like I did years ago. Perhaps you've attended a church in the past, but when it comes right down to it, you lost interest because...

...the people weren't very friendly, and you weren't comfortable there

...the sermons were boring and weren't relevant to you

...you couldn't relate to the music

...it wasn't clear where the church was going and how you could fit in.

When my wife, Carol, and I and a handful of folks began North Way Christian Community 20 years ago, we wanted to start a church where everyone would feel welcome, and where we could all learn together. We thought that attending church could be truly enjoyable. We wanted to be part of a church where we could be ourselves, and where we could meaningfully connect with friends and with God.

Our dream was to become a church where...

...people are genuine and friendly

...we can learn something new and be encouraged each week

...we can serve together and reach out to our community

...the worship is exciting and powerful, with upbeat contemporary music

...our kids are well cared for in a safe environment where they can have fun and grow

...there is a clear purpose to the church, and a place for everyone.

I've got some great news! Our dream is now North Way, and these priorities have become North Way's expression of what we think God's family was intended to be. We don't want to be a part of religious institutionalism and posturing; we just want to discover God together. And that's why North Way is built on solid Biblical principles... nothing more. We certainly don't have all the answers, but we're willing to learn from each other and grow together.

We also think all these great things are just too good to keep to ourselves! We'd sure love it if you would join us as we discover God's love. Stop by and see if we really are different from what has kept you away from church.

And please bring your kids. They have a special place in our hearts here, and we have a fun and fulfilling experience waiting for them - just ask our kids! Blessings to you and your family on your journey. We hope to see you soon.

Pastor Jay Passavant

At the same time new visitors were being welcomed so amiably, new members were challenged with a thorough and intentional process of integration. Over the years, North Way had experimented with many formats and durations of membership classes. At one point, the new members class was four weeks, but that didn't seem like enough. It went as far as a 12-week course that gave the time to go beyond sharing information to really getting to know the people attending on a personal level. 12 weeks ended up being too long, mostly on account of younger families who struggled to stay after church with their children so many weeks in a row. Yet even when slightly shorter, it remained a structured assimilation process.

One thing that required careful balance when seeking to welcome first-time visitors and challenge long-time members was the weekend teaching. All along, Jay had sought to balance a rich Scriptural offering with practical application. That balance remained but shifted slightly toward the more practical. It also shifted to be slightly more structured than charismatic, according to Roy Thompson. Roy, who had been drawn to North Way primarily because of Jay's teaching years before, says that while Jay's teaching changed somewhat in nature, the basic premise was never altered.

"There are things you can do when there are a hundred people that you can't do when there are a thousand," says Roy, "But I'd have to say that the basic thing, the basic premise that Jay teaches on has not changed at all. Still strictly Biblical, strictly Christ is the Lord, Son of God… Everything's in the Bible, that's where it comes from, that's the book that we work from. He's not into all this humanistic… all this other stuff. So other than working a little bit differently from the point of numbers out there, I don't think the basis of his teaching changed. What he preached was a little different, but the core, the reason, the theory, the philosophy, the theology behind it hasn't changed."

A sidebar in the *The Observer* offered examples of sermons with practical takeaways that went to the Bible for every point. These messages were both welcoming to new visitors and enriching to faithful members. Topics included: 5 Essentials for Great Relationships, 5 Principles for Financial Stability, Bringing Out the Best in Your Kids, and God's Plan for Managing Stress.

Perhaps the biggest development at North Way during these years was the expansion of individual church ministries. With new facilities and a growing congregation of connected and equipped members, the church was ready to reach the community in many new ways, and the key would be using the gifts of the members themselves. This was also one of the main topics of *The Purpose Driven Church*. Warren said, "Every church needs an intentional, well-planned system for uncovering, mobilizing, and supporting the giftedness of its members" (367).

When people came to North Way, the leadership made it clear that joining a small group would be vital to them being cared for. This had been the premise from week one when 90 people showed up to the information meeting at Northway Mall, and the leadership had continued this emphasis as the church grew to 2,000. Facilitating small groups wasn't where they stopped, however, as they knew healthy members need outlets to serve as well.

One of the important functions of North Way's membership classes was to help people identify their giftings and get them plugged into serving. Some people who came to North Way already had a ministry they were involved with, and the staff would ask how they could support and equip them. Others came with a passion for a specific ministry that already existed and just needed to get connected. Still others came with a heart for a certain topic that wasn't being addressed, and the staff would recommend that if God had given them a passion for it, He might be calling them to lead a new effort.

The number of unique member-run ministries at North Way grew during these years to 100. When people came with a good idea, the staff would coach them and provide a space, but would encourage them to lead and pray about how God could use *them* to meet the need they saw. If there was a need *in* the body, the staff was confident that God would provide the solution *through* the body.

Ephesians 4:11-13 says:

> And He himself gave some to be apostles, some prophets, some evangelists, some pastors and teachers, to equip the saints for the work of ministry, to build up the body of Christ, until we all reach unity in the faith and in the knowledge of God's Son, growing into maturity with a stature measured by Christ's fullness. (CSB)

While these verses were key in every step of Jay's pastoral career, he saw them become even more vital during this season of expansive ministry. Jay says, "I can't overstate how important that passage became. In that culture, like most, ministries were considered to be the work of the professionals. We educated the people to realize, no, ministry is what happens in the lives of people who yield to the Lord and seek to serve God themselves."

In a church North Way's size, this sentiment didn't mean that pastors had little to do. Jay says that it actually became a huge challenge to equip all of the people who were eager to serve. He says, "Even if a church ministry wanted to meet just once a week to have a ministry to recently divorced mothers, which was a definite group of people that we saw all the time, we'd have to have the space for them, and we'd have to have childcare for them. It just got to be gigantic: the logistical support that was needed to support these ministries. They didn't just happen on their own. But they all wanted our validation. They wanted to be able to say, 'We're a ministry of North Way, and we meet in this room at this time.'"

Jay was intent on not categorizing some ministries as more important than others, especially considering that the high-profile ministries were only possible through the ministry of others behind the scenes. He says, "I was aware of the danger of different classes of Christians. I hated that idea. To me there was only one class of Christians, and that was *servant*. Everyone was a servant, with just a different calling."

Roy Thompson's leadership of the building project offers a perfect example of this ideal. After growing under Jay's teaching, it became his desire to be there for the church and to have God use him. Roy says, "One of Jay's principles, which I agree with: you have an idea, we'll take a look at the idea — it might not fit in, but if it's a great idea you'd better step in and be ready to lead. Everyone feels like they have to go to the head minister. They need a ministry to do everything, they're going to sit back and volunteer to help. That's not how a church runs; that's not how it ran back in the New Testament either. The book of Acts was not just one person running it, it was everybody coming together, everyone throwing all their goods in... so that's been the philosophy that Jay started, and I think it's been the right philosophy."

Of the many ministries started and led by lay members, there were support groups listed for 12-step recovery, post-abortion recovery, and sexual abuse support. There were support groups for children from high-stress homes, for troubled marriages, and healing after separation or divorce.

Community outreach ministries included everything from a food bank to classes for developmentally disabled adults. The high school and middle school ministries were listed, along with men's and women's Bible studies, a group for mothers of preschoolers, and get-togethers and support for families with single parents. There was a Pioneer Club, described as a Christian scouting program and a Precept Bible Study, which was open to all Christians who desired an intensive study of the Bible. Priority Two provided emotional support, gift assessment, and leading-edge proactive job search skills for persons who were unemployed or in an employment transition.

Opportunities to use one's creative gifts and talents included volunteer teams for signing, musicals, banners and flags, dance, drama, orchestra, choirs, ladies' ensemble, costumes, creative arts, set design, stage construction, sound, lighting, photography, video, and computer/media graphics. One could serve in KiDZ Little Blessings Nursery, KiDZ Critterland Preschool, KiDZ Ventureland Elementary, or KiDZ Fourth & Fifth Grade. One could volunteer at the LifeLines Resource Center bookstore or the LifeLines tape ministry. Happily married couples could meet with engaged couples to help prepare them for marriage, and there were opportunities to support young mothers. There were missions trips and groups for intercessory prayer.

Any Bible studies mentioned in the last paragraphs were in

addition to over 100 small groups, which covered a broad range of topics and age ranges.

Readers who have attended North Way for some time will likely remember taking part in or being blessed by one or more of the ministries above. Each ministry requires servant leaders and volunteers. There are many stories that could be told of all that God accomplished through each person and ministry.

Paul and Linda Gregg were one of the original couples on the Servant's Council and were the ones to start and oversee North Way's food bank for many years. Linda also volunteered as part of the flag team for worship and served in production for the weekend services.

Susie McCabe, who was worship staff at the time, says that Linda went above and beyond in many areas. Linda worked alongside Susie by overseeing the social aspects of North Way events; from decorating, to getting food donations, to organizing teams to serve food, and managing many details.

Susie says of Linda, "She was so gifted in hospitality and used it constantly to create a warm environment for our gatherings. She was a leader that took charge and was very dependable and welcoming to all. She was such a blessing and continues to be a great friend even though they relocated to be near their sons, one of whom had Cystic Fibrosis and was a best friend to my son, Bryan. Their whole family was deeply involved all through the many years at North Way."

The purpose-driven model would eventually break down to some degree for North Way, especially as North Way embraced a strategic shift that will be discussed in the next chapter. Leadership had learned much from Saddleback's example, but Jay felt strongly all along that North Way should never become a clone of any other church. There were great people on staff at North Way, Jay says, who pushed to follow the purpose-driven model even more closely and to do things exactly like Warren did. Some churches did follow this path, but Jay felt that North Way should have its own personality.

Warren actually felt similarly and said in the book, "The application of your purposes will require months, maybe even years, of praying, planning, preparing, and experimenting... The end result in your church will look different from Saddleback and every other purpose-driven church." (137)

There are sections of Warren's book that have little underlining in Jay's copy, while others seem to be just what Jay was looking for. One thing I have noticed about Jay throughout our conversations is that he learns with humility from countless sources. He has an uncanny ability to find good things all over with very little judgement of a whole source or person based on pieces he doesn't find useful. Even today, he actively listens to sermons by young pastors from a wide range of churches. Jay eventually got to know Rick Warren personally, and one of the pictures that Jay had in his office was of him and Warren together. "I had a great deal of respect for him," says Jay, "Still do."

Speaking of Jay's ability to learn from a wide range of people, he also had a desire to stay connected to the other churches in the area. He felt that unity in the broader body of

Christ was something Christians were called to cultivate, so he led an initiative to bring together about a dozen pastors from the North Hills. Initially, they gathered every other week to pray for each other. It settled into a monthly thing and continued for several years.

After building relationships together as pastors, they organized multiple events for all of their churches to gather. One of the events was held at the Pine-Richland High School Stadium, and between all the churches, there were many thousands of people who gathered together to pray and intercede for their community, their country, and for Christ's church. Each pastor had a role in it, and at one point they had people turn in prayer circles.

Jay says, "By the grace of God, I had a sensitivity to those things. One of the potential negatives of a large church is that it overshadows and overwhelms a lot of smaller churches that can't afford to do different things, and that creates a sense of disunity in the body of Christ. By me reaching out to pastors, my heart was never to take their people; my heart was to support them. But that takes effort; that takes commitment. Whether it was a joint outreach event, or a prayer focus, or a concert, it was about *What can we do to minister together?*"

In 1991, the same year North Way bought the property at 12121 and began planning to build, significant effort and funds were put into a church plant in Coraopolis. North Way sent multiple valued staff members along as part of the launch team and looked forward to having a sister church that could carry what God had been teaching to a new area in the region. Within two or three years, however, the church started to take a different approach and eventually fell mostly out of touch. North Way realized that without stronger ties and specific expectations of the relationship, a church plant would have the freedom to change however it desired and to do its own thing.

Once the building project was complete and North Way was growing rapidly under the purpose-driven model, the leadership realized that the congregation would eventually outgrow the building at 12121. Rather than thinking about breaking off into more church plants, the leadership got thinking about continuing to grow at the current property.

"A key day in the life of North Way," says Mac McCabe, "was when the elders gathered outside the 12121 building, were split into four groups, and asked to walk around the periphery of the 13-acre property. Each team was to stop and pray for 15 minutes toward communities in the North, South, East, and West, then regather and report what the Lord might have said."

This took place at the elder's meeting in May of 2000, and what followed illustrates how prayer was so important to North Way's journey. After nearly an hour of prayer, Jay asked, "Do any of the groups feel any particular impression from the Lord during this prayer time?"

Mac recounts, "The big surprise was when each group prayed to the North; God spoke clearly that we were to *purchase 46 acres for sale*. That God-inspired decision has had a huge impact on the church."

The adjacent 46-acre lot was for sale, so Jay asked Jack

Lightbody to go check it out. The owner said, "In two weeks we were going to divide this into 15 three-acre lots."

"In two weeks?" Jack said.

They said, "If you're interested, we can wait. $4.6 million for the whole lot."

North Way was still in the middle of paying off the building. The building wasn't yet full of attendees, but attendance was growing and leadership knew that if they didn't move on those 46 acres, they would effectively be saying they would never need more than the 13 acres they owned at the time. This was the final piece of adjacent land, as another large lot had just sold to a strip mall.

Jay had to go back to the church and say, "We want to go ahead and buy this property, not for now, but for the future. Because if we don't, we're basically saying, 'God, all we can trust you for is what we have here.'" Jay says this was one of his most difficult challenges, but the church agreed to buy it.

Jay explains how they got the church excited about the purchase. "What we did to help the church visualize what could happen is we put together a couple flatbed trailers where we thought the future building would be (where Allegheny Health Network stands now) and had them dump a large truckload of sand as close to Route 19 as we could, back off the road 50 feet. We had every person who was praying for somebody to come to Christ through North Way plant a flag in that dirt. What that did was it personalized a level of interest. Close to 1,000 flags planted in the dirt said, 'We believe God is not done with us yet.'"

Now North Way had a lot of land and no money, but it had a large new parking lot space. The area was growing popular quickly, and the church sold one small piece of the property to a restaurant, where Walnut Grill stands now, for $1,000,000. The leadership didn't have any immediate plans for an addition to the building, but in a developing area they at least had the option and could continue to grow joyfully knowing any growth would not have to be limited.

We will pick up on this development for future vision in the next chapter, but the rest of this chapter will zoom in on some of the most impactful areas of ministry that grew during and came out of this time. The stories and developments of these ministries are best dealt with one topic at a time, so readers will want to keep in mind that start and end dates might overlap slightly with other sections. All of the ministries discussed, however, will show some of the great things that were accomplished during the years of expansion as a result of North Way's care for everything God provided.

A letter that was shared as a part of North Way's celebration of its 20-year anniversary depicts how leadership and members saw their calling and service to these ministries:

Dear North Way family and friends,

We've come together tonight to celebrate 20 years of God's faithfulness! Throughout scripture, the practice of celebrating the favor of God serves as a reminder of two things: His presence in our lives and our complete dependence upon him!

The journey over these past 20 years has not been an easy one. But, as with any adventure, there have been thrilling moments, great sacrifice, and a mysterious sense of destiny that just cannot be shaken. Along the way, your faith, encouragement, support, and most of all, your prayers, have sustained those of us who have had the privilege of leadership. On behalf of all of us who have served in some capacity, we say thank you for being such a gracious and understanding body of believers.

For the times when you served and nobody was looking, the times you shared when no one responded, the times that you prayed and even wept when no answer seemed forthcoming, I say, may Jesus Christ be praised.

It's always been our heart's desire that God receive all the glory for the work that He's done here at North Way. As we celebrate 20 years, let's unite together with praise and thanksgiving for being called to be part of... Changing Lives, Making History.

With love for each of you,
Pastor Jay and Carol Passavant

CAR CRUISE

It was Jay's father, Jack, who initially planted the bug in Jay's ear to consider using North Way's new parking area as a place for a car cruise. Jack had been involved in car restoration for years and had been to several local cruises in Beaver and Allegheny counties. Jay loved cars as well and went to cruises with his dad on occasion. Jack kept bugging Jay, saying, "This is an ideal location, ya know — the way things are set up here with the parking lanes (and so on) — you could make it look nice."

Jack passed away on April 21st, 1998, and North Way held its first car cruise in the Fall of 2000. Though he didn't get to see it while still on earth, Jack would doubtless be proud to know all that would come out of his idea. The first cruise was held on a Saturday in early October. "Don't ask me why we waited til so late in the year," says Jay, but it turned out to be a perfect Fall day and more than 200 cars showed up. There was a great amount of interest and support leading up to the event; Jay had no problem getting food vendors and volunteers to do everything from printing handouts to helping the cars park. Just like their first Sunday service in 1981, those involved didn't know what to expect, but 200 seemed like a healthy number for a first go.

North Way tried the event again the following Fall, but this time it snowed and hardly any cars came. This failure made the organizers sit down and prayerfully think, "Alright, what would happen if we got serious about this and tried to do something on a regular basis?" One of the elders asked, "What do you mean by regular… once a month?" Jay said, "No, something like this needs to happen every week."

The next year, in 2002, the first cruise was on the first Friday in May, and it continued every Friday evening, weather permitting, until the last Friday in September. *Five months!* North Way brought in a DJ and some food vendors to run a fun, family-friendly event. The cruise averaged a steady 200 or more cars through the whole summer and began to develop a reputation.

The cruise kept the same summer schedule, May to September, for close to five years, but the organizers realized eventually that it was too many weekends for the volunteers. Each summer the number of volunteers would start strong at first, but dwindle to a fraction by September. To keep from burning out the volunteers, they shortened the schedule by a few weeks so that it would start on the Friday before Memorial Day and end on the Friday before Labor Day.

By the fifth year, the cruise was averaging 500 cars a week. Now that they were taking up a much more significant portion of the parking lot, sound needed to be dispersed beyond the front of the lot. The organizers decided to invest in some new sound equipment in order for people to be able to hear the announcements and music. Each year, they dedicated a limited portion of church outreach resources to get more equipment, so as the event grew, so did the quality. They also built a website just for the cruise and did some online advertising.

By 2007, and for the next five years, "We became *the* place," says Pastor Jay. On a good night, North Way had 1,000 cars in the lot and spectators parked on the furthest reaches of the property — the land the church had bought on faith in 2000. The prayers that the land would be used to reach many in the community were answered differently than anyone expected. A larger church building didn't go up on those acres, but the empty space provided an opportunity for people to be accepted and affirmed week after week at the car cruise.

Eventually, on some of the big nights — big nights being the season opener, the 4th of July, the grand finale, and an occasional special event like "horsepower night" — the cruise would bring in over 2,000 cruise cars. This made North Way's cruise one of the largest weekly car cruises in America. In fact, Jay did some research to see if there were any other places that did more than 2,000 cars. He couldn't find any.

In 2008, the Starlite Car Cruise earned North Way a creative outreach award from The Christian Broadcasting Network. For four hours every Friday night, North Way was able to bring people together on its property. It had quickly been recognized as a great place to bring your family and hang out. There was a play area for children with inflatables and other activities. There were 15 or more quality food vendors, a great DJ, and occasionally some live music.

The Car Cruise had two principles that were surprising to most people — first, there was never any admission cost, and second, there was never any preaching. The cruise was an opportunity to invite people to come to church, but there was never a time where someone would stop the music and say, "Okay, Pastor Jay is going to come and preach now."

The event simply began to be known as a great place to go on a Friday night with your family. For the church to provide that to an entire community without any specific agenda was unheard of and at the same time completely natural. Jay remembers more than one Pine Township commissioner stopping him at the cruise — where they had come just to hang out — and saying, "This is the best community event in Pine Township."

The event was safe, appealed more or less to all ages, and harbored a very positive environment. There was no drinking on the premises, and the church building was open for people to use the bathrooms or take a break from the sun when it was particularly hot outside. Each week, simply by offering a family friendly event, North Way reinforced the positive public image that the church was a place that was open to the people of the community. You didn't have to be religious to attend, and you didn't have to be a member of the church to feel at home and use the facilities.

"It's really difficult to overstate how positive that was," says Jay. "North Way's reputation in the community as a place that was welcoming to others, regardless of their church or spiritual background, became a very positive message."

As a byproduct of this simple emphasis on welcoming and serving the community, people did start showing up at church other times. Not right away — from visiting the car cruise on Friday to deciding to try a church service that coming Sunday

— but over the course of months or maybe a year, people would start to feel at home and reach out for more. North Way had a number of "side door ministries" that provided a service to people that could act as a bridge between the car cruise and actually becoming a part of North Way.

This was less of a tactic and more of a discovery along the way. When asking people in new members classes how they had come to North Way, leaders began to hear, "Well, my first time was the car cruise. And then after that I saw that you had a marriage class (or a parenting class, or the job transition ministry with Charlie Beck)..." These classes and ministries, which were available to anyone, not just to church members, were often a great next step for attendees of the car cruise. They would go from Friday night, just for fun, to a side door opportunity that met a need, to eventually choosing North Way as their church home.

Very often people at the cruise would ask for counseling, and since North Way had established a professional counseling center in 2002, volunteers had a high-quality, Christ-centered place to send people for care. Sometimes the need was urgent, and there were always a couple elders there who could meet with anyone that very night. Again, this wasn't a tactic or even a publicized opportunity; it was just the intentionality to respond to whatever ministry moments arose.

Jay says, "I did not require for there to be a direct link for people coming to church and the investment in the car cruise. To me, we were investing in lives by just being there and demonstrating God's love to people by providing an outlet for something they enjoyed doing." The cruise allowed for innumerable opportunities to minister that didn't directly benefit North Way but benefited the Kingdom.

North Way had managed to find an outreach where anyone could feel welcome while still being aware that this was an event put on by the church. It was clear that the church wasn't renting out its parking lot to a car cruise: these were the church people, and they were simply offering something to the community in the name of Christ, whether or not people came to church. "The average person is not just going to go to church," Jay says. "Relationship building is the key to help people, most often; to get down to their heart issues."

Each summer was fruitful and satisfying to the team. The majority of the work fell on the shoulders of volunteers, and Jay never assigned a staff person to run recruitment or organization. It was a team effort, and the volunteers loved being a part of it. The organizers would begin recruiting volunteers around the first week of February each year. Volunteers would show up from a number of churches and organizations besides North Way, including a healthy contingent of car club guys. "Everyone wanted to be a part because the cruise had a reputation for being family friendly and run with excellence," says Jay.

As a cruise that was both family friendly and run with excellence, they were able to steer clear of the things that typically caused car cruises to fail. At other cruises it was common for people to drink too much and get rowdy, and it was also common for the organization in charge to not invest enough to have a good sound system, a good DJ, good vendors, or to have bathrooms figured out. North Way believed it was offering a real service to the community, so the organizers wanted to do it well and host an event that all could enjoy. Through the years of experience, they figured out what was important and what was not.

On occasion, there were people who tried to "game the system" when it came to alcohol. Jay says, "They would put their beer in some kind of Coca-Cola cup, but our guys were really good — they'd say, 'You know what, I'll just assume maybe you didn't know that we have a zero-tolerance rule on drinking.' And they'd sheepishly say, 'Okay, well I'll dump this.' So it never became an issue."

In typical Pittsburgh fashion, rain was often in the forecast, but didn't always show up when expected. Tough calls would have to be made by 1 or 2 p.m. on particular Fridays so that vendors could know whether or not to purchase their meat and other fresh food products. Sometimes, despite a cloudy forecast, it would be a clear, sun-filled day. The best days, however, were when a clear forecast and the reality matched up — this was when incredible numbers of people would come.

On decent nights with 1,000 cruise cars, there would be 6,000 to 7,000 people in attendance. And on exceptional nights with 2,000 cars, it could easily be 10,000 people. Sometimes the parking was so full for attendees that volunteers had to put things on hold and deliver announcements regarding how to come and go from the parking lot to make room for others.

Even with such large numbers and over 17 years of opening

up the property to the community, Jay says there was never a serious injury at the car cruise and never a serious complaint. Some people in neighboring apartments said it was loud at one point, but North Way adjusted accordingly and never had an issue bad enough to think of cancelling.

The cruise was a place where families could become comfortable spending time on church property on a regular basis. While many standalone outreach events might allow a church to send a positive message and touch hearts for one specific moment, the cruise managed to help people form a fruitful habit. With this in mind, there were a couple unique features each week to keep people coming back, as well as to interest new people.

First, there was a specific kind of car featured every week. Week One might be Corvettes, Week Two: all Mopar products, Week Three: Mustangs, Week Four: pickup trucks. This wide range of features brought cars and attendees from all over, and once they came once… they were hooked. Jay heard people countless times around the grounds on their cellphones saying, "Dude, you gotta come out and see this. I've never seen a car cruise like this."

Another reason people kept coming back was for dash plaques; a little piece of metal, about the size of a business card, with the date and a picture of the featured car or vehicle. Most cruises would give away plaques to the first 50 people, but North Way gave away 300 or 400 on the first Friday of every month and at the season opener and season finale. "People loved those things," says Jay. There were people who collected them and came out just to get them.

The organizers chose not to do a 50-50 like most car cruises, but instead, as part of their budget, they gave away cash awards, usually three times a night. The first would be for $50, the second for $100, and if you were willing to stay until the 9 p.m. drawing, you could win $200 dollars. Jay says, "Well, $100 to some of these guys was like, *holy cow*, they would drive 1,000 miles. It was something else." The crowd didn't have to buy anything to enter the drawings; they just had to fill out a little clip of paper with their name and email. This allowed North Way to build the email list for the cruise, and the drawing really got people engaged. Typically, a young person would be invited to pull out a random name, and read off, "Is (so and so) here?"

The team approached the cruise as a creative and sustainable outreach to the community, and it was exactly that: creative and sustainable. The last few years the cruise took no money from the church at all — it all came from sponsors. There was a person who went around in a funny outfit with a donation basket, and on a really good night that person might get $75. The team found this funny and almost a bit frustrating, considering that most cruises charged a $5 entrance fee. Car cruises are often used as fundraisers, and on a night with 6,000 people, $5 a head would have been significant, but that was not the point for the team.

On a typical Friday at the cruise, even if you weren't a car enthusiast, it was a great place to walk around and talk to people. If you found a car that you liked, you'd quickly find that whoever was sitting in the lawn chair in front of it would love to talk about it. An unending supply of pleasant conversation starters between neighbors is no small phenomenon.

If you walked up to Jay by a yellow Plymouth Convertible, you might say, "Well, that's pretty nice, what year is that?"

"It's a '46." he would respond.

You might say, "Well, how'd you end up with that?"

And then Jay would start telling you about his dad… "He restored 11 cars in his last 12 or so years of life, and this is the last one he restored before he passed away. And, there's an incredible story about this car because when my dad came back from WWII, where he served in the Pacific theater, he married my mom, who was his high school sweetheart. And he went out not long after and ordered this exact car: a yellow 1946 Plymouth convertible. And, I don't know, a month or two, a couple months after he ordered it, he discovered my mom was pregnant. And that completely changed their plans. My dad would always say, 'You never know what I had to give up to have you.'"

"So he gave it up?" you might ask. "And then went back and rebuilt one?"

"Not for 40 years! He rebuilt it a long time later. I really chuckle because this is the one he gave up to have me, and I've had it for 20 years now, since he died."

It is easy to see how quickly a meaningful conversation could start, passing on great stories from neighbor to neighbor.

When the Transformers movie came out in 2007, Jay received a call from Detroit about showing a certain gold

Camaro. "We were wondering if we could bring the Bumblebee and show it at your event," they said.

"Well, yeah of course," said Jay, "Why would you pick us?"

"Because you're pretty widely known as the biggest event of its kind anywhere."

Jay was very patriotic, so on the opening Memorial Day weekend and on the 4th of July weekend, there was always a raising of colors and a salute to veterans.

Since the event drew a wide range of people, a wide range of ministry opportunities arose. Jay says, "We did not attract simply the people who looked just like us. We attracted people from all over the city." One of the small sub-ministries that was going on at the cruise for years was called the Single Moms Garage.

North Way got the word out to the city ministries it supported that if they had a single mom who they were trying to care for and she needed any help with her vehicle, she could bring the vehicle out to the Wexford Starlite Car Cruise. North Way had a team of guys who would inspect the car and do repairs for free. Sometimes the car was too far gone to be able to help, but they would give the single mom an investment of $100 to help in looking for a new car.

Over the years, North Way pursued and obtained corporate sponsorships from large companies, including Geico, Comcast, and the Baierl Family of Dealerships. Based on the donation level, each would be called a bronze, silver, gold, or platinum sponsor. Baierl agreed to donate something beyond cash. North Way would find a person, perhaps a single mom with children who desperately needed a vehicle, and then Baierl would look over its huge stockpile of cars to find a used car that was in good shape that had just passed inspection. Together, Baierl and North Way would make a little presentation of the car right there at the cruise at no cost to the overjoyed family.

On numerous occasions, people would pull Jay aside and share what the cruise had meant to them. He'd be walking by, or driving his golf cart, and a father would pull him aside and say, "You're the guy that started this, right?"

Jay would reply, "Well, indirectly; our team, but I headed up the team…"

"Well, I wanted you to know: my son and I hadn't talked for three years until I said to him, 'Hey, you wanna get together and build that Mustang I've had in the garage since 1968?'"

The goal of bringing the car to the cruise might allow a father and son to reconnect and eventually heal their relationship. "This cruise is the reason why my son and I are back together again and talking," the father would say. A safe and simple space and a neutral and mutual interest was all that some families needed for life-changing breakthroughs.

The cruise was also a good place for singles and folks who weren't connected. It was a great place for a date or a place to show up by yourself and meet other singles. "Is that a spiritual purpose? I don't know. Probably not, but it certainly was a need we were meeting," says Jay.

Jay shares a memorable illustration of the culture of the cruise: "One of the more vivid images in my mind was: this one particular night, it was a nice warm night and I remember, we had a thing we did once or twice a year called the Blessing of the Bikes. We averaged about 100 motorcycles every Friday night, but on the Blessing of the Bikes we'd get 200 or more motorcycles. And I have an image in my mind from one of those nights when I saw two guys — big physical guys with all kinds of tattoos, leather vests, long hair pulled back, beard — walking right alongside this six-year-old kid, and it wasn't their kid, and just talking. Just seeing people stepping out of their stereotypical fears and accepting each other for who they were..."

In 2017, the cruise held its final season. Jay ran a calculation based on average attendance from 2000 to 2017 and estimated that over 500,000 people had attended over the past 18 years. Jay made a T-shirt for the final cruise in 2017, which says, "Wexford Starlite Car Cruise: over half a million served."

The name, readers may notice, was not "North Way Car Cruise." It was named for the Starlight Drive-In Theatre which had served families for many years before North Way bought the property. People from past generations had gone there to see movies, but when it went out of business and North Way bought the property, it was not so the church could hold its own private club on the spot. North Way opened the property back up to the community.

Jay says, "I would say that unquestionably it was one of the most effective things that we did to reach our community with some expression of: 'we care about you and your family.' And we had a steady stream of churches from all over who would come and ask if they could just see how we did it because they wanted to try to do something like that in their communities. Strange as it may sound, I just think God had His hand on it. Because there were a lot of churches that tried to do it, tried it for a month or two, and it just didn't work."

Jay notes that it is fair to say cruises, by their nature, tend to draw an older crowd because baby boomers were the ones who really benefited from the muscle car era. The muscle car era, roughly from 1962-1972, was when everything from Mustangs, to Camaros, to Mopars became insanely popular, he explains. The idea was: a lot of horsepower, a lot of speed, not a lot of frills, not a lot of stuff you didn't need. Since most of the people enthused by that era are getting up in age, Jay expects that the cruise phenomenon will decline.

There are some other things taking their place now, however. Jay continues to attend car events in the Pittsburgh region and enjoys something called "Cars and Coffee" in Warrendale. Cars and Coffee is not associated with a church but makes for a fun place to go every other weekend in the summer. Rather than being mainly restored cars like Starlite was, the cars at Cars and Coffee are mostly new and exotic supercars like Ferraris. There isn't any drinking allowed there, but they also don't play music or allow you to sit down with a lawn chair in front of your car. The culture of these events is quite different and they might not be as laid back as the Starlite cruise was, but Jay feels that they continue to demonstrate the value of offering a place to meet people and be with family. He takes his grandson there most Saturdays that it is open.

After the close of the Starlite at North Way, the organizers passed on some of the equipment to Victory Family Church, just up Rt. 19 in Cranberry Township. Victory is calling it the "Victory Starlite Cruise" now, so it has lived on. "We graciously handed it off, and I give John Nuzzo credit: they wanted to do it on a Friday, but he would not let them start it as long as North Way was doing it," says Jay. "That just eliminated any kind of competition, and that's why we donated as much of it as we could to them."

Jay concluded our interview on the car cruise by saying, "I was saddened to see it finally have to end, but I didn't let that overtake the incredible joy of the total 18 seasons, if you count 2000. 18 seasons of opening our church home to the general community, expecting nothing in return. That's what we did, and it was just a real blessing."

WORSHIP

Even with a new building and unique outreach opportunities like the car cruise, the fuel behind North Way's ministry and expansion continued to be the passionate pursuit of the art of worship. To express the breadth of this pursuit during these years, we turn now to worship director Susie McCabe. As we saw in previous chapters, Susie started as a volunteer, then became a staff member, and ended up writing her own original worship songs. This era, however, is where we will be able to share some of her deepest insights and some of North Way's most powerful events.

Before stepping into the role of worship director in 1987, Susie had demonstrated many years of faithfulness and had been stretched by supporting multiple worship directors. She didn't plan to draw only from what she had already learned and tried; rather, she continued to search for God's heart through worship with prophetic vision. Susie saw church music as a wineskin — a delivery system for the gospel wine — that needed ever to be renewed. In a writing of hers from her first years as worship director, we read:

> This is not news, but we are still out searching for a used wine skin that will do and there is none. God wants to build our experience of Him from the foundation up. It is not a remodeling job He is doing but an original work; not a replica, not a print, but an original. We must start with a new tapestry and allow God to paint. Our form has become the veil; God rent the veil but we hold it taut.

(To read more from this writing see Appendix Four)

Susie sought, with Jay, to find how God was moving across the country. If something new was going on, they wanted to see if and how North Way could step into it. They took trips with the staff to Saddleback Church in California and to Willow Creek Community Church in Chicago. During the Brownsville Revival in the '90s, they went down to Brownsville Assembly of God in Pensacola, Florida.

Susie says that their search for how to keep current was all about keeping up with what God was doing, making sure they weren't missing out on something He could use to change lives. While worship directors today doubtless have an easier time seeing what is happening around the country and across the world thanks to YouTube, Spotify, and church live streams, Susie says that the firsthand experience they gained on these trips was invaluable. There in the midst of a worship service, they would ask God, "Do You want us to do this at North Way?"

When it came to leading worship on weekends, Susie describes seeing herself on a constant vertical/horizontal pendulum. On one plane, she would be worshipping God and listening to His direction personally, on the other she'd be paying attention to what was happening in the room and seeing how she could step in and nurture. She and the band had signals for repeating choruses and remained constantly aware of what was going on.

Having served in worship at North Way during the '80s, Susie had already seen and led many necessary adjustments to accommodate the needs of the congregation as it grew. In the earliest years, the worship had been deeply charismatic as the smaller crowd had allowed for broad participation in spontaneous worship. As the crowd at North Way grew, however, it had been more difficult to cultivate such free-formed worship.

From the stage, Susie was able to see times where the front of the room was very active, while the back of the room seemed to be wondering how they could join the party. Upon such realizations, the worship team would gradually adjust, searching for the best ways to reach maximum participation. Susie's goal was for everyone to be able to resonate with the music and for everyone to be able to join in. Susie continued to write songs, expressing meaningful Biblical truths with tunes that everyone could go out of church humming.

Beyond the congregational worship, Susie was able to organize more diverse musical selections for weekly Sunday specials, which they called "ministry songs." Susie loved harmony and coached women's and men's ensembles on various songs by Glad and 4Him. As she worked with Jay to design each week's service, she would recommend dance and drama elements as well. She would organize a drama presentation for the service every three weeks or so. "We always looked for moments where someone would be encountered in a different way. Jay never wanted every week to be the same, and he really pressed us to that creativity."

Susie focused a significant amount of her effort on "mining gifts" and developing leaders. For weekly worship, she cultivated and rotated three strong worship teams. At Christmas and Easter times, when North Way put on large productions that would involve several evenings of shows, Susie invested in 10 volunteer ministry leaders who would oversee certain focuses of the production, including a drama director, an orchestra director, a costume designer, and a set designer. Michael Knaub directed many of these productions, and together they would lead teams totaling 250 volunteers.

Countless hours went into the Christmas and Easter productions, both from staff and volunteers. For Susie and some members of her team, these productions often meant weeks of 60 to 80 hours; staying up until 2 or 3 a.m. to plan and being up again at 8 a.m. to rehearse. Often, whole families would volunteer their time. "Why?" Susie says, "Because they felt like they had a part in what God was doing."

Starting with all the volunteers inviting their family and friends to attend the performances, a reputation began to grow in the community that a North Way production was not to be missed. People from the community and people from other churches started coming to see what North Way put on each year. Eventually, the events would draw crowds totaling 10,000 to 12,000 each year. Multiple years, the Christmas programs were held at Heinz Hall. These productions were not only edifying to believers, but they were the first exposure to church and the gospel for many unbelievers.

"They were profound and very well done because Jay had a very high — and I did too — expectation of excellence," says Susie. "And when these productions came together, I would just sit back and just say, *Oh my gosh, I can't believe God did this.*"

Susie describes her job as one of weaving together tapestries: seeing each thread come together, saying *yes* to one thing and *no* to another, figuring out logistics for where to build sets, where to have makeup done. The whole church had to be on board with the big productions. "Talk about the body of Christ," she says. "Working together and every part being important, whether someone was watching the animals (we used live animals) or cleaning up after them, or a soloist with a major part... to see all these threads: that was my job, just to pull them all together.'"

Susie was constantly researching musicals and dramas that North Way could pull off, but one year for Easter a unique idea came to her in the middle of the night. "He literally woke me up and said, 'This Easter I want everyone to feel my pain.' And He laid out what it should look like, and He gave me songs, and I'm just thinking, *Woah, I gotta write all of this down.* And we had 400 people come to Christ that Easter. It was one of the most powerful things that we've ever done."

In the process of such productions, Susie would discover talents within the congregation and then cultivate those talents to serve in Sunday worship. She says that her favorite part of her job was seeing people realize for the first time that God could use them for His glory. She says she treasures to this day each memory of finding someone with a great voice and picking a song for them that would allow them to minister, maybe even to change someone's life through a song.

"I think the greatest joy for me — and this was my passion — I wanted other people to experience the fulfillment of stepping into God's call, of stepping into being used by Him. There's nothing more fulfilling than knowing God's saying *this* and watching Him work. And to see the power of God made manifest," Susie says. "And we had, I'll tell you, we just had some powerful things because when you use the gifts of the body of Christ, He provides them. He makes them available."

If North Way hadn't invested all the necessary time into these productions that called for great numbers of volunteers, Susie wonders how many gifts would have remained in the crowd and never would have had a chance to be used or nurtured. Knowing the leadership was open to the gifts of the congregation, people brought a wide range of ideas to Susie. Some ideas she could use on Sunday, and some she couldn't. But if she couldn't find a place to use it, she'd create a special event where they could use it.

Besides the large annual Christmas and Easter productions, North Way teams would produce dinner theaters like Uncle Phil's Diner, under the direction of Ruth Harold. Ginger Pillar directed the dance ministry, which put on evening events. JoAnn Hoover created men's and women's vocal ensembles, and they did carol sings and other specials. North Way had a choir and an orchestra, both directed by Mickey Knaub, and they remained on call to support any events God called North Way to do. Susie says that so many volunteer leaders led well and gave people a chance to use their gifts.

Beyond the walls of the church, North Way held several Freedom Festivals around July 4th, which gave many a chance to use their gifts to reach the community. North Way would host many big-name Christian artists at concerts held indoors and out, introducing a broader crowd to worship. "We really wanted to do outreach in the community and city, so we would hold concerts to bring people inside the walls of the church, trusting God would use it to bring people to Himself," says Susie.

Wanting the worship teams at North Way to be fully equipped both in hearts and talent, the church hosted inspiring worship conferences including Hosanna! Integrity Conferences and Maranatha! Conferences. These and many other multi-church events allowed North Way to continue to support the growth of worship across the Pittsburgh region.

In the mid to late '90s, Susie worked with a particularly talented group of about 20 young people, many of whom had participated in North Way's productions of the *Seeker* musicals while elementary students. Now that they were teenagers, they needed a different focus. They formed a team with Matt Griffin as their leader, along with his brother, Drew. Julia Dawson (later Allan) was a key member, as was Susie's daughter, Cameron.

The group served regularly in worship services and began to dream of having special events. Susie looked for musicals for them to do, and after they performed their first, once they had some experience, they came to her to ask for more freedom to put together their own productions. Susie told him to go for it. They started coming up with their own dance and drama specials for the church services and began composing music.

The youth wrote their own musical from scratch called, "What if Mary Were My Friend?" Set in modern times, the musical explored what it would be like if Mary went to your high school when she became pregnant with Jesus. Musical numbers expressed various reactions to her story and asked the audience how it would have treated her in modern culture. The youth wrote the script and songs. They came up with the choreography and managed all the drama elements. Susie says they felt strongly about the message and gave it their all.

"The pieces they came up with were... I can't even describe... they were over the top; they were professional," she says. "Not sloppily done. Matt Griffin was a drill sergeant!" As they accomplished more and more of the musical work on their own, Susie mentored them on a deeper level. "I taught them community; I taught them how to work out their difficulties together, how to work, how to work hard and feel that pride of accomplishment knowing that you're ministering to the Lord."

Some of these young people went on to major in music, including Cameron and Drew. Drew would study viola performance at Carnegie Mellon University and then at The Juilliard School in New York City before joining the orchestra for the national tour of Les Miserables. Susie feels that North Way was a vital experience for those who went on to careers in music.

About her own personal journey during these powerful years of worship ministry, Susie says, "There's something about serving God that requires humility, because it isn't about you. That's why God had to keep teaching me. There were a couple markers in my life that God taught me: 'choose not to be offended,' and, 'Lord, make me gracious.' In all things be gracious because you don't know what a person's experiencing. It really does require a laying down of your life. I know there's a balance to that because you don't want to be a doormat either, but I find that God can use laying down your life more than he can use asserting stuff that maybe doesn't need to be asserted.

"And believe me, if you talked to some people who worked

with me, I was very demanding, very high energy, very high excellence, so I demanded a lot and I didn't… sometimes I cringe at some of my memories. But those were growing moments for me, because you're not perfect. I tried to have short accounts, so I knew if I hurt someone I was there saying, 'Forgive me, that wasn't right… I don't know where that came from.'

"I've gone through different inner healing things because we all have squishy spots, and I wanted to sort those out. I didn't want to continue to act in ways that weren't godly… and by staying through the long haul and going through the rough patches, those things have a tendency to be kind of worked out by God. But if you never rub and you never stumble then you never grow."

Until around 2001, 20 years after North Way began, Jay was active every week choosing the songs and putting the services together. For all these years, almost every production position was filled by volunteers. Susie began to find it difficult to equip everyone for their roles if Jay didn't choose the music early enough. Susie encouraged Jay that he might need to hire a pastor of worship who could take that responsibility off of him. While Susie was happy to stay on staff assisting and leading worship, they agreed that having someone in this position would be best for the growing needs of the church.

At this point, North Way hired David Watts. David came from a solid Baptist background and had strong organizational skills, so Jay quickly felt comfortable focusing more of his time on the sermon and other responsibilities.

Susie says, "My last event to plan before David Watts came to be worship pastor was for Steve Green. He had come before, and it was a privilege to work with him. He made a point of pulling me aside to affirm my leadership and all that God had done, knowing I was passing the baton and stepping aside. That encouragement made the transition so much easier, and I handed over the leadership."

North Way would eventually add more staff worship leaders, especially when branching out into other campuses, but this overseeing pastoral position for the music has continued. David was followed by Rob Burkey and then (and today) by Billy Bob White.

Susie retired from North Way in 2007, after 12 years as worship director. She says she still misses it to this day. A remarkable prose piece she wrote at the time she stepped down shows how deeply she loved her job. She considered it to be "the loss of a love," speaking of the creation of music and weekly offerings but especially of the ability to cultivate the talents of others and see them minister. Please refer to Appendix Four for her full note on retirement.

Though she saw her retirement as a loss, Susie soon realized that God had plans in store for her in the new season. Less than a year after she retired, her daughter Shannon went through a difficult premature birth and her newborn daughter had to spend nine days in the hospital. Susie was able to be there to help without a care or a concert on her mind. As Shannon was stepping into her ministry at North Way over the following years, Susie was able to help by watching the grandchildren. "God knew that I was going to be needed," says Susie.

Mac and Susie's three children are all in ministry today. Shannon Libengood is the oldest and currently serves as North Way's Executive Director of Spiritual Development. Bryan is the second born and currently serves as North Way's Pastor of Transformational Urban Leadership. Cameron, the youngest — after majoring in voice in college — went on to earn her Masters of Divinity and is a chaplain at Mount Sinai West Hospital in New York City.

As Susie reflects on her demanding job as worship director and the paths of each of her children, she says, "The fact that they're in ministry is a shock to me because I thought I ruined it for them." Susie always knew how easy it was for worship leaders to fall into being a facade on Sundays and prayed about this regularly. "Lord," she would say, "I just want to be the same person with the church family that I am with my home family. Don't let there be this double standard, and cover me, cover my kids." Susie let her children know that they were the most important thing and attended all of their events she could.

Mac and Susie's family grew together through the pressures of the ministry environment. Serving on the Elder's Council for 16 years, Mac was able to understand and help Susie work through frustrations. Susie describes ministry as an especially challenging place because of all of the expectations from so many people, but even when she felt she couldn't meet everyone's expectations, she kept her family top priority. Shannon, Bryan, and Cameron gained an inside view of ministry life and often served alongside their parents. While they knew the challenges, they also got to see firsthand that it can really work; that it can be healthy and that they didn't need to be afraid of it. "So I guess we equipped them in a way," says Susie.

"I'll tell you, it's humbling more than anything to see God's faithfulness," she says. "It almost brings me to tears that God was so faithful. And then you see this legacy. I see Bryan with his girls — they're in their teens and one's already thinking she wants to be a missionary. Shannon's daughter has been thinking she wants to be a missionary to Cambodia since she was 10!"

Mac and Susie continue to attend North Way, and Susie is thankful that they never felt God offered them a chance to leave. As a result, they have a lifetime of relationships and keep close to many friends through Bible studies and worship nights. Susie and Carol Passavant go for walks together almost every day. "When you're faithful through the rough times, there's just a lot of richness that you develop from that obedience to just stay the long haul. I don't think people know the beauty of the long haul, and it just creates so much brokenness when you walk away. I think God rewards that faithfulness in staying with it."

MISSIONS

A FAX RECEIVED FROM PASTOR JAY

It is difficult to describe our experience… the conditions are indescribable… to see how many people live in <u>filth</u> and squalor with little hope for anything to change, breaks the heart. Open sewers, "homes" that are 12 x 12… usually <u>one</u> meal a day, etc.

Our Bible School is a wonderful contrast. The people are clean and happy. They have food and shelter. Abraham has taken in seven "Bush Children" — little ones whose parents became Christians in distant villages but wanted "<u>better</u>" for their kids. They are precious.

Abraham was very thankful for our gift. He pledged it to church-planting pastors around the area.

Pray for our transportation on ground — it is unbelievable… <u>even</u> for me!

Love in Jesus,
Pastor Jay

Jay pointed out in one of our interviews that churches that are big into worship experience often tend to ignore outward mission. For North Way, however, worship and missions were both essential and worked together. It is important to note that while North Way was pulling off large worship productions, it was doing so with hundreds of volunteers who were led by very few paid staff members. Even while North Way accomplished great things to bless each other and the community at home, significant financial priority was able to be placed on others abroad. Jay continually reminded North Way that God would never disappoint when their focus was on others, and the natural outworking of being involved in what God was doing at North Way was a desire to further His work around the globe.

As North Way grew and expanded, several short-term missions trips exposed Jay to greater opportunities for North Way to develop its global missions efforts and partnerships. One trip Jay went on was funded through World Vision, an organization that figured if they could get pastors of growing American churches to see first-hand what was being accomplished overseas, it would more than pay for the trips in eventual support — which it did.

Jay saw the expertise of World Vision, along with others like Compassion International and World Evangelism Crusade, and was impressed with how well they stayed involved with those they sent. They weren't the type, as Jay puts it, "To send them off and say, 'God bless you, we'll see you at the rapture.'" For the first several years, North Way partnered with these agencies to support missionaries around the world and even sent people from the congregation to be trained by them before going into the field.

Over time, however, Jay and the elders came to the understanding that North Way might be able to do just as good of a job, or better, at sending and supporting its own missionaries. The administrative costs of those organizations were substantial, and North Way considered what it might look like to bring all the finances in house and become its own sending agency. This would be a significant undertaking, not only initially with training the missionaries, but also going forward with sole responsibility for them and their spiritual well-being.

North Way went for it and gained the legal authority necessary. This move required a full-time missions head with one support person. Mark Geppert, who had been serving as missions head part-time, handed over the reins to Charlie Beck. Charlie's career background was actually with the railroad, but he had great spiritual maturity and ended up serving as an elder at North Way as well. Charlie had already started a ministry, Priority Two, for unemployed people in Pittsburgh and became well known as a guy from the church who would sit down with you and help you rethink your career direction and redraft your resume.

Jay says that while that ministry wasn't missions in the traditional way of going and sharing the gospel, it was important to include unconventional thinking when it came to missions. North Way rolled that ministry into Charlie's job description as missions head and eventually even held conferences around it.

Operating its own missions agency, North Way's recruiting began to take off. Members from a great diversity of backgrounds stepped up to say, "We're not sure how this happened — it hasn't been in our family or anything — but we're feeling called to the mission field." Typically, people would come forward with a burden for a particular region, and Charlie would start by helping them discern just where they should go.

It was up to North Way to offer the training necessary for these folks and to stay in touch with them to validate their work. North Way made a commitment to see every missionary once a year, whether by going to the place where they were serving or by having them return home for a visit. Some missions partners were international, some were national. The national partners tended to be in cities that were highly unchurched, with great opportunity for church planting.

One of North Way's earliest homegrown missionary couples was Sam and Ruth Shock. They began working in Southeast Asia in 1990, and North Way became their sending agency. In such a region where family was the essential unit, orphans and abandoned children faced devastating odds, often suffering poverty and malnourishment. By 1999, the Shocks had helped found the Foster Care Network, which went on to care for over a thousand children, helping them transition into foster homes and adoption. More recently, they have established Hope's House, which offers long term medical care to rescued infants and children.

Every North Way member was encouraged to consider a short-term missions trip. Through the '90s, North Way would organize somewhere between four to ten different trips a year. Some trips were made up of students from the youth group,

262

some were made up of adults who would take time off work to go. Jay says that this was a wonderful statement of support to the missionaries they had sent, but that maybe even more importantly, it forever touched the hearts of the people who went on the trips. When they came back, even if they didn't become full-time missionaries, they became very aware of the call to evangelize in their own lives.

Jay would talk about how, "God doesn't want an audience; He wants an army." With all of North Way's focus on caring for those God sent, North Way members had access to great speakers, vibrant small groups, and powerful worship. It was vital, however, that members had opportunities to share and serve out of all that they were taking in. Jay uses an analogy about the Dead Sea to explain this.

"One of the remarkable things that you experience when you go to the Holy Land," he says, "is you take a day trip down to the Dead Sea, maybe a two or three hour ride by bus, and what you discover is this huge body of water with one main inlet. But then you notice, strangely, that there's no way for water to get out of it. Therefore, just based on the soil content and so on, the water gets down there, gets locked in, and it just gets overloaded with salt.

"You just float on it. You can literally go in and pick up today's paper and lean back and read the paper. I did, and it's a wonderful, experiential picture of what happens when you have all kinds of input in your life and no output. The tributary that feeds into the Dead Sea is the Jordan river. That's intriguing because the Jordan upstream near Jerusalem is where everyone gets baptized when they go to the Holy Land — it's fresh water."

Jay would often challenge North Way members to find outlets. Whether it be locally in their neighborhoods, workplaces, or schools; in their city, or maybe overseas; they needed to have an outlet *somewhere*. Jay would get frustrated with people who would show up to every service and meeting, "Bibles in both hands," taking no responsibility for any kind of service or ministry outside the church. They'd say things like, "We want more of the Spirit… we want more of the gospel… we want more Scripture."

Jay would ask where these members were investing what they were receiving, and he'd often hear in return, "Ah, we're not called to do that. We're not called to be missionaries… we're not called to be evangelists."

"Yeah, no, you *are*," he'd respond. "We're all called to share the gospel. It's not just for the chosen. If you're looking up here at these pastors and thinking they're the ones that are going to do everything, you're missing it."

With even further pushback from folks with demanding jobs and busy family lives who didn't believe they had any time to give, Jay would say, "At least live your life in such a way that it gives you an opportunity to talk to people. If people see something about your life different enough that they're curious, you might have an opportunity at work to go out to lunch with somebody and just talk about how much your faith means to you."

Though some could not be convinced, the missions trips

that many went on continually added fresh perspective and fueled North Way's heart for missions. Each team that was sent on a short-term trip would be brought up to the front and prayed for before they left. And when they returned, they would be given time to share what they did on their trip, along with a few photos. This regular practice of seeing normal members from the congregation sharing up front had the powerful effect of inspiring others. Members who had never gone were left to wonder, "Why not me?" while those who were supporting financially were given the chance to say, "Wow, our giving does matter here."

North Way eventually realized it needed to set a maximum number for supported missionaries in the field. The typical plight of missionaries is to be supported by small gifts from many churches, making it difficult to see all the churches involved and to receive substantial focus from any of them. North Way didn't want to get to this point and wanted to be able to offer substantial support and a substantial relationship with all those sent. At least one weekend a year, North Way would invite all its missionaries back off the field and host a weekend where the missionaries could get refreshed and reconnect.

Charlie Beck and his wife Sharon founded MTEC International (Mobilizing, Training, Equipping, Connecting to the Nations) in 2008 and transitioned into full-time missionary work in 2011. With MTEC, they train and mentor students at colleges and universities with the goal of raising up the next generation of missionaries and evangelists. When the Becks made this transition from missionary support staff to supported missionaries, a new missions head was needed.

Shannon (McCabe) Libengood had joined North Way's staff in 2005 and took over Charlie's position in 2011. Shannon had spent two years after college teaching English as a missionary in China, followed by six years as a dorm assistant at the Dalat International School, a boarding school serving children of missionaries in Malaysia. These experiences gave Shannon a foundation in missions that complimented all she had learned about ministry from growing up at North Way.

Though it would fill many more books to relate the work of all the missionaries who North Way partnered with over the years — and I pray those books are written! — I would like to share just a couple stories. The following letter was posted by Jay on his blog June 25th, 2019, after the passing of one of North Way's faithful missionaries: Dr. Abraham Pothen (the same Abraham spoken of in the fax at the start of this section). In this post, Jay gives a beautiful overview of Abraham's work. Rather than retelling that story, I will include Jay's full post word for word.

ABRAHAM POTHEN: HIS LIFE AND LEGACY

It was well over 30 years ago that I first met Abraham Pothen. It was following a worship service at North Way Christian Community in Wexford that I noticed our Missions Director moving toward the platform in the front of the worship center with a couple that I did not recognize who appeared to be of Southeast Asian or Indian descent.

Charlie Beck took his time and graciously introduced me to Abraham and Molly Pothen for the very first time. Charlie told me something about the recent journey of faith of Abraham and Molly, and I sensed the depth of their love for Christ and humility of spirit.

Charlie shared with me that Abraham had come to western Pennsylvania to study at a local Bible college, but soon discovered after a couple of months that he was in fact farther along in his education than most of the professors at his school. This was not an arrogant statement, but an honest evaluation of the devotion and giftedness of young Abraham.

We talked briefly and arranged to connect within the next few days to discuss Abraham's future education and training opportunities. Because I had recently completed my Doctor of Ministry degree from Fuller Theological Seminary in Pasadena, California, I was blessed to have personal connections with Dr. Peter Wagner who had recently been appointed as the Director of the School of World Missions at Fuller Seminary.

Dr. Wagner agreed to consider Abraham for admission into Fuller Seminary but offered no assurance because

Abraham did not have some of the theological credentials normally required. Nonetheless, we were overjoyed that several weeks later we received affirmation that Abraham had been accepted into the program and could begin in the next semester.

Of course, Abraham and Molly needed financial support to undertake this level of theological and ministry training. Somehow, I knew that this was going to be one of those seeds of faith that we would plant into soil that would yield a hundredfold return.

When I sat with Abraham to express our willingness to support him I remember asking him for just one promise and that was that he would return to India upon the completion of his studies and not relocate to the US because he didn't have the credentials to get a teaching position here. Both Abraham and Molly vowed that they would return to their native India upon the completion of their studies because it was God's calling upon their lives.

At least six years had passed when I got notification that Abraham received his PhD from Fuller Seminary in Missiology with honors; I was overjoyed! I called Abraham to congratulate him and he told me before I even asked that Molly and Abraham and their young family would be leaving for India in two weeks! (I later discovered in a conversation with Dr. Wagner, Abraham Pothen was the single greatest student he'd ever had in the school of world mission… this was good soil, indeed!).

The challenges that faced Abraham and Molly when they returned to India were enormous. They began to gather other highly committed believers to rally behind Abraham's vision of establishing a bona fide Bible college training center in the west coast city of Alwaye, India.

Abraham was faithful to establish spiritual relationships and to model a life of devotion to Christ and the gospel in such a way that many others were drawn to share in this vision despite the fact that nearly 90% of the population in India is not Christian.

Abraham lived sacrificially because the cost of acquiring property and establishing ministry facilities was equal to or even more expensive than doing the same things in the states.

However, Abraham moved ahead wisely and with great faith every step of the way. Through the support of his friends at North Way and a few other ministries, and the sacrifices of those to whom Abraham ministered, Doulos Theological College continued to grow in attendance and fruitfulness.

It was in the spring of 1994 that I made my trip to India to visit Abraham and Molly and their growing family, Emanuel and Grace, who also reflected a deep humility and love for Jesus, with a warm and engaging joy of heart.

Even though Abraham's passion was to train pastors and send them out to plant churches in neighborhoods throughout the region, he also did everything within his power to meet the needs of the outcast, forgotten, and hurting people in the oppressed culture of some of India's more impoverished areas.

I recall that when we took a two-day trip to visit some churches away from the compound, I saw young men and women in love with Christ and the power of the gospel but living with just the bare essentials necessary to sustain life and have a little left over to share with others.

Abraham and Molly and their growing team of dedicated staff established a boys and girls home to care for orphaned or abandoned children near Doulos Theological College. They had many ways of providing food and other essentials to people who had little or no resources. My heart was both broken and filled by my experience during the trip to the Pothen's.

Abraham was a man of profound integrity. His word was his bond and his actions always reflected his biblical convictions which he taught and preached with passion and consistency.

Abraham and Molly were also devoted prayer warriors

who would regularly communicate about the spiritual and physical needs that their lives and ministries were confronting as they gave everything to be faithful to fulfill the calling.

In the midst of all of this, Molly continued her education at Fuller Seminary through online classwork as she too wanted to become all she could be for Christ and in support of her beloved Abraham.

I don't think that any of us imagined that not 30 years later there would be nearly 600 churches planted out of the Doulos training center reaching throughout most of the states in the nation of India. It's reported that nearly 60,000 believers now gather in churches that are pastored by a graduate of that initial vision of Abraham and Molly!

The training center has grown substantially, and many others have come alongside Abraham to continue to expand the outreach and improve the quality of training so that the gospel might be shared and disciples might be raised up throughout this enormous nation of 1.2 billion people.

Perhaps the greatest joy of my relationship with Abraham and Molly is to see the maturity, humility, faith and courage of his two children, Emmanuel and Grace. The mantle that has been on Abraham's shoulders for many years has been shifted to those of his son who has raised the vision to reach the 21st-century culture of a nation that is expanding in education and technology while still dealing with profound inequities and limitations.

Grace continues to serve alongside the family while continuing her education and growth as an intern in North Way's ministry here in Pittsburgh.

My prayer was that I would be able to share my thoughts with family members and the faculty and staff of Doulos and other leaders that Abraham had so greatly affected. For physical reasons, I was not able to do that. Nonetheless, I want to be clear that no other relationship with a national ministry leader from another country taught me more about what it meant to follow Jesus with no regard to circumstance or limitations and with full confidence in God's ability to hear and answer prayer.

I will greatly miss my brother Abraham, but I know that his life will continue to inspire and challenge countless others through his legacy of family and faithful disciples that he has trained up through his ministry of Doulos Theological College and Training Center. May the Lord Jesus bless those who remain with a double portion of Abraham's anointing in the years ahead. May Molly, Emmanuel, his wife Allison, their two children, and Grace find great peace in knowing that their husband and father proved faithful

272

to the glory and honor of his calling in Jesus Christ.

With love and profound appreciation for a lifelong
friendship,
Pastor Jay

Readers may have noted how Jay's time at Fuller gave him the connections to help set the Pothens on their way. Don't forget that it was Jay's discipler from college, John White, who had encouraged Jay to apply when he wasn't even sure if he should go into ministry. Jay's leap of faith back in Chapter One ended up being important not only to his own path and the start of North Way, but also to the spreading of the gospel around the world.

Also notice how Abraham's legacy is carried on by his children and grandchildren as missionaries and North Way staff members. Grace Pothen completed her internship at North Way and is now on staff as Missions Coordinator. It is remarkable that while we have examples of North Way staff members whose children have been called to the mission field, we also have examples of North Way supported missionaries whose descendants have become North Way staff members.

Bruce and Kathy Bain's son, Daniel, has been serving as a missionary in Central America since 2005, where he met his wife Jessenia. Daniel and Jessenia keep up an active blog, where you can find the history quoted below and much more about their ministry. Jay says that whenever North Way has sent people on trips to where the Bains serve, invariably those people have come back moved by what they have seen. "It's the real thing," says Jay.

As much as this book in your hands covers many of the main events in North Way's history, it is really about recording how the faith of a few has coincided with the faithfulness of God to bring much fruit in Pittsburgh and across the world. Below we hear from the son of one of North Way's original couples, who were involved in the years of preparation and continue to serve faithfully today.

The LORD called me (Daniel Bain) to move to Nicaragua in 2005. After graduating from USC with a business administration degree, I served with Manna Project International-Nicaragua, leading various after-school programs and community development projects. The LORD taught me a lot through MPI, including my introduction to La Chureca.

During my second year with Manna, I found the LORD planting my heart in La Chureca, the community of 200 families that lived in the Managua city trash dump. (In 2013 they were all given new housing outside the dump and better jobs, praise God!) When I first entered the dump, it was such a raw physical picture of what most of "life" looks like from a spiritual perspective, as people dug through garbage, trying to find value in the trash that surrounded them. They made their living by recycling and selling what they found in the rubbish. It

made me think of what U.S. culture would look like if
you pulled back the spiritual veil behind which the
American Dream hides – digging through superficial
garbage, trying to find value in life. It made me marvel
at how much God loves us. Little 3 year-old Reynaldo
(home page photo) would be naked and absolutely
filthy from head to toe, and yet I would joyfully pick
him up and hug him and hold him when he would
come running, desperate for love. Despite how filthy
we get pursuing "the cares of the world, the
deceitfulness of riches, and lusts of other things," God
still loves us and longs to hold us, and clean us up, that
we may have Life (Mark 4:19).

Also in that second year, I began a friendship with Brad
Corrigan, who was in the process of starting a non-
profit called Love, Light & Melody (LLM). After much
prayer, the LORD made it clear that we were called into
His Work with the families in La Chureca together,
though Brad was based in Denver. Some of the scripture
He led us with was Isaiah 58 & 61, 1 Samuel 2:1-10, and
Psalm 36:3-6. I also prayed and asked God for someone
to walk with daily in this ministry, given that I didn't
think it best to minister alone. Actually, God thought
that first: "It is not good for man to be alone" (Gen 2:18).
Jessenia was the answer to that prayer, though neither
of us understood in 2007 that it was a lifelong answer
to that prayer.

Jessenia was born and raised here in Managua. She was finishing her civil engineering degree when I met her, though her heart was also quickly shifted the first time she stepped foot in the dump. Her first time in the dump she walked in alone, in a cute outfit, past the drug addicts and drunks, through the swirling gauntlet of trash trucks, right into Alejandra's house (Reynaldo's mom), where a drunk neighbor was threatening people with a knife. That's a brave woman! God gave Jessenia a vivid dream to confirm His plans for her, and my spirit also witnessed to its message. Clearly, the LORD had gone before her to prepare the way.

After two years of being friends and serving together, in God's timing He opened our eyes to see that we were made one for the other. We knew from day one of our relationship that we would be married, and we did just that on the first of the year, 2010.

As we were walking alongside many families in La Chureca in 2009, the LORD put it on Jessenia's heart to open a children's home. While parents struggled to make changes in their lives, the children suffered the consequences of the brokenness in the family and society. After a lot of prayer with the board of LLM and many steps of faith in response to God's direction, we opened Casa Libertad y Sanidad (Deliverance & Healing House) on April 1, 2010.

For the first two months, Jessenia and I lived in the

home full-time to establish the rules, schedules, and expectations for everyone's new life together. The children were unaccustomed to consistent rules, schedules, and expectations, and we adults made many mistakes trying to establish consistency. Casa Libertad y Sanidad is now well-established, and while we continue to learn and grow, we thank the LORD for the peace and wisdom He has given to provide the children with the stability they need in the home.

For the first 4 years (and the 2 before the home) God provided for Jessenia and I and the home through Love Light & Melody, for which we are incredibly thankful. Since the start of 2014, we are independent missionaries, learning to trust more and more in His Hand of Provision.

While Jessenia and I supervise the home and handle all administrative affairs, we do not live there. Two Nicaraguan women, Victoria and Angela, are the current full-time care-givers. We are very thankful for them and to them for the sacrifice they make by ministering to and loving these children who are not their own. In addition to loving, nurturing, and disciplining the children as part of the team, they do all the cooking and house-cleaning, freeing Jessenia and I to manage things like spiritual direction, teenage girls, grocery shopping, and homework.

The children all attend a Nicaraguan Christian school,

and we are blessed to have them there. Upon returning from school, they eat a snack and tackle their homework. When they have finished homework, they play. They like that part. Then it's dinner time, teeth-brushing, bathing, chill-out, and bed time. We sometimes do activities on Saturdays, and other times we just relax. On Sundays we go to church together, and often go to the park in the afternoon.

The children go home to be with their families during school vacations, and once a month when there are no vacations, so that family ties remain constant. We also do monthly programs with the parents, seeking to raise them up in their identity in Christ as well as teach them to be more responsible parents. We pray that they would know Jesus, their Rock, and establish their families' lives in and on Him.

L.A.M.P.

As North Way cared for all those who God sent, the church increased its capacity to reach the world. From serving the community of Wexford through the car cruise, to blessing other churches through combined worship events and productions, to partnering with missionaries around the globe, it did all it could to look out for more than just its own members.

There was one area, however, where leadership felt they

had room to grow. After the great success of the Christmas banquets, they wanted to find more ways to show just how deeply they cared for the whole city of Pittsburgh. North Way had struck up relationships with many dynamic inner-city pastors and ministry leaders, but still the church could have a bigger impact.

Jay decided to go right to the top and managed to arrange a meeting with Tom Murphy, the mayor of Pittsburgh. At the meeting with Murphy and one of his top associates, Jay simply asked how a church like North Way — a healthy, relatively large suburban church from just outside the city limits — could serve the city of Pittsburgh. Jay wanted to communicate in clear and agreeable terms that North Way wanted to help address the needs of the city and used a wording like, "What influence can we have to help the city become a better place to live?"

Mayor Murphy reflected for a moment and said, "Well, right now I have two thoughts of things that we really need. Number One is that we need a more aggressive economic development strategy for incoming corporations so that they would be more interested in coming here — you could seek to meet with business leaders and people who are considering investing in Pittsburgh about making a commitment to Pittsburgh with their business." Jay's eyes glazed over on that one, but the mayor went on.

"Number Two," Murphy said, "Our city schools are struggling to meet the needs of our students, and we are in very serious need of turning around a declining quality of education and school outcomes." Right away, like a light switch going on, Jay knew that this was a place where North Way had potential for lasting impact.

Jay said, "Well, Mr. Mayor, I know you're not asking me to make a decision right now, but I'll tell you, door number two is probably where we're going to go." As soon as he walked out of the meeting Jay made a call to a young woman he had met named Erika Jones. Erika worked for the school board and was also a Christian. Jay and Erika had met briefly through one of North Way's other missions; she was eager to help.

The two sat down for a meeting, and Jay shared his desire for North Way to help with the Pittsburgh schools. Erika said, "Well, we have this thing called L.A.M.P, the Learning Assistance and Mentoring Partnership." She went on to explain how the L.A.M.P. program had been created by Family Guidance (a Christian organization in Cranberry that has been working to mentor students in Pittsburgh since 1964). L.A.M.P. was a collaborative effort between Family Guidance and Pittsburgh Public Schools to pair churches with city schools for one-on-one student mentorship.

Jay said, "Hey, is there a place that we can talk to them about their spiritual life?"

Erika said, "Well, not on school grounds, but anything off school grounds, yes, you can do that."

Jay met with the creators of L.A.M.P. and found out they had already established the protocol to get authorization from the state to go into the schools — one of the more complicated administrative pieces of the whole effort. The next part was choosing just the right school to pair with North Way. Erika prayed about it for a couple weeks and said, "Jay, I think I know the school that would be a great match for you. Meet me at 7430 Tioga Street."

The address Erika gave Jay was for Pittsburgh Faison K-5, on the border of Homewood and Wilkinsburg. When he showed up, it wasn't hard for Jay to see that this was as different from the suburban world of the North Hills as they could possibly hope for. He immediately said, "I think this is going to work. I can imagine how our people would fit in here."

The teachers at Faison had already become skeptical of mentorship programs, since well-intended people had come on numerous occasions to help and had only lasted a few weeks or perhaps a couple months. That had been bad for the students, probably worse than no help at all. When Erika paired North Way with Faison, Jay knew he would be making a firm request at North Way. Right out of the gate, Jay told the church, "If you commit to this, I'm asking you to say you're at least going to do this one entire school year."

With Erika's help, North Way and L.A.M.P. worked out many details for North Way's volunteers and the signup process for the students as well. Family Guidance helped with the state clearances required for the volunteers and provided training and support. The volunteer list grew slowly at first as Jay was up front about the fact that anyone who signed up would be spending two or three hours every week in Homewood (plus travel) for a minimum of a year, entirely as a volunteer. "You can write the word 'sacrifice' over this," Jay said.

Right from the beginning, however, the ministry was a win-win. Jay says that the students warmed up to the volunteers, and as soon as the teachers saw that North Way wouldn't bail after a few weeks or months, they too warmed up because they knew they needed the help. The volunteers loved this personal and simple way to have an impact on the lives and futures of at risk-students, and the list of active volunteers eventually grew to well over 100.

Volunteers could meet with students at Faison during lunchtime on school days or off school grounds on the weekends. Some mentors/mentees would meet at the basketball court, some in the art studio. The mentors became involved in the lives of the students and were able to share Christ with them. The application process would pair mentors with students that had similar interests, skills, or hobbies, but perhaps the most important aspect of the program was simply providing a consistent and healthy relationship that the student could count on.

After the first year, North Way put Bryan McCabe in charge of the L.A.M.P. outreach. Having grown up with his parents in staff and eldership positions at North Way, Bryan already understood the concept of sacrificial ministry. Bryan had earned his bachelor's degree in Physical Education from Malone University and then his Masters in Education Administration from California State University, Fresno. When he lived in California, Brian gained some experience teaching PE and coaching wrestling. Working in the inner city with a large Hispanic population, Bryan felt a stirring in his heart as he saw the effects of Latino gangs.

Moving back to Pittsburgh to be close to family after completing his Masters degree, the timing ended up being perfect for him to step into leadership at L.A.M.P. Brian was married with two young daughters and moved his family right next to the school in Homewood with the sentiment, "If I'm going to be here, I'm all in."

North Way's web page on L.A.M.P. answers some frequently asked questions, including one on whether or not mentorship actually makes a difference. The answer is:

> YES! Over the past (14+) years, L.A.M.P. mentors have been able to witness their mentees improving their academic performance, reducing their number of school absences and disciplinary incidents, the Faison School has achieved higher standardized test scores, and numerous L.A.M.P. mentees have graduated high school and college. Most rewarding is that surveys of L.A.M.P. mentees have shown that by being in the program, they have experienced significant growth in their relationship with God!

L.A.M.P. has remained one of North Way's top local missions priorities since 2006. In 2019, North Way expanded to work with schools in Beaver County, matching volunteers with students in the Ambridge and Rochester districts. When Jay set out to get a meeting with the mayor, he had been looking for an opportunity for the church to show and grow its heart for the city, and that's exactly what came of it.

One of Jay's and North Way's long-standing ideals — that church leaders were to be about equipping the saints to do the work of the ministry — took one of its fullest applications here, with the training of not just one or two mentors from the congregation, but hundreds. This work in the schools could not possibly have been accomplished by the church staff alone, even with great financial support. As North Way effectively cared for its members and provided opportunities for them to serve, the impact on the city was multiplied immeasurably.

CHAPTER SIX:

CHANGE

After a season of rich growth and ministry expansion, North Way found itself at a crossroads of strategy. It had never been the goal to become a mega church, but to make disciples. As disciples were made, however, *mega* growth just continued to happen.

The church had been sitting on the extra property it had bought in faith years before, knowing that a significant addition would allow North Way to continue to grow in its current location. As leadership considered what it might cost to add to the building and use the land to the fullest potential, they found themselves looking at the possibility of a $25,000,000 facility. Though it wasn't difficult to envision and drawings and initial plans were made, Jay says that nobody quite had the stomach for that option.

Traditionally, growth beyond a comfortable size would suggest a church plant might be in order, but North Way's experiences with that route left the leadership wondering if there was another way. While the plant of West Ridge Christian Community was a successful one and West Ridge continues in ministry decades later, North Way had hoped that the two churches would maintain a more active relationship and reach the city with one unified vision.

Another piece that was in play at this crossroads was North Way's heart for the city of Pittsburgh, as demonstrated by programs like L.A.M.P. The mission had never been just to the North Hills, and if North Way truly had a desire to win the people of the city at large, that would imply that it would seek wider access to and provide resources for the city.

The leadership of North Way was well aware that Pittsburgh is not a city where people will typically travel long distances to do anything. Pittsburgh doesn't have a beltway like many similar cities, nor does it have convenient public transit in the North Hills. Those traveling from beyond the North Hills will find themselves doing two things that Pittsburghers are often said to avoid, if possible: crossing rivers and going through tunnels. Jay says, "There's a reason why native Pittsburgh people always talk about the city in terms of its four hills. *Are you from the North Hills? South Hills? West Hills? East Hills?*"

It would be a serious decision not to focus on continuing to build larger at 12121, and the Elder's Council also felt they needed to consider alternative strategies to the traditional church plant. Over several months, North Way had been following developments in the electronic revolution, though no one had imagined how pervasive the internet would become to culture and daily life. While they knew the church couldn't jump on every cultural phenomenon, North Way couldn't ignore this one, especially with a school like Carnegie Mellon

University in its backyard.

One unique approach was that of Craig Groeschel, who at the time was just a few years into founding Life.Church. Groeschel started with the idea that people would be willing to attend and participate in a church service even if the message was on video. Though the original church campus of Life Covenant Church was in Edmond, Oklahoma, he and his staff saw the whole nation as their mission field and were willing to use a video message as a way to unite bodies from all over.

Until the turn of the millennium, the technology for video broadcasts was not high enough quality for many church attenders to stick with it. It was too grainy or too unpredictable, sometimes breaking down in the middle of service and making it all too obvious that one was watching a video and not a live sermon. As the technology improved, however, and especially as high-quality live streaming became possible, the leadership at North Way was paying attention. When it became clear that the technology had the ability to deliver a product that people would find engaging rather than something they would just put up with, North Way began to factor this tool into ideas for the future.

Roy Thompson was willing to help again with a physical addition at 12121, but he was on board with whatever direction the church decided. He went to Jay and said, "Jay, someone's gonna have to make a decision. We're either gonna have to expand here — put in a whole new sanctuary to fit another two or three thousand people — or you're gonna have to do something different. You can expand another branch or do whatever." North Way decided to pursue its first off-site campus, and Roy began to develop a smaller addition for 12121.

The model Jay and the elders landed on was a hybrid between live and video. People would attend in person, be greeted by volunteers, and participate in a live worship experience. A campus pastor would guide them through different segments of the service, while the children would participate in in-person kids ministry. The only thing that would be different was that the message, most of the time (at least 45 times a year), would be on video.

A key resource as they began to pursue this idea was Jim Tomberlin, who had just spent five years developing the multi-site model for Willow Creek Community Church and founded MultiSite Solutions in 2005. Jay took a majority of elders to visit Willow Creek to see how it worked. The idea of a multi-site church connected by video sermon was new nationwide, and Jay says it would have been easy for North Way to find themselves, "Up willow creek without a paddle." As with the purpose-driven church model, North Way wanted to learn from a successful concept, not be a clone.

As other churches began to pick up the idea, it became clear to North Way's leadership that this wasn't just a fad, and that it was going to be around. With widespread agreement that the potential benefits were very real, the next question became: *What part of the city would seem to be the most likely to engage in a multi-site campus?*

In surveying North Way's weekly attendees and the information the church had on them, it was clear that Oakland had the highest concentration of regular visitors from the same zip code of any other town or community North Way could identify. This was reflective of the professional community North Way was attracting from Oakland along with a large number of students from the six major colleges and universities in that area. Jay and the staff already found it astonishing that so many college students were managing to make it out to Wexford for church, and they considered how many more they might reach if city-dwellers wouldn't have to make the trip.

The demographics of Oakland, with its young professionals and students, made it more likely that attendees would be receptive to a video presentation compared to some of the more traditional communities around Pittsburgh.

Author's note: by the time I showed up as a freshman at CMU in 2009, I was already accustomed to watching sermons on YouTube and on desiringgod.com. Though I had never experienced a video message at a church service before North Way, I was aware that John Piper was using this technology at Bethlehem Baptist to reach multiple campuses. My grandparents attended one of the campuses of Bethlehem, and I figured that if the video message didn't bother them, I could appreciate it as well.

Jay says it didn't take long to discern that Oakland was North Way's number one option for a campus launch. Sewickley offered a second option, but not a close second. In the initial research, leadership was not able to find one successful new church started in Oakland within the past 20 years. "That blew us away!" says Jay. There had been attempts, but none had worked out. There were newer campus ministries, but no successful church plants.

After choosing an area, the next task was finding a building. At first, they thought, "We'll just hook up with a church that's not being used, or we'll find some campus facility," but it turned out to be much more difficult than they had imagined. After a substantial search, they found a recently vacated Chinese restaurant for sale and bought it outright. It was in an ideal physical location, right on the edge of South Oakland on McKee Place. Its primary limitation was that it had (1) parking space. Anyone who was driving in would have to find a place to park on the street or in a garage, but the location was easily walkable or bus-able for much of the community, including students and professors from the colleges and medical staff from the nearby hospitals.

Jay remembers going door to door during the foundational stage of the Oakland project to gauge the interest of people who lived within a mile or two of the building on McKee Place. He or another member of the launch team would ask each person if they attended church. The answer was most often, "No." They would ask if the person would be interested in a local church, and the answer was most often, "I dunno." And finally, they would ask what it might take for them to give it a try and would offer some information.

Jay knew that skimping on the quality of the video was not an option, but the technology was expensive. While the purchase of the building was hefty, none of the elders expected that would be a losing proposition. Even if the campus experiment failed, property in Oakland had little likelihood of depreciating, especially considering that they would leave the building in much better shape than they found it. Convincing the elders of the added cost of the HD technology, however, was not so easy for Jay — until they saw it for themselves.

Jay says, "When the screen came down, if it was done right, it looked like a full-size figure standing on the stage. In fact, in the early history of Oakland, Carol took one of the Wednesday meetings of the seniors to stop by the Oakland campus and just see it. They had the guys play a greeting from me on video, and a number of the seniors were heard to say to one another, 'I didn't know Jay was gonna be here!'" The technology was effective.

Jay coached the crowd at Wexford on how to help make it more natural for the other campus, encouraging them to share their enthusiasm throughout the message. "How you respond gives the freedom to the rest of the churches to respond. So, if you hear a point that you want to clap or you want to say *Amen*, just do it!"

Oakland's first campus pastor was Mike Arnold. Mike, with the support of his wife Rochelle, spearheaded much of the new effort. The launch team was deliberate and took its time, knowing that if this idea worked it could soon be followed by other campuses. North Way still held the property at 12121 and didn't immediately abandon the idea of a large addition, but Jay says that within a couple years, "We knew that the handwriting was on the wall; that this was the direction that we were going to go."

Jay continues, "We were told by countless people that it would never work because it was students and they wouldn't give any money — all of which was true — but that didn't keep us from knowing God wanted us there, right?" Though the young congregation at Oakland didn't have the means to fully support their campus at first, they were encouraged to give, and Wexford was able to make up the difference.

Still, one of Jay's leadership convictions was that people needed to own their decisions not by voting but by giving. "Without sacrifice, they don't own the vision," he says. North Way set up Oakland with its own missionaries that it would support out of its own giving. Daniel and Jessenia Bain were one of the first couples supported by the young campus.

Ray and Marcia Speicher decided to check out what was going on with this new venture for North Way. Marcia says, "Whatever the flavor the Holy Spirit decided to use with all of us, when Ray and I first visited the Oakland campus, it was like being back at the youth group at Memorial Park. It felt just like it! It was such a blessing to see that the worship was front and central and that hearts were still hungry to do that. Even though styles of ministry change, it's all about worship."

Ray and Marcia could also quickly see that the Oakland campus was full of people who had either struggled to find church fellowship or who had never gone to church before. "That seems to me to have been the core of what North Way's *always* been about: reaching the unreached. Thinking about how North Way started, it started with outreach to junior high and high school kids. Then, North Way was founded on reaching out into the community. That doesn't allow a whole lot of room to get stagnant and old. If your vision is always to be reaching out, you don't just grow old together and get curmudgeonly."

Roy Thompson says he was perfectly happy with the decision to go multi-site, especially with the universities and the hospitals close by in Oakland. Rather than pursuing the building of a new sanctuary at 12121, Roy headed up a smaller addition of an annex that now houses the connect center. He was able to dovetail the roofing for the annex to match and made it look like part of the original building.

Roy also talked with Jay about launching a campus in Sewickley, where he had lived his whole life. They put together a hand-selected team of six couples, including Roy and his wife Karen and Mac and Susie McCabe. Each couple on the team had to not only be committed to establishing a church in the community of Sewickley, but also be willing to leave 12121 to make the new campus their home. Mac and Susie felt that being part of that new campus would be similar to all they had experienced in the early years of North Way, so they felt they could add a helpful perspective.

Jay met with this group regularly for 16 months. Their goal was to meet every week, and they came close, other than some weeks in the summer when people were on vacation. The team prayed for the vision of the new campus and was integral to the property search.

Roy advocated for the possibility of meeting at the YMCA.

He worked out there regularly and was on the board of directors, but for some reason, the Y said no. Jay and Roy knew the Y had the facilities necessary and the time on Sundays as well. It also had the legacy as the "Young Men's Christian Association," but still it declined.

The team got rejections from five or six venues. Churches said "No," and the movie theater in town said "No." Roy had some pull at a local school, and gave that a try. Finally, they received as "Yes," and found a win-win situation at Osborne Elementary School. The space worked well for North Way on Sundays, and the school received a steady income stream. North Way was self-sustaining and came in and out without making any messes. The parking was sparse, similar to Oakland, but that could be worked around.

Sewickley was a very different neighborhood from Oakland. Most church-goers expected a church to own its building and expected that building to have a steeple. After attending the reputable St. Stephen's earlier in life, Roy had to get used to talking about North Way with people in the community and hearing, "Oh, you're that church in the school." Whether a borough was churched or unchurched, North Way found that there were people who were hungry for genuine community.

Scott McCabe, after decades on staff as a pastor at North Way, became campus pastor at the Sewickley location. And while Roy felt that the school worked well, he began looking on day one for a permanent home for the Sewickley campus.

Once North Way fully embraced the multi-site approach, the property surrounding 12121 that it had bought on faith was now more than it would need going forward. The church had been able to use it for the biggest years of the car cruise, and then it was able to sell off various pieces for considerably more than it paid years earlier.

North Way found several strong advantages to the multi-site model. One of the most immediate and recurring benefits was that people perceived each campus as a local church. Rather than focusing on creating a megachurch experience in one location that would draw people from long distances, individual campuses could focus on the same values of personal discipleship and fellowship that had given North Way such a strong start.

When people from Oakland or Sewickley could come to an actual building in their community rather than traveling 40 minutes to Wexford, Jay believes it was much easier for people to connect. "Consequently," he says, "they'll sacrifice for it. They'll serve the mission of that local ministry, and they're much more likely to invite their friends."

Another less obvious reason the model worked well was that while each campus had its own campus pastor, that pastor was not required to preach on a weekly basis. Jay suggests that depending on the preacher, a good sermon takes a minimum of 15 and a maximum of 30 hours of preparation. Without that weekly responsibility, Jay explains, "That immediately now provides an additional opportunity for the pastor to work on leadership development, community building, discipleship, and small groups — all the things that the church needs to be a healthy, well-rounded, growing body. He can be more engaged without the worry or without the expectations he'll prepare a message every week."

When the benefits of a local church building came together with the benefits of a video message, what was created was a personal experience under a unified vision. Jay saw this unity as the most important element, especially after North Way's previous church planting experiences. Jay says, "In effect, our goal was: no matter where you went to church on Sunday, whatever campus you went to, you would essentially have, essentially, the same experience. I mean there'd be different things, nuances of leadership styles... not all the places did the same music exactly, but the message that all campuses were getting was: *Hey, this is what the Lord was saying to us as the church, this is the direction we're going, this is what we're excited about*, and that has proven to be the case."

Another benefit of keeping the campuses connected to Wexford, as seen later, was the ability to gracefully handle staffing issues. Jay says that the devil worked hard to try to bring the new campuses down, and there were multiple circumstances over the years that would have likely been too difficult for a new independent church plant to handle. With the unified board of elders, however, things were able to be handled with grace and truth, and support was able to be offered out of Wexford's experienced staff.

Jay says, "Christians seem to be really good at shooting their wounded, instead of healing their wounded," and says that leadership tried to handle any issues with integrity and love. "We weren't unscathed, but I like to think God redeemed us through those circumstances."

Another benefit of the multi-site model was that while Jay had always welcomed other regular voices in the pulpit, he now could develop a true teaching team. The team was comprised of multiple pastors out of Wexford and multiple campus pastors who had the gift and desire to teach. Being part of this team allowed campus pastors to be a part of the formation of each teaching series and to offer perspective from their ministries at their individual campuses.

Some churches that pursued the multi-site model during this time and since have done so to allow more campuses to hear from a famous voice, perhaps with the added motivation to provide a church experience in a more local setting. Jay says that North Way's teaching team, however, "Sent the message to the church body as a whole that you didn't have to have just one anointed person to be hearing from God; that other people could hear from the Lord and under that same anointing and same conviction share God's message."

While Jay was a gifted teacher and visionary, he desired to cultivate a culture at North Way that wouldn't be disappointed if it didn't happen to be him preaching on a particular week. Jay once visited a church with a famous pastor, and was astonished to see what happened when another man stepped up to give the message. A large chunk of the audience actually got up and walked out. "That blew me away! Rude as can be. It's so silly to think, *I can't possibly hear anything from this person...*"

The teaching team rotated weekly, working through topical series and books of the Bible. Each teacher would take a chapter or subtopic, depending on his gifts and experiences. Other voices were welcomed on occasion as well, sometimes from within the church, sometimes as a guest speaker from without. Several times a year, each campus pastor would have the opportunity to preach live to his own campus. This allowed campus pastors to address issues that were more unique to the regions and demographics of their campuses, and it also kept them growing as teachers.

Another invaluable benefit of the teaching team was that it prepared North Way to thrive under new leadership. As North Way became more and more accustomed to learning and growing from multiple regular voices in the pulpit, the congregation was well prepared for a *seamless succession.*

North Way's handling of its first senior leadership transition was perhaps one of its greatest achievements. However strong a foundation had been laid and no matter how many great ministries had been launched, this test had the potential to make or break North Way's future. As Peter Drucker said, "There is no success without a successor."

Jay approached his possible stepping down as Senior Pastor with the knowledge that the failure rate of church successions was 70% in the first three years. In fact, Jay's first attempt at finding a successor nearly ended in disaster. After a serious step back, Jay pressed on with the elders in a way so organized that it deserved its own book.

Jay wrote that book, one that detailed the journey North Way went on and that offered insights for other churches facing this vital but seldom taught topic. The book is titled *Seamless Succession: Simplifying Church Leadership Transitions* and was published in 2015. Jim Tomberlin from MultiSite Solutions wrote the foreword. Though North Way members would benefit from reading Jay's whole book, I will include some major points as they relate to this important chapter of North Way's history.

Seamless Succession details seven steps in the succession process and provides a chapter on each - 1. Initiate, 2. Cultivate, 3. Communicate, 4. Investigate, 5. Integrate, 6. Celebrate, 7. Evaluate.

In the first chapter, it is not surprising to see that copious amounts of prayer and planning were involved. As Sue Dawson said about another moment in North Way's history, "Some of us got together and prayed because we knew that's how you started something." The careful establishment of a transition team and the addition of a devoted prayer team were foundational to everything that would happen going forward.

The second chapter addresses the importance of *cultivating* a climate where the congregation would be receptive and even enthusiastic about the season of change. The teaching team was key in accomplishing this culture at North Way, and while Jay's book is aimed at being practicable for churches of many sizes and styles, this is one place where he makes a firm recommendation: churches with a single prominent voice should take steps toward including others.

The third chapter focuses on the importance of *communicating* with the congregation in a clear and exciting way. North Way had good practice on this after multiple building projects and campus launches. The transition team played a vital role in earning the trust of the congregation as it welcomed and responded to feedback on any and all concerns along the way. Jay writes:

What you are asking the church to do in a succession is to accept and graft in something different, other, new. Chances are the congregation is aware that this is more than a decision about a new leader or an isolated personnel event. They know that the new leader means a new season and that things may look different than they used to. Things will change, and those changes will affect them. They may not be quick to articulate it or even be able to articulate it, but many members of the congregation may be concerned that the church they have come to love may drastically change. Consistent, positive, and well-placed communication does a great deal to foster a sense of ownership in the process, and relieve the fear that arises with the realization that things are changing. It leads the congregation to receive the decisions of those who have been delegated the responsibility to make them with a sense of appreciation and support, not skepticism or negativity. (44)

The fourth chapter of Jay's book details the transition team's *investigation* into first: the needs of the church, and second: potential candidates. Here Jay writes:

Assessing the church's needs should come *prior* to the search for suitable candidates and/or any assessment of the strengths and weaknesses of any potential in-house candidates. The whole investigation process can be shortchanged if the needs of the church are not taken into account prior to the search. It's far easier to figure out what you're looking for *before* you begin your journey and thereby bypass a great deal of confusion, time, and heartache. (53)

When it came to the needs of North Way for the next season, Jay shares openly in his book about his own leadership strengths and weaknesses. While he says it might be tempting for churches to search for a younger version of a senior pastor they already loved, Jay recommends that differences are key to filling in existing holes in ministry and leading the church to new kinds of growth and maturity. Jay says:

Under my leadership the church has grown with the natural bent towards vision. As a result, we have a wonderful abundance of vision in a number of areas of ministry. The flip side of this strength, however, is that it's easy to develop a natural deficiency in following through with these initiatives... When we began to assess the church for weaknesses, we noticed that there were several areas of ministry and staff that could greatly benefit from someone with a high capacity for administration and management, able to address some of the weaknesses in the church that arose during my years as senior pastor... This identified need in our church for administrative follow-through became a core strength the transition team looked for in a potential future leader. Vision was still an important quality to us, but we also recognized the necessity and benefit of hiring someone who had a desire to develop clear support strategies and help implement already-existing visions. (54-55)

The next step after drafting a description for the new leader was to interview in-house candidates. Jay believed that a current member of North Way's leadership was clearly preferable to an outside hire. Raising up leaders was one of North Way's long-standing ideals, and the transition team quickly identified four staff pastors who would make excellent candidates.

North Way's process for considering these candidates included a "rather exhaustive questionnaire, including everything from theological questions, personal background, and experiences, to a self-analysis of perceived strengths and limitations" (57).

This step was not rushed in any way, and the process, while exhaustive and exhausting for each candidate, was designed to grow each of them as leaders within North Way, whether or not they received the position. The transition team agreed to hire an outside agency to help analyze the leadership strengths and weaknesses of each candidate from an unbiased viewpoint. The feedback they received was helpful to the candidates and to the search. Jay writes:

> The best part of the outcome was not just that we found a very capable and committed person within the group of four, but that all the men continued on in their service to their respective campuses after learning that they had not been selected. In my view, this was an exemplary demonstration of humility and self-sacrifice. (60)

While Jay offers some advice in his book for circumstances where an internal candidate is not chosen, he and the team were thrilled to have found someone with many years of ministry experience at North Way who excelled at organizational leadership and much more.

> It's hard to do justice to the positive shift within the transition team when we knew with certainty that the candidate God had been directing to us was someone

that we already knew well and all that remained was to prepare the candidate and the congregation for the most important season of transition. We were still pretty far from the finish line, but the critical decision had been made! (61)

The team's choice was Pastor Scott Stevens. Scott was not just a North Way guy; he was a quintessential Pittsburgh guy. He brought a love for North Way and a love for the city of Pittsburgh, along with deep humility from nine years on the pastoral staff at North Way — first as Family Pastor and then as Executive Pastor. Stepping into Jay's overseeing and visionary role would be a significant change for Scott, but one that the transition team planned for.

Jay starts the fifth chapter on *integration* by saying:

In late April of 2011, the transition team made their unanimous recommendation to the Elders' Council to extend the position to Pastor Scott. Scott prayed about it with his wife and closest mentors and accepted the call. The Elders' Council agreed that a brief announcement should be made to the congregation communicating our joy and excitement, peace and unity, in the unanimous decision of inviting Pastor Scott to accept the position of senior pastor, the public transition would not occur until September 30th, 2011, nearly a five-month runway where I (Jay) would remain in my position and focus my best energies and helping Scott, the staff, and congregation prepare for the official transition. (63)

After starting the church from the ground up and cultivating life-long friendships amongst faithful and founding members, Jay and Carol's influence on the acceptance of Pastor Scott was powerful. Beyond the elders and staff, there were many individuals in the church who held key roles in continuing the vision of North Way financially and others who carried great relational sway. Knowing it would be essential for Scott to build relationships with these same people, Jay and Carol came up with a personal way to connect them. Jay says:

I believe it to be absolutely true: you very likely will not support someone you don't trust. And, it's nearly impossible to trust someone that you don't know. Therefore, Carol and I made it a priority to introduce Pastor Scott and his wife, Tina, to about one hundred people that we invited to our home over several nights. These gatherings were informal, relatively brief, and included a great deal of interaction amongst the people who were invited. (50)

Jay and Scott met at least once a week during these months and supported each other as they both moved into new territory. Jay helped Scott become more familiar with some of the duties Jay had been in charge of for years as Senior Pastor, and they were able to talk one by one through many of North Way's ministries. As hoped, Scott's strong gifting for *administrative follow-through* complimented Jay's visionary bent, and they were able to discuss places where pruning ministerial focus might lead to future health within North Way.

During the months of integration, Scott was also able to preach more often. Though he hadn't started out as a regular member of the teaching team, North Way's model allowed for a gradual and natural process for his voice to gain acceptance from the congregation.

Though I was brand new to North Way at the time, I remember one week at the Oakland campus on McKee Place that must have been during this season of transition. Scott gave a powerful live message on the use of an "Ebenezer" in the Old Testament. Scott's sermon highlighted the importance of remembrance and of memorializing what God has done in your life. Jay talks of the same concept of a corporate altar in Chapter Six of his book: *Celebrate.* He makes a case for rest and observance, saying, "This principle of celebration is one of the most undervalued and even altogether unobserved stages in church successions. In an action entirely unlike God, we skip right past the seventh day of creation" (75).

Agreeing with Jay on the Biblical case for celebration, North Way held three events to celebrate the leadership succession. First, it held one to celebrate the departing Senior Pastor: Jay. The event was by invitation and included 300 key members who wanted to share appreciation for Jay's decades of leadership. The celebration was held downtown, symbolic of North Way's and Jay's heart for the city. Jay says:

> The evening was a mixture of humor and emotion, from a screen show that included 30-year-old photographs revealing just how different many of us have come to appear on the outside to the testimonies of quite a number of people who came from other cities and careers simply to add their words of Celebration and remembrance of what God had done.
>
> With all glory to God, I will never forget the deep inner joy of that experience and the unmistakable sense that we had made a statement not just about a man or one person's gifts, but rather about the power of God to change hearts, create community, and design destiny in those who trust in him. As in the feasts and celebrations of the Old Testament, this also would serve as a bedrock of faith for those who were present who were being called to lead the community in its next season of growth in the grace of community and mission. (77-78)

The second event was for the whole church and was held outdoors at 12121 so people from all the services at all three campuses could be included. There was ample time for sharing stories and good food. Everyone present celebrated God's work over North Way's 30-year history and also celebrated His guidance through the succession process. Jay took the opportunity to publicly thank the transition team for its selfless service as well.

Jay believed that these events were vital not just to the succession, but also to honoring God. "Celebration is not a sinful indulgence but a part of what it means to worship an extravagant God! Our redemption story should set celebration at the very core of who we are and all we do." (80)

The final event celebrated the new Lead Pastor — the title Scott preferred to Senior Pastor — at a Sunday morning service. As Jay brainstormed on the most effective way to "pass the baton," he considered Scott's favorite sports. Jay tells the story in his book as an example of an effective transition, but it's a piece of history well worth sharing here as well.

Most of our congregation knows that Pastor Scott has two great loves in athletics. First, he's been a fan and participant in the age-old sport of good, old-fashioned boxing. Though a set of boxing gloves may have had more use going forward, it is Scott's other love, the hometown major-league baseball franchise known as the Pittsburgh Pirates, that provided me with a nearly perfect object illustration. I immediately saw the image of a pitcher's baseball glove that was symbolic of when a relief pitcher took over for the starter. It was in no way a perfect image as Scott wasn't coming in for any inning or two, or even to be a "closer." He was, however, coming in to relieve the starting pitcher and to continue the game in a seamless and effective way.

Probably about eight weeks prior to this transition service, I began making a connection with the Pirates organization to provide me with an authentic baseball mitt worn by one of the team's relief pitchers. The image of a healthy, strong reliever coming in to secure the win for the team was on auto-replay in my mind every day leading up to that service. As I finished my brief remarks that morning, I turned to the congregation and said something like, "Now please demonstrate your full support by welcoming our new Lead Pastor, who's coming into this position with a strong arm and heart for our mission, Pastor Scott!"

As I pulled the beautiful game tested baseball glove out of the bag, the congregation exploded with enthusiastic applause, and I could tell that Scott not only got the image, but felt their affirmation and support as he took his new position. It was one of those rare moments that one can plan for and think about for a long time, and yet it actually exceeded my expectations in terms of its impact and allowed Scott to begin his journey as leader from a position of joy and rejoicing.

As I stepped off the platform for the last time as senior pastor, I had every confidence that the Lord had directed us to identify the right man for this position at the right time. Now, over three years later, I have little doubt that anyone present then would remember a single word that was said by either of us, but nearly everyone would remember the baseball glove that Scott received as he came on to lead the team. (81-82)

The seventh and final chapter of Jay's book deals with the *evaluation* of the succession after the fact. This was a unique phase for Jay because he and Carol made the decision to stay at North Way, and Jay was welcomed into the role of Founding Pastor. While many congregations and pastors find it easier to move on separately after a major transition, Jay was able to communicate a message of unity in this role. He writes:

For those who had a long history with North Way, this brought reassurance that we were holding to our core values and commitments even though certain elements of style or even priorities might change in the upcoming months and years. For people that were new to our church, it gave them a profound sense of the deep foundation that had been laid over the previous thirty years and spoke volumes to the stability of this congregation that they were considering as their possible home church. If anything, I believe this enabled and possibly even expedited the congregation to embrace Scott's leadership with even more trust and appreciation. (88)

Jay shares the dangers of this arrangement of staying on after stepping down but suggests that they mostly lie with the departing pastor and can easily be solved by that pastor's willingness to stay out of daily operations and guard his opinions, only sharing input when asked.

We are proof that this relationship can result in health and encouragement while both pastors remain involved both in the local church and the greater community at large. It's an incredible statement of Christians loving each other through change rather than divorcing each other. I am in no way promising that this is easy, but it is very possible by the grace of God and in fact, I would say, incredibly rewarding to see the ministry not just continue on, but flourish under new leadership. (89)

Jay's new position included overseeing the completion of an extension campus of Trinity Evangelical Divinity School at North Way, a project started under his leadership five years previous. He was also assigned leadership and support for the volunteers of L.A.M.P. and encouraged toward personal mentorship of pastors throughout the church staff.

As a result of an effective leadership transition, North Way saw unhindered growth in attendance, giving, small group participation, and ministry service. Jay says that each of these areas grew eight to ten percent annually. "One could just sense the joy and excitement of the new chapters that were about to unfold" (92).

Having come through one of the greatest challenges of a pastor's ministry, succession, Jay reflects on its gravity and grace, but suggests, "Isn't this often where true greatness lies, caught in the balance between daunting earthly statistics and the relentless love and efforts of God to build His Church, especially when all odds are stacked against us?" (97).

To this day, Jay receives countless comments from ministry leaders around the city on their admiration for the continued thriving of North Way after the succession. For the Founding Pastor and his wife to continue to attend and feel welcome at any campus and for the church to never have experienced a split or fracture of any kind is almost unheard of, according to Pittsburgh pastors like Lee Kricher of Amplify Church and John Nuzzo of Victory Family Church.

The transition team was careful to *communicate* with the press through the process, so that the succession could be presented accurately to the general public as well. One article that came out during the middle of the transition shows the witness of the transition. It went with a large color photograph of Jay at the top of the staircase in the annex at 12121.

FOUNDING PASTOR PROUD OF GROWTH
After 3 decades, Passavant ready to watch North Way flourish under new leadership
By Adam Brandolph

Tribune-Review
March 17th, 2011

The Rev. Jay Passavant knows how to grow a parish.

Since founding North Way Christian Community with eight couples in 1981, the church's congregation has expanded to include more than 4,000 weekly attendees at three campuses in Pine, Sewickley, and Oakland.

"That was never the objective or goal, it was more a by-product of what we do here." said Passavant, 63. "It's not 'churchy' in the sense that there's a lot of formality. What we're preaching is Biblical, but I think people appreciate that it's relevant to daily living."

Thirty years since forming the church in a small building off Perry Highway, Passavant is transitioning over the next six to 12 months to founding pastor, a role in which he no longer will make final decisions affecting the church or deliver weekly sermons.

"Now's the time to give that mantle to someone else, see this thing multiply even more," he said.

A graduate of Washington and Lee University, Fuller Theological Seminary, and Grove City College, Passavant — whose great-great grandfather William Alfred Passavant, started the first Passavant Hospital in the Hill District in the 1850s — has been married to his wife, Carol, for 40 years. They have three children and four grandchildren.

Passavant prides himself on the expansion of North Way, one of the first nondenominational churches in the region. The Oakland branch opened in March 2008, attracting students and families from the city and its eastern suburbs. The Sewickley branch, which meets at Osborne Elementary School, opened in September. The church plans to open a fourth location in the East End by the end of 2012.

Passavant picked Executive Pastor Scott Stevens as his replacement. Stevens is a nine-year member of the church who served as a family pastor for six years and executive pastor for three years.

"He's prepared and experienced," Passavant said. "He fits hand-in-glove with our vision."

As founding pastor, Passavant plans to spend time mentoring, bringing a seminary to the Pittsburgh area, finishing two books he's writing, and possibly visiting missionaries supported by the church in China, Honduras, and Turkey.

"Clearly, I'm not retiring," he said. "I have no desire to move to Florida to fish or ride a boat. It's not in my DNA."

With Pastor Scott at the helm, North Way went through a process of refocusing. After a long and fruitful season of expansive ministry, Scott's approach allowed the church to trim some things back and ask what was most important. The purpose-driven model helped assimilate large numbers of people and brought them into deeper involvement and commitment, but the leadership team also realized that the model carried less of an emphasis on North Way's original mission: making disciples, one at a time.

In 2012, a group of North Way pastors, elders, and other staff formed a team to study and implement a renewed focus on discipleship. Scott asked Kent Chevalier, Wexford's Campus Pastor, to lead the effort. Much like leaders earlier in North Way's history, the group read many books, visited other churches, and prayed about what God would have them do.

Pastor Kent, now Chaplain for the Pittsburgh Steelers, wrote the following about that process:

Through the strategic leadership of Pastor Scott Stevens, we landed on a definition of discipleship and how we would practice Jesus' last command at North Way.

A Disciple-Maker reproduces the character, ways, and mission of Jesus in others. We wrote this on a whiteboard and painstakingly wrestled through every word. We all agreed that this had to be an intentional journey with a few relationships at a time. One follower of Jesus would purposefully invest in a few people to reproduce what they had learned in them.

316

We trusted Jesus' original blueprint for making
disciples a few at a time. This is the long game approach
to disciple making and changing a culture. We believed
that if we invested in a few and journeyed slowly with
them to ensure a transfer of life, knowledge, and
obedience, we would see the multiplied impact of
discipleship in and through our church.

Kent and the team discovered several discipleship resources
and chose two to encourage North Way members to use in their
discipleship relationships. One was Dave Bhuering's book, *A
Discipleship Journey: A Guide for Making Disciples that Make
Disciple-Makers*. Bhuering, founder of Lionshare and host of
the d4 Conference on discipleship, was a personal mentor to
Kent and offered significant help and advice to the team at
North Way. The other book they chose was Greg Ogden's book
Discipleship Essentials, which emphasized the relationship-
building aspect of discipleship.

Within a few years, North Way created a full-time
discipleship director position in Wexford, followed eventually
by discipleship directors for each campus. Working alongside
campus pastors and other staff, these directors were tasked with
organizing small groups, equipping small group leaders, and
connecting members in one-to-one discipleship relationships.
*Author's note: reaching out for discipleship at North Way
during graduate school was a game-changer for me. Shout-out
to Dana Hunter at East End for connecting me to my wonderful*

friend and discipler Bob Connelly.

When Pastor Scott took over the Lead Pastor position, plans were already in place for the opening of a fourth campus in East Liberty. East Liberty was chosen with a desire to reach a new area and demographic, and leadership found a unique venue willing to house the campus: the historic Kelly Strayhorn Theater on Penn Avenue. As North Way sought to reach a more urban environment, and with the theater being just two miles from Faison K-5, Bryan McCabe was the perfect pick for Campus Pastor. He continued to oversee L.A.M.P. and shared the duties of Campus Pastor with Pastor Freedom Blackwell.

Freedom became a member of the teaching team, and he and Bryan worked together to reach a racially diverse congregation at the East Liberty campus. The East Liberty campus didn't turn out exactly as imagined, since the neighboring Bakery Square soon became home to new Google offices and luxury apartments for young professionals began to go up all over East Liberty. Though he continued to teach at North Way for years while fighting cancer, Freedom's final life's work was in founding House of Manna Faith Community in Homewood with the support of North Way and other churches, reaching the disadvantaged communities originally intended when planting the East End campus.

Freedom's obituary in the Pittsburgh Post-Gazette gives a glimpse into this man's life and faith, which so deeply impacted North Way:

OBITUARY:
REV. EUGENE "FREEDOM" BLACKWELL

Homewood pastor had passion for urban ministry

July 31, 1973 - Aug. 29, 2016

By Peter Smith

Pittsburgh Post-Gazette

September 6th, 2016

In what turned out to be one of his last sermons, the Rev. Eugene "Freedom" Blackwell sat earlier this summer in a simple chair in the parking lot of House of Manna, the church he helped found in his longtime neighborhood of Homewood.

By his side were the crutches he had been using since his left leg had been amputated due to the spreading cancer that would soon claim his life. A small group of congregants sat in folding chairs along with neighborhood residents for the casual Friday night service, drawn by the sound of gospel music and the scent of grilled burgers and hot dogs.

There, the former University of Pittsburgh football player told of his journey from the deadly streets of Chicago to his Christian conversion, how he visited church as a young boy and sensed a call to ministry but thought it would be boring. "Never tell God no, OK?" he told his listeners. What followed were years of risky living in and around Chicago and, later, Pittsburgh.

That changed with a powerful spiritual experience that, this time, prompted him to embrace a call to seminary and the ministry, most recently with House of Manna.

He said his story is not one of self-empowerment in which "I got off the corner, I'm strong," he said. "No, it's finding Jesus and being able to live like that."

Rev. Blackwell died Monday at 43 of complications from his long battle with bone cancer. He is remembered by colleagues for his ability to bridge racial, economic, and educational gaps and his contagious enthusiasm toward helping the needy.

"He had a fierce passion for justice and great faith," said the Rev. Sheldon Sorge, general minister for the Pittsburgh Presbytery. "He brought together beautifully the evangelical and justice components of the gospel."

Rev. Blackwell was committed to "tearing down the walls that divided people, the walls of race and age and all the walls we tend to put up in Christendom," added the Rev. Johnnie Monroe, retired pastor of Grace Memorial Presbyterian Church in the Hill District, where Rev. Blackwell attended. Rev. Blackwell later served as pastor of Bethesda Presbyterian Church in Homewood.

Alicia LaGuardia, who leads student ministry at House of Manna, said Rev. Blackwell's vision for the church was one that welcomed all regardless of how they were dressed or whether they had addictions or other problems. "Instead of having a traditional church where everyone feels they have to come in perfect, he wanted everyone to come as they were," she said. "He loved you like you were royalty."

Rev. Blackwell described earlier this summer how, even though he found success on the football field, he still faced temptations to "seek the money and seek the drugs and seek the attention from women. At the beginning it all seems good but … I was getting further and further away from God."

The pattern continued when he came to Pitt on a football scholarship. "I really didn't understand how much [my life] was deteriorating. One day I realized, 'I've got to get out of here.'" He moved from Oakland to live in Homewood with his grandmother.

She invited him to join her at a service at Carrone Baptist Church, just a couple blocks from where House of Manna eventually located. He described being overcome spiritually. "I started crying," he said. "I felt like God was saying, 'I'm calling you now.'"

He graduated from Pitt in 1999 with a bachelor's degree in natural sciences. In 2005, he graduated from Pittsburgh Theological Seminary with a Masters of divinity. He was ordained in the Presbyterian Church

(U.S.A.) in 2006. He also crossed denominational lines, including for North Way Christian Community.

He became founding pastor in 2009 of House of Manna, which has connections to Presbyterian and other church groups.

He flew to Portland, Ore., in June to the General Assembly of the Presbyterian Church (U.S.A.). There, he advocated for a proposal by the Pittsburgh Presbytery to start pilot programs in Pittsburgh and four other cities to address the "worsening plight of the African-American male."

Rev. Blackwell had been having difficulty eating and sleeping, but stood with the aid of crutches and made an impassioned plea that preceded the unanimous passage of the measure. "He caught enough people's imagination that people from around the country are contacting me and saying, 'We're going to do something in Eugene's honor,'" Rev. Sorge said.

Among Rev. Blackwell's survivors are his wife, Dina "Free" Blackwell, and their five children: sons Canaan and Elisha, and daughters Elizabeth, Alexis, and Jessyca.

Visiting hours with the family will be held Wednesday and Thursday from 11 a.m. to 1 p.m. and from 4 to 7 p.m. at House of Manna, 7240 Frankstown Ave. The funeral is scheduled for 11 a.m. on Sept. 9 at House of

Manna.

North Way's next campus was in Dormont in 2014, which reached a large urban population and was still several miles from any of the other campuses. The building the launch team found was a historic Presbyterian church. While the beautiful building added to the diversity of North Way's fellowships, the Dormont campus was still able to achieve a "North Way feel" through contemporary worship and the shared video message. John Reilly, who had multi-site experience from serving as Assistant Campus Pastor at the Oakland campus under Doug Melder, took on the role of Dormont Campus Pastor.

Around the same time, the Oakland campus outgrew the old Chinese restaurant on McKee Place. Despite offering four services every Sunday, 9 a.m., 11 a.m., 5 p.m., and 7 p.m., it could not fit all of the people who wanted to come. Pastor Doug Melder led a search for a larger space and found an old "gumband" factory with two floors and plenty of space for a sanctuary and kid's ministry. The congregation worked together on painting and other renovations and were proud of the new space.

Oakland's first building had limited space for kid's ministry, which had been okay since the majority of attendees were college students at first, but the new space allowed young families to feel comfortable attending the Oakland campus. As Pittsburgh became rated one of the nation's most livable cities and more tech jobs in Bakery Square caused students from

Carnegie Mellon and other universities to stay in the area after school, the new space was a great success. Dennis Allan became Campus Pastor at Oakland in the new location. Dennis had already been serving at North Way for several years and had met his wife Julia there. Julia is the daughter of Jay and Sue Dawson — North Way had started in her parent's basement.

In 2018, North Way launched the sixth campus in Beaver Valley. The building it found and renovated was instantly North Way's second largest facility, and its first weekend drew 800 people. Chris White, a pastor and church planter from Texas, was chosen as campus pastor and moved to Pittsburgh a year before launch to integrate and prepare. While Chris brought an outside perspective, other campus staff had been at North Way all their lives. Ceddie Conway became Worship Director at Beaver Valley, one of the first examples of a third generation North Way member on staff. Ceddie's grandparents, Chuck and Donna Conway were early North Way members, and Chuck was one of North Way's first elders.

While all these developments were taking place, Roy Thompson says he was looking for a more permanent home for the Sewickley campus from day one. In 2019, he finally found one. The location of the building he found provided extended access not only to Sewickley, but to Bellevue, Avalon, and more neighborhoods. The building was an old printing machine factory and perhaps bigger than North Way needed, but Roy ended up being willing to make the investment to purchase the building himself and rent most of it to North Way while using the other portion for his business offices.

Roy had been eyeing the place for four years, but had to wait for its pending sale to a lab company to fall through. "God held it open for us," says Roy. "First time I walked into it, I knew this was the place. It was perfect." After working on the initial 12121 building project and then on the addition of the annex at 12121, and as a faithful member of the Sewickley launch team and congregation, Roy was thrilled to continue to help North Way through a deal that will save a great deal of money. "Happy to be able to do it and put it together for the church," he says.

At the start of 2020, Pastor Scott passed the role of Lead Pastor to Dave D'Angelo in a succession as seamless as the last. Dave had spent the previous few years on staff as the Family Matters Pastor (the same role Pastor Scott had once held) and was found to be a strong internal candidate with experience and vision from other church leadership experience. Scott stayed on staff as Wexford Campus Pastor, making him the second Lead Pastor in North Way's history to "stick around" after stepping down from the position.

Scott approached the voluntary transition with great humility, and like Jay, looked to his next season with the spirit of Caleb, as spoken in Joshua 14:

I am still as strong today as I was in the day that Moses sent me; my strength now is as my strength was then, for war and for going and coming. So now give me this hill country of which the LORD spoke on that day, for you heard on that day how the Anakim were there, with great fortified cities. It may be that the LORD will be with me, and I shall drive them out just as the LORD said. (ESV)

~~~

Having arrived at this point in the history of North Way, we've come near the present, and in God's providential timing, we release this story on 1/21/21 to those who will write future chapters. I should say that this volume of history is limited in two ways. First — when it comes to the past — it is only representative, rather than exhaustive. We have followed the personal stories and perspectives of some key individuals, but there are literally thousands more to be shared which will surely bring inspiration and encouragement to all who will listen at the dinner table and in small groups.

Second — when it comes to the future — there are events in the works even during publication that are daily becoming part of North Way's story. Exciting developments in new campuses and leadership roles are happening. Challenges are being faced that few can yet imagine looking back on. I pray that each reader will be blessed by this work, but that they will look beyond its pages to learn more from the past and expect more from the future.

Grant and Rosalie Smith, who we met in Chapter One, have

remained members of North Way over the years up to today. After asking them a number of specific questions about their time at North Way, I welcomed any additional thoughts they might want to share. Grant's words below are a fitting close to this final chapter, so that Pastor Jay might share his own reflections to conclude.

All I can say, as I look back on the years of life together in this church, is that it has been an amazing ride, seeing what God has done. We have had a lot of ups and downs over the years, but He has remained faithful to keep us on track. The size of North Way and its impact on the Pittsburgh community is a bit overwhelming, except for the fact that God has done it. Clearly, we need to keep our focus on preaching and teaching the word, on prayer, evangelism, and growing deeper in our corporate and individual lives.

EPILOGUE
BY DR. JAY PASSAVANT

Reflecting on the past 40 years of life at North Way, I'd like to offer readers from our church and beyond four summarizing principles of all that has contributed to our health and success: strong spiritual foundations establish freedom, disciple making is organic, God's grace empowers effective ministry, and this all leads to a sure faith in the future. These principles are not about a particular strategy and certainly not a style of ministry; rather, they are principles based upon careful study of God's word, the benefit of many years of experience, and the confidence that God is still working by His Holy Spirit to expand His kingdom and grow His church which will share His presence and His reign for all of eternity.

The primary foundation leading to spiritual freedom, as seen throughout the story of North Way, is prayer. The importance of prayer can never be overstated, and real commitment to the practice of prayer is something that is not so easy to develop, let alone sustain. I believe with absolute certainty that the birth of North Way was in part a result of the sustained prayers of faith from saints who would not let go of God until He gave a clear answer. After establishing a steady stream of intercession two years before North Way even started, we could not imagine moving ahead without continuing our daily morning discipline of corporate prayer. Though that practice has morphed through the years, prayer remains in our church not just an awareness, but a commitment to a joyful discipline that is the essential way that Kingdom rule is established in and through our lives.

I'm not a fan of only praying prescribed prayers or any particular kind of determined pattern or outline. It is possible that these formulas may stifle our connection with the Lord. In our history, when we met for corporate prayer, we relied on the Lord's Prayer to give us a framework in which to include worship, declaration, repentance, petition, spiritual warfare, and the declaration of God's glory and future dominion. Still, we let the Spirit lead. Our times were never dull and boring; they were different every day and never ceased to raise our expectations of the Lord's presence and favor.

In addition to prayer, worship is another foundation on which to establish a healthy church. Acts 2:42 says that the early church "devoted themselves to the breaking of bread." Some translations interpret this as meaning that they shared meals together; however, that practice is specifically mentioned later on in verse 46. Other translations elevate this reference to the sharing of holy communion. In that sense, coming together to break bread is a practice of worship.

It's essential to be clear that when we speak of worship it is not simply what we practice on a Sunday. Worship should be a part of each time the church comes together in various contexts. So too worship can be found in the consistency of a lifestyle that honors God in word and deed and reflects the character and heart of God in relationships with others in acts of service.

Perhaps the most important component of the worship life of our church was the commitment we made to help equip each believer to understand that they had a "ministry to God" through the practice of worship. The glorious thing about praise is that it is communal, never becomes old, never loses its sense of mystery and majesty, and never ceases to remind us that God is so much greater than we are and always able to sustain us no matter what life brings.

The third foundation encapsulates and contextualizes the others. The word of God is so profound in its breadth and depth that literally thousands of books have been written on the topic. Without a strong scriptural foundation, we are setting aside one of the primary means that the Lord has given His church to grow in faith, make wise decisions, and live effectively as citizens of the Kingdom of God while here on earth.

At points in North Way's history, we made a practice of giving a brand-new Bible to every person who responded to an invitation to receive Jesus Christ as Savior and Lord. On numerous occasions over the years, I've been greatly blessed when I encountered someone who had received Christ at North Way, was given a Bible, and took the time to share with me how God had changed their life as a result of that decision and the sustaining strength they found in growing in their relationship with the Lord through reading, studying, and sharing God's word.

John 1:14 says, "The Word became flesh and made His dwelling among us. We have seen His glory, the glory of the One and Only, who came from the Father, full of grace and truth." There is incredible importance in understanding this verse properly. As a church, we have not allowed the word of God to become more central to the church's core identity than the Word of God, Jesus Himself, Who is full of grace and truth! Nonetheless, it has been critically important to stay rooted in the inspired word of God, particularly in our culture which increasingly tends to reject any form of absolute authority and leaves even the most important moral decisions up to one's individual preference. I'm deeply grateful for those who continue to teach the word of God and for all those who study and apply it to their personal and family lives on a day to day basis. May it always be so!

The final foundation from which a healthy church can expect blessed freedom in God's goodness is authentic community. One of the most natural and greatest joys of being a part of the North Way journey from the beginning was the experience of building an incredible number of caring lifelong relationships.

From the beginning, we didn't just meet to plan more meetings and have fun. Instead, we learned how to pray, worship, study, and serve together and to experience God's love as we all navigated through our various decisions and directions in life. When we formed small groups, it was not just a "program" which gave people a responsibility of meeting week by week to accomplish a certain task; rather, the groups became places of discovery where people could open up transparently with others and find acceptance, love, forgiveness, support, wisdom, and the true joy of learning how to walk closely with the Lord through the daily responsibilities of life.

One of the most important ways of training leaders was to tell them, "Once people know that you care for them more than for what they do, they will give you their very best in both." Authentic relationships are vital for community leadership and service. It has to be seen at the highest levels of leadership. People will not entrust themselves to leadership if they sense that the leaders don't share the same level of openness and transparency that is demanded throughout the church body.

I cannot think of anything more gratifying to me than to see that our small group ministries continue to flourish at every level and at every campus of North Way some 40 years after we began as one small group in Jay and Sue Dawson's basement in January of 1981. I've often said that North Way was a church of small groups before it ever was a church of weekend worship.

With a community established on the foundations of prayer, worship, the word of God, and authentic relationships, our second principle naturally extends from the health and life of the church: disciple making becomes an organic process. Over the years, I've read a number of well-written books on the practice of "discipleship" or "making disciples," which reference the Great Commission as the foundation for this theme. I remember attending at least three separate seminars that were supposed to be instructional about how to disciple others or, in some cases, taught discipleship as a way of advancing the kingdom of God through the local church. But in North Way's success, we never really came up with any kind of replicable formula for making disciples.

As the Servants Council studied the gospels, it became absolutely clear that the strategy Jesus pursued in establishing His kingdom was to invest His life into the lives of other men, particularly the twelve that He called to be His disciples. Jesus' message of salvation was learned; it was experienced through knowing Him. The full expression of the Gospel message as read in the Bible only came through the mouthpiece of the disciples after Jesus' resurrection. At the heart of North Way's foundation, establishment, growth, and reproduction as a church was that making disciples is something that takes place naturally and consistently through personal relationships, small group life, and regular ministry involvement.

There are countless stories that are not contained in this volume of people who volunteered to serve or help in a particular ministry simply because it was something they felt they wanted to do or were interested in. Only later did they discover a long-lasting network of relationships that was built around that ministry, which deeply affected their own spiritual growth as disciples of Jesus. In ways too numerous to count, disciples were made at North Way... but they were made by the grace of God through our natural relationships.

Running in and through the other principles vital to North

Way's history of health and growth is the rich bounty of God's grace. Grace is the difference between working in our actions, words, and disciplines to gain acceptance from God compared to the free gift of salvation based solely on the incomprehensible love of God, that which seeks us out and imparts to us the forgiveness and redemption that we desire.

No possible explanation exists for the relative efficacy and influence of North Way Christian Community other than the fact that God chose, by His grace, to allow His favor to rest upon us and to bless us beyond anything we had ever imagined, let alone prepared for. This expression of God's power through grace has worked itself out in three specific attitudes and operational convictions: flexibility, creativity, and risk taking.

From the very first days when we were gathering in homes during the week and in a rented banquet room on Sunday, every single week required an attitude of flexibility. In so many ways I was grateful that it was never easy. It helped to fashion in us a sense of resolve that no matter what the circumstances were, we could prevail over them if we pulled together with a joyful confidence that we could overcome these obstacles by the grace of God in us.

Hand in hand with the first value of flexibility is that of creativity. We discovered early on that there was often more than one way to give expression or meet a need than had been traditionally understood both in the operation and ministries of the church. We also engendered church-wide creativity when it came to giving personal testimonies on a regular basis. The stories of others became an important part of identifying the dynamic work of God that transcends a weekend's message in ways that a single preaching pastor could never accomplish.

Creativity was demonstrated in so many areas of our ministry. It was first discerned to be an essential part of learning to do "more with less." We soon discovered that God had poured out His spirit of creativity on so many people in various areas of service and ministry. As we've moved more wholeheartedly into the digital age, the historical creativity of the church has now manifested itself in incredible ways through video production, internet resources, and a commitment to excellence that has been woven into the fabric of our culture. There is only one Creator, but Ephesians 2:10 states that we've been created in Christ Jesus to do good works. We are stewards of God's good earth. We are co-creators of our blessed future.

Operating alongside flexibility and creativity within the power of God's grace is what the world would consider to be risk taking. Even a cursory reading of the book of Acts shows that early believers were courageous, bold, and willing to take whatever risk necessary to fulfill the Great Commission and to establish themselves in communities of faith meeting both in the temple courts and house to house.

When a handful of people are motivated to leave the security and stability of an established religious tradition in order to embrace something entirely new and unproven, there is an enormous sense of risk. We did this when we formed a church outside of a formal denomination. The reason I include the matter of risk taking under the theme of God's grace is because without the grace of God we would have stumbled badly and perhaps fallen woefully short of the plans God had for us. Risk for risk's sake, outside of God's provision, is not what I'm talking about. In retrospect, God's providence is what empowers and validates the risks we take in faith.

I'll never forget the profound recognition of God's hand at work on April 30, 1985, when we took a leap of faith and offered a price for our desired building that was underneath what we had previously offered, substantially less than we knew several other bidders could easily afford. As the years went on, the risk taking jumped to ever greater levels. As we acted in faith in the small decisions, God increased our faith for the larger ones. He proved faithful in the early risks, and we trusted Him even more as the risks became much greater than we could ever manage taking on our own. Along the way we discovered that God seemed pleased when we were willing to risk all that we had on all we knew Him to be.

As I write this, we approach the 40-year anniversary of the founding of our amazing church. It's with incredible gratitude and humility that I say with a deep level of confidence that our mission of establishing a local church that would stand faithful to the Kingdom of God and spread the gospel, not just for our generation but for our children's generation and their children and beyond, is clearly in view. By developing the values of North Way Christian Community with a balance of scriptural faithfulness and spiritual power, we have been able to navigate through many changing dynamics and the administrative oversight that is required as God adds significant numbers to our growing spiritual family.

One of the unchanging principles that we have never failed to consider was that early prophetic word: "I will send you all who you will care for." It continues to work itself out in consistent and growing small group involvement and the recognition that authentic relationships are foundational to the life of a growing disciple of Christ.

The working of the Holy Spirit has best been described as a pendulum that swings rather than moving in a rigid, straight line. Even though North Way's commitment to the Spirit's leading has caused some frustration for those who fall on either side of His centering line, it seems to have allowed our church to embrace people with various religious backgrounds without sacrificing an unrelenting desire for God's very best for our lives. This commitment inevitably draws us back to dependence upon the Holy Spirit, a recognition of the power of prayer, the priority of wholehearted worship, and faithful biblical teaching.

We have now completed two successful primary leadership successions. I have such great admiration for the leadership that Scott Stevens provided for eight and a half years. And one of my brightest moments in this past year was to stand on the platform on January 5, 2020. The Elders Council invited Carol and me to stand with Scott and Tina to officially embrace Dave D'Angelo and his wife Brooke as the new Lead Pastor for North Way's next season of kingdom growth. That service was a powerful experience for all who attended, to see the visual expression of unity and anticipation surrounding this second succession of primary leadership.

Dave brings a passion for biblical fidelity along with an openness to Holy Spirit led experiences that will empower our congregation and equip it to "prepare God's people for works of service, so that the body of Christ may be built up until we all reach unity in the faith and in the knowledge of the Son of God and become mature, attaining to the whole measure of the fullness of Christ" (Eph 4:12-13). To see the unity around Dave's leadership with gratitude for his high level of energy and desire to build consistency and fellowship between North Way's campuses, I have growing faith in the future of God's purposes being fulfilled through the life of our young church.

As I write these words, we are still navigating a global pandemic that has made leadership and personal ministry very difficult; nonetheless, we continue to believe God has a call upon our church. We've adapted by using digital media to stay connected and to proclaim the gospel with anticipation that in the coming year and those beyond we will be greatly blessed to see untold thousands of people around the globe reached with the hope of the gospel of Jesus Christ because of the faithful ministry of the saints who have been connected by the Holy Spirit in this one band of believers who 40 years ago committed themselves to one another and to reaching our world one person at a time… 1-2-1-2-1

All glory to God!
Dr. Jay Passavant

338

REFERENCES

Brandolph, Adam. "Founding pastor proud of growth." *Pittsburgh Tribune-Review.* March 17, 2011.

Galle, Deborah. "Church opens joyfully." *PG North.* October 16, 1994.

Gerberding, G. H. *The Life and Letters of W. A. Passavant.* The Young Lutheran Co., 1906.

Jelinek, Janet. "In search of God's heart: North Way Christian Community offers love and acceptance." *North Journal.* March 5, 1992.

Ovenshine, Gordon. "Christian body builders pump crowd." *North Hills News Record.* January 11, 1991.

Passavant, Dr. Jay. *Seamless Succession.* Xulon Press, 2015.

Passavant, Jay. "Stop Strife Before It Happens." *Ministries Today.* January/February 2002.

Phillips, J. B. *The New Testament in Modern English.* Geoffrey Bles, 1960.

Smith, Matthew P. "McCandless Church to Build a Multimillion-Dollar Complex." *The Pittsburgh Press.* December 20, 1989.

Smith, Peter. "Obituary: Rev. Eugene 'Freedom' Blackwell / Homewood pastor had a passion for urban ministry." *Pittsburgh Post-Gazette.* September 6, 2016.

340

Snyder, Howard A. *The Problem of Wineskins.* Inter-Varsity Press, 1975.

Snyder, Howard A. *The Community of the King.* Inter-Varsity Press, 1977.

Warren, Rick. *Purpose Driven Church.* Zondervan, 1995.

APPENDIX ONE:
DISCUSSION QUESTIONS

Bruce Bain, one the founding members of North Way Christian Community, has been leading small groups in the church for 40 years. From that wellspring of experience, he has provided the following reflections and questions pertaining to each of the chapters in 12121.

The questions are written to be used in small groups, but each reader can also dwell on these considerations on their own. After reading each chapter, before engaging in conversation, the reader should dwell on what points stood out and what ideas they will be taking from their reading.

CHAPTER ONE - PREPARATION

Pastor Jay stated, "I am the result of the prayers of my forefathers."

1) Do you feel you are a self-made person, or can you see how others have positively contributed to who you are? Who helped shape you?

2) Who might have prayed for you? Thank God for them, and if possible, thank them personally.

3) Who have you prayed for in the past? Who are you praying for now?

Elsie, Jay and John White, and then Jay and Carol all experienced beginning, growing, and expanding in their relationships with the Lord.

4) What are ways you see God beginning, growing, and expanding in your life?

5) Where is God leading you to have wider, long-lasting influence in some area of your life?

CHAPTER TWO – LAUNCH

The launch of North Way was preceded by persistent prayer, which helped in overcoming persistent obstacles. The early meetings of *the 9* consisted of worship, discussion, and prayer on repeat (Rom 12:12, Phil 4:6, 1 Thess 5:17).

1) What specific concerns in your life need persistent prayer at this time?

Small groups are core at North Way: no one alone, from a single original group to hundreds of current groups.

2) Are you in a small group? What impact have small groups had in your life?

The *original 9* found great direction in their foundational scriptures: Acts 2:42-47 and Eph 4:12-16.

3) What are foundational scriptures for you and why?

CHAPTER THREE – ESTABLISHMENT

In the first years, North Way developed its own unique personality: worship, small groups, leadership style, and solid core values. Follow Jesus; Do life together; Engage and influence culture.

1) Consider writing your own core values: for your life, for your work, for your family.

Another core principle for the church was one particular word from the Lord – "I will send you all you will care for." Caring for people brought people together.

2) What are ways; small, medium, or large; that you can care for those whom God has brought into your life?

CHAPTER FOUR – GROWTH

North Way tried to buy The Bradley House, but had to go into waiting at St Teresa's before God opened the door. Have you heard a "No" or "Not yet" from God? Are you at St. Teresa's, waiting and cold? Press on and don't give up.

This chapter has BIG events:

- Home group ministry greatly expanded.

- Blaine Workman became a pastor in a city church.

- Susan Geer cast vision for the Women's Choice Network.

- Michael Geer founded the Pennsylvania Family Institute.

But big events have small beginnings, so do not despise the day of small beginnings (Zech 4:10).

- There were only four home groups in 1981.

- Blaine left his CPA career to become a youth pastor.

- Susan went to a conference.

- Michael returned to school for a Masters degree.

1) What are the small steps you are afraid to step into?

CHAPTER FIVE – EXPANSION

Becoming a large church was not a goal of North Way, but expansion was the result of the leaders focusing on one core scripture. The call and purpose of church leaders is "…to equip the saints (believers) for the work of ministry…" (Eph 4:11-13) and help provide opportunities to serve. Examples are…

- The Car Cruise grew and reached a half a million people because volunteers gave time and effort and cheerfully welcomed all who came.

- Worship under Susie McCabe grew as she "mined the congregation" for talent and interest. She gave many an opportunity to use their gifts.

- Short term mission trips provided opportunities for non-missional individuals to expand their view of the world and of God's purpose for them.

- L.A.M.P. ministry was an opportunity to serve the city, continuing and expanding the effect of the city Christmas Banquets.

1) Often the *equipping* occurs in the *doing*. What areas of service or ministry is the Lord leading you into?

Regarding faithful, long term commitments, Susie McCabe said, "When you're faithful through the rough times, there's just a lot of richness that you develop from that obedience to just stay the long haul. I don't think people know the beauty of the long haul…"

2) What beauty have you seen through your persistence and obedience in the long haul with the Lord?

CHAPTER SIX – CHANGE

North Way and its leadership experiences change often, including the big changes of switching to the multi-site model and changes in leadership. But not only is God in the changes, He may be directing changes. Pray for God's direction amidst the changes you are facing.

Each chapter of this book, PREPARATION, LAUNCH, ESTABLISHMENT, GROWTH, and EXPANSION, and each chapter of life, they all have to do with CHANGE. Whatever change you are going through, trust God in it. The words of Grant Smith, one of the *original 9*, are very appropriate to ponder, lean into, and apply: "The size of North Way and its impact on the Pittsburgh community is a bit overwhelming, except for the fact that God has done it."

1) What are the things you are trusting for God to do in your life?

2) If you are in an overwhelming chapter, are you trying to work it out or trusting that God will do it?

APPENDIX TWO:
HOWARD SNYDER AND THE SERVANTS COUNCIL OF 1981

"This age to which we have come may be the most strategic one for the effective proclamation of the Biblical gospel" (26). Howard Snyder begins his book, *The Problem of Wineskins*, by comparing his culture of the 1970s to that of the 1st-century Roman Empire, a time when the early New Testament thrived.

Snyder saw the world to be increasingly urban and city-driven, as it was under the Roman Empire, more so than most centuries in between. He saw the world becoming increasingly driven by one culture and language (Western and English), as it was by the Roman Empire and the Greek language. The ease of modern international travel hearkened back to the 52,000 miles of roads built by the Romans, and he saw cultural interchange through mass communication to be again at the forefront.

From these observations, Snyder argues that if the early church could spread the gospel all over the world in the 1st century, the church should be able to employ similar tactics to influence the similar late 20th century. Snyder also draws parallels between the spiritual conditions of the 1st century and the late 20th century: the spread of humanism, practical atheism, and existential mysticism; the rise of new religions and cults, a fascination with astrology, the exultation of experience over reason; even moral degeneration.

While it would be easy to be frightened by such signs of moral decline, Snyder encourages, "Rather than be dismayed, perhaps we should look at these indications in another light. For we as Christians know that the true church of Jesus Christ can never be in any real danger of extinction. Institutionalized religion may decline. Immorality may grow. But even through these things God may be preparing a new revolutionary outbreak of the gospel that will once again alter the course of human history. Christ came 'in the fullness of time,' when the stage was set. And God is setting the stage today for a great moving of his hand — perhaps the last great moving in the world's history" (35). For this moving, Snyder believed the gospel would need new wineskins.

Taking "a new look at old wineskins," Snyder starts with the Mosaic covenant in the Old Testament and describes its three essential elements as sacrifice, priesthood, and tabernacle. He seeks to show from Scripture how all three are fulfilled in Christ, who became our once-for-all sacrifice, our eternal high priest (expanding the priesthood to *all* believers), and our full access into the presence of God.

Snyder believed that the early church lived in this freedom for over a century, to incredible affect, but that the church faced continual temptation to reinstate the old elements. "Returning to the spirit of the Old Testament, she has set up a professional priesthood, turned the Eucharist into a new sacrificial system, and built great cathedrals. When this happens, a return to faithfulness must mean a return to the profound simplicity of the New Testament" (58).

In good company with the author of Hebrews, Snyder contends that while the elements of the Mosaic covenant were of vital significance, the church has a better version. The tabernacle, a tent where God's glory could reside, was only a temporary substitute for the body of Christ and the eventual plan for God's presence to dwell in the hearts of believers and with His people in glory for all eternity (Rev 21:3).

In the next chapter titled, "Are Church Buildings Superfluous?" Snyder's answer is an unabashed, Yes: they are superfluous. He goes far beyond saying they are not theologically essential and recommends that they have been actually detrimental throughout much of Christian history. "Our church buildings witness to the *immobility, inflexibility, lack of fellowship, pride,* and *class divisions* in the modern church" (73).

These critiques may seem harsh, but Snyder was writing about the same status quo of mainline denominational churches that North Way was departing from. Snyder allows that a helpful use of church buildings is possible, but recommends that many of the local churches of his time would be better off abandoning their buildings altogether and meeting in homes instead. "A fine church building may simply attract the Pharisees and repel the poor" (72), he says, and, "Those really committed to Christ and his church will meet anywhere" (74).

North Way would one day accomplish great building projects, designing and renovating buildings to become functional hubs of ministry rather than sacrilegious temples of exclusivity, but this would only come after many years of minimalism, mobility, and creativity. At the start, the Servants Council felt that whole system needed to be challenged, and Snyder's book helped them tackle the radical questions that needed to be asked.

Next, Snyder asks, "Must the Pastor be a superstar?" By superstar, he was speaking of the rare dynamic leaders that seem to be equipped and effective in every area of church ministry. While we may be thankful for these leaders, he points out that if this is to be the standard, there are not enough such superstars to go around. Beyond a shortage of such leaders, he suggests that churches built on the talent of one pastor may find themselves simply looking on and that many gifts and hearts may be squashed in the process. But, he counters, if the body is to be a body, with each member performing its role, then God may provide all of the needs of a church through the unique giftings of the Holy Spirit (1 Cor 1, Eph 4).

Though Jay seemed to have a talent in a number of areas for leading people, he had learned well before the start of the Servants Council that leading meant training others to do ministry, not just doing all the ministry himself. Grant Smith says that one of his greatest encouragements as a member of the Council was that Jay, "didn't wear the pastor label strongly at all." With the eventual development of the teaching team, campus pastors, etc., the leadership model at North Way would differ greatly from many congregations that follow a single imposing personality.

The next part of the book discusses "Biblical Material for New Wineskins," starting with a chapter on what the Greek NT calls *koinonia*, or Fellowship of the Holy Spirit. Snyder describes *koinonia* as an inestimable gift and vital pursuit. It is not only fellowship *with* the Holy Spirit, but, "That fellowship *among* believers which the Holy Spirit gives" (93). He describes it further as the kind of closeness Christ modeled with his twelve apostles in the gospels; the atmosphere of the early NT church in Acts; a foretaste of the joy of heaven; a picture of the unity of the Father, Son, and Holy Spirit; the oneness Jesus prays we would have with each other and with Him and the Father in John 17.

According to Snyder, seeing the experience of *koinonia* as the goal behind church structures offers great freedom in those structures. A spiritual truth is at the forefront, rather than a physical blueprint, and, "We are free to create those structures most conducive to the mission and need of the church in our time, within the broad outlines of the biblical vision of the church" (95).

Several implications for churches are available from a study of *koinonia*, Snyder recommends. He starts with what might seem obvious: since *koinonia* is a collective experience, priority must be placed on gathering. With the first step of physical proximity in place, communication between believers should be pursued, so these gatherings should encourage churchgoers to do more than stare at the backs of each other's heads. If fellowship is to truly be of the Spirit, Snyder recommends, "The church must provide structures which are sufficiently informal and intimate to permit the freedom of the Spirit" (97). For, "Where the Spirit of the Lord is, there is freedom" (2 Cor 3:17). Lastly, Snyder says that *koinonia* should involve learning together in the Word, as promised by Christ in John 14:26: "But the Helper, the Holy Spirit, whom the Father will send in my name, he will teach you all things and bring to your remembrance all that I have said to you."

Snyder recommends that the togetherness, communication, freedom, and active learning aspects of *koinonia* can all be experienced, perhaps best, in home groups. He quotes Robert Raines, who said while speaking of *koinonia*, "Worship is indispensable as the weekly meeting of the Christian community. But it is effective only as the total sharing of all the people of the friendship in Christ they have known between Sundays" (98).

Next, in a chapter called "The People of God," Snyder talks about the church's peoplehood and the implications of being a called and chosen people. 1 Peter 2:9-10 says, "But you are a chosen race, a royal priesthood, a holy nation, a people for his own possession, that you may proclaim the excellencies of him who called you out of darkness into his marvelous light. Once you were not a people, but now you are God's people; once you had not received mercy, but now you have received mercy" (ESV).

While Snyder suggests that the Fellowship of the Holy Spirit may be best experienced in small groups, he sees the large group gathering as the best way to realize and experience peoplehood. "This is one reason why small-group fellowships, essential as they are, are not in themselves sufficient to sustain the life of the church. The individual cells of the Body of Christ must *see* and *feel* their unity with the larger body" (107). Snyder believes this feeling of being part of a *people* and a *movement* can give us courage and hope as we are scattered throughout the city during the week.

These meetings of peoplehood may extend beyond Sunday services to occasional meetings of thousands; Snyder even references the camp meetings of the previous generations. Beyond being saved at Camp Hollow Rock, Jay had with youth staff seen the beauty of this large gathering concept at the Jesus Festivals and at Vision '77. It was never the goal of North Way to become its own people separate from the wider church of God, and for many years leaders organized city-wide worship events, inviting and involving other churches.

One of the most important and thought-provoking chapters in *Wineskins* is on "The Place of Spiritual Gifts." Snyder declares, "One cannot understand what the New Testament means when it speaks of the church unless one understands what it teaches about the gifts of the Spirit" (130). He believed that individual gifting was an area where institutionalism was diminishing the creativity and uniqueness the people of God should display. As they read Snyder's challenges, the Servants Council knew it would be simpler to delegate the work of the ministry to the clergy — but they were after what was Biblical, not just what was the least messy.

Snyder points out several tendencies of the church regarding spiritual gifts, starting with the common belief that they are *not valid for today.* To come to such a conclusion, he argues that one must limit the application of the New Testament. He points out, for example, that we apply 1 Corinthians Chapters 12 and 14 to the operation of the early church, but would never consider throwing out Chapter 13. "Gifts and love go together — in the twentieth century as in the first" (130). He suggests that our tendency to deny their validity comes mostly from fear rather than Biblical understanding and argues that by ignoring this topic simply because it is difficult, we are in danger of "impoverishing the church" (131).

The best place for the use of spiritual gifts, Snyder recommends, may be the small group, where freedom and flexibility is typically greater than at the worship service. He points out the tendency to confuse spiritual gifts with innate abilities and explains that though these gifts often have roots in our personalities, they should be understood as *gifts* which are given by the Holy Spirit to the believer. The other extreme is possible as well, assuming that if one has a particular skill or talent before conversion, it cannot be a true spiritual gift. Snyder says, "A spiritual gift is often a God-given ability caught on fire" (133).

The most common and serious tendency *Wineskins* covers related to spiritual gifts is that of *exaggerating some gifts while depreciating others.* Snyder points to the way most discussions on gifts end up becoming debates on speaking in tongues as a clue that we are missing the point. "The tendency to think of spiritual gifts only in terms of the more spectacular gifts such as tongues, healing, or prophecy is an aberration which must be avoided. All gifts are important, all gifts are necessary and all are given by God for the common good" (134).

Snyder suggests that the lists of gifts found in places like Ephesians 4 and 1 Corinthians 12 were not intended to be exhaustive but are instead representative of broad categories that may include countless possibilities. "Any ability ignited and used by the Holy Spirit — whether in music, art, writing, intercessory prayer, homemaking, hospitality, listening, or whatever — is a legitimate spiritual gift. If God has given the gift, then it is good and is intended to be used. The biblical teaching is plain: 'As each has received a gift, employ it for one another, as good stewards of God's varied grace… in order that in everything God may be glorified through Jesus Christ (1 Pet 4:10-11).'"

Snyder quotes David Mains, saying, "Every true member of the local church has a minimum or one gift, and most people have many. Since no one has every gift, and everyone has at least one, there exists an interdependence among the members of the church. Scripture teaches (1 Cor 12:22-25) that the less spectacular gifts are more necessary than the showy ones. In other words, the church can go a long time without a miracle, but let it try to exist without acts of mercy or contributions!…How disabled the body of Christ has become because our primary purpose for church attendance has been to hear one man exercise his gifts, rather than to prepare all the people to develop their gifts for ministry, not only within the church but also to society" (135).

One final thing Snyder diagnoses is *the tendency to divorce spiritual gifts from the cross.* By this he means that the faithful use of gifts will involve sacrifice. He points to how Jesus publicly demonstrated many gifts and fruits of the Spirit, and yet, "The faithful exercise of his ministry led him not to the throne, but to the cross" (136). In light of Snyder's challenges, the naming of one's spiritual gifts may be less like a fun exercise in understanding one's personality and more like a costly call to action and divine purpose.

This topic of spiritual gifts is one of the reasons the council was starting a new church. They believed in the working and the gifting of the Holy Spirit and were not willing to sacrifice these gifts. Ray Speicher says the council was united by a passion for the work of the Holy Spirit, from the youthful couples to matured members like Grant and Rosa Lee Smith and a Marine officer like Jay Passavant. They believed this emphasis was not just for certain churches with certain extra-emotional people — the emphasis was Biblical and essential to the whole Church.

Having mentioned the importance of small groups throughout the book, Snyder also dedicates a full chapter to this topic as a basic and essential structure of the church. He details several advantages of the small group structure, including their flexibility, mobility, and inclusivity; their effectiveness at evangelism, ability to divide into more small groups as they grow, minimal need for professional leadership, and ability to adapt and support any existing church structures.

When talking about the inclusive nature of small groups, Snyder shares this quote by Elton Trueblood: "When a person is drawn into a little circle, devoted to prayer and to deep sharing of its spiritual resources, he is well aware that he is welcomed for his own sake, since the small group has no budget, no officers concerned with the success of their administration, and nothing to promote." This concept of welcoming each individual for their own sake and helping them find a home through small group fellowship has been vital at all points in North Way's history.

Snyder speaks of how urban mobility and technology are changing the way we operate in society. Church has become one box to check on a list of many compartmentalized priorities. We race from one distinct world to the next throughout our weeks, rather than living in close and continual fellowship and community. It is not likely we will even run into our brothers and sisters throughout the week unless we make time for it. Small groups, he recommends, may help church life be a way of life.

Along with their possibilities for fellowship and community, Snyder suggests that small groups offer one of the best opportunities to learn from the Bible. "The crucial fact is that something happens in Bible study in a small group that does not happen elsewhere. The Holy Spirit gives the unique gift of *koinonia* which makes Bible study come alive" (145). While sermons can be very helpful, Snyder says that in a small group one must confront God's word face to face and has the ability to wrestle with its demands in a group of people who know and care for them individually. This may not happen right away, Snyder allows, or all the time, but he suggests that the pursuit of this supernatural Bible study experience will be well worth the time and effort.

If readers of this book who attend North Way have ever wondered why North Way always seems to be harping on joining a small group, hopefully they will begin to see why. During college I was only a casual weekend attender for years and would complain that nobody even knew me, blaming the large structure of the church. I tried a couple of small groups, but didn't feel I fit in, so I continued attending on Sundays, expecting to survive on 90 minutes of fellowship a week. I do *not* recommend this path for any extended period of time.

I have had friends leave North Way for other churches where they immediately find they fit in better and begin growing. They compare and explain why a different sermon style or musical style has been a better fit for them, but I typically observe the biggest difference to be that the new church finally got them to join a small group. If one only attends on Sundays, they cannot expect to receive all of the components of Christian fellowship and growth — in my experience, it's that simple. So let me humbly ask once more: reader, are you in a small group?

In a chapter called "Church and Culture," Snyder describes two views on church that he believes both miss the mark of effectively engaging culture. First, the church could be seen as an earthly institution that must operate entirely within the bounds of earthly society. Second, the church could be seen as purely mystical, not to be bound to any earthly limitations or dimensions. The problem, he suggests, can be either immortalizing the wineskins or denying their usefulness completely.

While speaking of church within culture, Snyder asserts that the Bible does not speak of the church as an institution, but rather as a *charismatic organism.* "The church is, first of all, a spiritual organism, which may, secondarily, have some organizational expressions" (157). Snyder suggests it may be most helpful to make a distinction between the church and the parachurch structures that coincide with it. All that is not speaking of the church as the actual, global body of Christ may be seen as comprising parachurch structures — not only things like Billy Graham crusades and interdenominational meetings, but denominations themselves.

When viewed in their proper and secondary light, Snyder says, church organizations, programs, and denominations can be valid and helpful: expressing the varied personalities and cultures represented in the body of Christ and carrying the wine of the gospel to the nations. It is when traditions are sacralized and mistaken for the church itself that they become harmful, he says.

A proper view can actually bring great freedom and legitimacy to church denominations, suggests Snyder. "If such structures are not themselves the church and are culturally determined, then whole volumes of controversy and polemics lose their urgency and become merely secondary. Widely varying confessions are freed (at least potentially) to concentrate on that which unites them — being the people of God and carrying out their kingdom tasks — while relegating structural differences to the plane of cultural and historical relativity" (161). According to Snyder, setting aside stale structures would not only allow the Servants Council to pursue fresh ones, but would allow them to partner in the future with many different churches!

Snyder, himself a Methodist, dedicates a whole chapter to John Wesley as an innovator of church structures in the 1700s. He speaks of how Wesley took the gospel beyond the existing church structures of his time, even championing "class meetings" that were at their essence small group home Bible studies. In this chapter, Snyder says, "Church history reveals a recurrent tendency to absolutize and institutionalize the large group, wedding it to a specific building and form, while at the same time neglecting or even condemning the small group. Virtually every major movement of spiritual renewal in the Christian church has been accompanied by a return to the small group" (164). *Note: Snyder is still writing today and in 2014 published a book called "The Radical Wesley: The Practices and Patterns of a Movement Maker."*

Any member of North Way would do well to find a copy of *The Problem of Wineskins* and read it in full — better yet, study and discuss it in your small group! Check eBay; the book is out of print. Readers may find the final chapter to be a bit dated, where Snyder looks at the rapid acceleration of society and technology in the '70s and suggests that his would perhaps be one of the final generations on earth. He does offer a relevant insight here, however, saying that the early church also believed that Jesus would return in their lifetimes. According to Snyder, a belief that our time is short may inspire us to spread the gospel like they did and allow us to take part in God's grace toward many future generations.

Readers will also benefit from *The Community of the King*. Though it was of secondary importance to *Wineskins* to the Council, the amount of underlining in Pastor Jay's copy shows that it was very formative and would be well worth a read by anyone who wants to dig deeper into the spiritual roots and heart of North Way.

The *Community of the King* digs deep into the heart of the church; her identity, God's plan for her, and her role in the accomplishment of Christ's kingdom. While *Wineskins* was irreplaceable in helping the council rethink and reimagine church structure, *Community of the King* took them to the next level of understanding the nature and mission of the church they were structuring. Snyder covers the theology of a wide range of topics on the life and growth of the church and includes several more drawings to illustrate concepts.

The fact that the Servants Council took time in just three months of preparation for North Way to study not just *Wineskins*, but *Community* demonstrates that they were dedicated to more than just how this new congregation would operate. They wanted to get the heart right. They wanted to understand what it would mean to be a real community so they could live it out.

Here is one quote from *Community of the King* that I cannot pass up. Jay's copy of the book lays completely flat to this spot. "Spiritual growth occurs best in a caring community. There are spiritual truths I will never grasp and Christian standards I will never attain except as I share in community with other believers — and *this is God's plan*" (75). That first sentence sounds an awful lot like, "We here at North Way believe that life change happens best in small groups."

APPENDIX THREE:

WHITE PAPERS ON BAPTISM, ORDINATION, AND THE HOLY SPIRIT

There are thriving churches in Pittsburgh and around the world with different views on all three of the topics included here; however, the leadership of North Way believed it was vital to know where they stood as a church: why it believed what it believed and practiced what it practiced. Included here, these statements may continue to serve and inspire current members of North Way.

Just as North Way was at the time these were written seeking to reach its members with fresh study and articulations, each new generation must study these topics for itself. The hard work and findings represented here may offer a healthy jumpstart. Even as these topics must be articulated anew in response to new movements in the church and in society, a revisiting of the work and methods of previous generations may offer wisdom for our time.

BAPTISM

The "catch phrase" mission statement of North Way Christian Community is *Freeing People to Follow Jesus.* North Way is not about getting people to join the church or about making people religious. Instead, the preaching, teaching and leadership of North Way seeks to invite every person to live a new life by following the real and present person of our Lord, Jesus Christ. Following Jesus is a decision to submit to the new life that God offers through his son, Jesus Christ. One step that is very helpful in making this decision a reality is to follow Jesus' example and be baptized in water.

Baptism at North Way is not a religious rite for the sake of looking religious or faithful. Those who decide to follow Jesus have decided to live the new life that Jesus offers and baptism is an *outward* expression of that *inward* desire to live a new life. Baptism is also a *public* expression by the individual, which tells everyone of this decision to follow Jesus; they have accepted Jesus as the Lord of their life. Baptism is a marker for the believer that the old way of life is dead and they have a new life ahead.

The Bible refers to baptism using different analogies and descriptions. John the Baptist preached a baptism of repentance for the forgiveness of sins. He also said that he himself baptized in water, but Jesus would baptize with the Holy Spirit (Mk 1:4, 7-8). Jesus commanded his followers to "Go and make disciples of all nations, baptizing them and teaching them..." (Matt 28:19). Peter the apostle told new believers to "Repent and be baptized...for the forgiveness of your sins" (Acts 2:38). Paul speaks of baptism which washes away sins (Acts 22:16) and that in baptism, the believer dies to sin (Rom 6:2). Paul continues in Romans and shows that baptism is an identification with the death and resurrection of Jesus Christ.

What is baptism? What does it mean?

Sin separates us from God. There is nothing that any person can do to remove the guilt of sin because our own death is required to pay the penalty of our sin - the wages of our sin is death (Rom 6:23). Knowing that we are lost in this state of sin, God sent his son, Jesus (Mk 10:45), who took our sin upon himself though he himself is without sin (2Cor 5:21; 1Pet 2:22). He took our sin and died (our sin dying also) upon the cross. What must we do so that the death, the price Christ paid, can be our salvation? (Rom 4:25; 5:8-10)

If you confess with your mouth that Jesus is Lord and believe in your heart that God raised him from the dead, you will be saved. For it is with your heart that you believe and are justified, and it is with your mouth that you confess and are saved. (Rom 10:9-10)

Salvation is an act of faith, where we confess that we are sinful and unable to save ourselves - we need to be redeemed by God and for God. We accept God's love for us, expressed through the sacrifice of Jesus Christ and we give our lives to God. When we proclaim that Jesus is our Lord and Savior, God accepts us into his family.

Baptism is the symbol and expression of all this. Baptism is the outward expression of my choice to stop living for myself and be given new life by God. I die to myself so that I might live in the new life that God has for me to live. This is what Jesus means when he says, "If anyone would follow me, let him deny himself, pick up his cross and follow me." (Mt 16:24; Mk

8:34; Lk 9:23) Or as Paul said, "I have been crucified with Christ. It is no longer I who live, but Christ who lives in me." Gal 2:20. To confess Jesus is Lord means that I give up my life, die to sin, accept the death of Christ as my own death, receive my new life from God and resubmit it to the Lordship of Jesus Christ.

Paul describes this connection between baptism, sin and new life in Romans 6:1-14:

> What shall we say, then? Shall we go on sinning so that grace may increase? By no means! We died to sin; how can we live in it any longer? Or don't you know that all of us who were baptized into Christ Jesus were baptized into his death? We were therefore buried with him through baptism into death in order that, just as Christ was raised from the dead through the glory of the Father, we too may live a new life.

In baptism, we have a great picture and symbol of our death and resurrection as a participation and identification with Jesus' death and resurrection. In baptism, we die to sin. Jesus took all our sin upon himself as he went to the cross and died. Jesus' death is a sacrifice and sin offering to God (Rom 8:32; Heb 9:26; 1Jn 1:7-8). In baptism, we identify with the death of Christ by going into (being buried) in the water.

> If we have been united with him like this in his death, we will certainly also be united with him in his resurrection. For we know that our old self was crucified with him so that the body of sin might be

done away with, that we should no longer be slaves to sin— because anyone who has died has been freed from sin.

Now if we died with Christ, we believe that we will also live with him. For we know that since Christ was raised from the dead, he cannot die again; death no longer has mastery over him. The death he died, he died to sin once for all; but the life he lives, he lives to God.

In baptism, we also identify with the resurrection of Christ by being raised up out of the water. Therefore, we do not merely try to live a new life - we are raised to a new life. Our "salvation," our new life, is not about us trying to live in the newness of Christ, it is about depending on God to lead us in our new life. Verse four, above, declares that "Christ was raised from the dead through the glory of the Father..." Jesus Christ did not raise himself and no one can baptize him or herself. Dying to sin and being crucified with Christ is our decision, but we must be raised up to new life by God. No one goes to the waters of baptism alone. The pastor or leader is there in the water to act as God's representative to raise the believer from death to life. Likewise, no one lives their new life to God by themselves. We need to be in fellowship with one another.

The third member of the Trinity, the Holy Spirit, is also present and active in baptism and in the believer's life. The Holy Spirit is the power of God that raised Jesus from the dead (Rom 8:11). That same Holy Spirit is also given to the believer. The Spirit is the seal of our salvation (Eph 1:13-14a; 2 Cor 1:21-

22) and the power in us to overcome sin.

> In the same way, count yourselves dead to sin but alive to God in Christ Jesus. Therefore do not let sin reign in your mortal body so that you obey its evil desires. Do not offer the parts of your body to sin, as instruments of wickedness, but rather offer yourselves to God, as those who have been brought from death to life; and offer the parts of your body to him as instruments of righteousness. For sin shall not be your master, because you are not under law, but under grace.

As you count yourself dead to sin and offer yourself to God, you seek the new life God is giving and live under the grace of God through Jesus Christ, not under the old covenant law, which can not free us from sin and death.

Believer's baptism

The Greek word for baptize means to dip or immerse. Being fully immersed in water is the best symbol of the description of baptism above, as a burial (Rom 6:4). Likewise, the picture of one being raised from the water is also an apt symbol of being raised to new life.

In that the mode of baptism as described above, is that of immersion in water, the belief within North Way is that "baptism should only be administered to people who believe in the Lord Jesus" (Dr. Jay Passavant, Senior Pastor). In other words, those baptized should be old enough to know personal failure and sin, and be mature enough to understand Christ's death, and be responsible enough to decide to follow Christ as Lord. Therefore, North Way does not baptize infants, however, North Way does recognize and pray for the children and their parents as they are brought forward for baby or child dedication.

Many adults do request baptism even though they were baptized as infants or young children, when their parents so presented them. Since infant baptism, as practiced by many churches, is not believer baptism; since these are coming as adults to receive believer baptism, North Way will baptize them according to their profession of faith. Being baptized as adults multiple times, however, will be discouraged.

Romans 8 (New International Version)

Therefore, there is now no condemnation for those who are in Christ Jesus, because through Christ Jesus the law of the Spirit of life set me free from the law of sin and death. For what the law was powerless to do in that it was weakened by the sinful nature, God did by sending his own Son in the likeness of sinful man to be a sin offering. And so he condemned sin in sinful man, in order that the righteous requirements of the law might be fully met in us, who do not live according to the sinful nature but according to the Spirit.

Those who live according to the sinful nature have their minds set on what that nature desires; but those who live in accordance with the Spirit have their minds set on what the Spirit desires. The mind of sinful man is death, but the mind controlled by the Spirit is life and peace; the sinful mind is hostile to God. It does not submit to God's law, nor can it do so. Those controlled by the sinful nature cannot please God.

You, however, are controlled not by the sinful nature but by the Spirit, if the Spirit of God lives in you. And if anyone does not have the Spirit of Christ, he does not belong to Christ. But if Christ is in you, your body is dead because of sin, yet your spirit is alive because of righteousness. And if the Spirit of him who raised Jesus from the dead is living in you, he who raised Christ from the dead will also give life to your mortal bodies through his Spirit, who lives in you.

Therefore, brothers, we have an obligation—but it is not to the sinful nature, to live according to it. For if you live according to the sinful nature, you will die; but if by the Spirit you put to death the misdeeds of the body, you will live, because those who are led by the Spirit of God are sons of God. For you did not receive a spirit that makes you a slave again to fear, but you received the Spirit of sonship. And by him we cry, "Abba, Father." The Spirit himself testifies with our spirit that we are God's children. Now if we are children, then we are heirs—heirs of God and co-heirs with Christ, if indeed we share in his sufferings in order that we may also share in his glory.

Lead header on Baptism in search on NW site:

Publicly declaring your decision to follow Christ through baptism is an important step in your spiritual journey. We believe that baptism is an outward expression of the grace of God in the life of a believer. It is symbolic of salvation, not a part of it. Therefore, anyone professing a personal faith in Jesus should be baptized.

ORDINATION

The government of North Way Christian Community (NWCC) is established according to biblical principles and the guidance of the Holy Spirit. The Scripture is the primary guide for establishing the governing body for NWCC. This governing body consists of elders and pastors.

The NWCC board of elders consists of individuals recognized by the congregation and existing elders, who are mature believers with biblically defined character (1Tim 3:1-7; Tit 1:6-9). Prior to becoming elders, they would normally already be caring for and exercising leadership within subsets of the larger congregation. Therefore, it is not by mere appointment or elective voting that one becomes an elder. North Way is looking for people of mature faith, biblical character and spiritual leadership to become an elder and leader of the congregation. As spiritual leaders within and over the congregation one of the responsibilities of the elders is to appoint and ordain pastors for the church.

The pastors of NWCC are individuals who have received a personal call from God to pastoral ministry and who are recognized by the elders as operating within that call. The call of God and the gifting for ministry is confirmed through a process of training and ordination whereby that person becomes a pastor within the body of Christ.

What is ordination?

To ordain means to appoint, to establish, or to invest with the functions of a minister, priest, or rabbi. The Scriptures include various examples of ordaining and appointing. The purpose and design of ordination at NWCC is drawn from these scriptural examples.

The first instance of ordination in the Scripture is seen in the consecration, anointing and ordination of Aaron and his sons as the high priests of Israel. Their ordination is described in the 29th chapter of Exodus and includes the laying on of hands, consecrating and anointing them, and the sacrifices given which God required to accept them as his representatives for the people of Israel. Likewise, the Levites, in Numbers 8:5-22, were ordained for their service to God and to Israel in the tabernacle. They were consecrated and commissioned with sacrifices and laying on of hands. Thirdly, Joshua was appointed to succeed Moses and lead Israel. The Scripture recognized that he had the Holy Spirit within him and was commissioned to lead Israel. Moses declared this by laying his hands on Joshua in the presence of the priests and all the people. In this way,

Moses gave his authority to Joshua, so the people would obey him - Numbers 27:15-20.

Though all members of Christ's body are ministers of the Gospel, there are various offices of ministers within the church as described in the NWCC By-Laws. The Ordained Gospel Minister is that office of pastoral ministry wherein the minister is commissioned not only to minister the gospel to the congregation, but is set apart for that purpose and paid to perform that function within NWCC as well as to represent NWCC in the local community. The acceptance of God's call to pastoral ministry and leadership is not an elevation of spiritual rank over the rest of the congregation, but rather the acceptance of responsibility to serve God, to serve God's people and God's purpose in this local expression of God's body. The pastor takes on the responsibility of leading the congregation to be a visible expression of God's presence in the community. God also gives authority to the leaders to lead and guard the flock (Heb 13:17).

The official recognition and confirmation of God's call on an individual to pastoral ministry is established in an ordination ceremony, whether in front of the congregation or within a smaller setting of members of the church. Elements of pastoral ordination include prayer and the laying on of hands. Ordination is also the statement of the church to the state, which fulfills the legal requirements, so that the person is recognized by the state as a pastor who can perform marriage ceremonies as well as sets the tax status of the pastor for employment by the church.

Significance of laying on of hands

As seen in the examples from scripture above, the ordination "ceremony" must include prayer and the laying on of hands. What does the Bible mean by this phrase? The Greek word, *epitithami*, means *to put upon*. When hands are *put upon* in scripture, it is often translated lay (hands) on. Physical contact is a part of laying on hands, wherein a connection is established as a conduit to transfer from one to another. Throughout the Old and New Testaments, the hand is a symbol of power or authority, strength or might. The laying on of hands imparts the authority and spirit of one to another, such as Moses to Joshua, Moses to Aaron and Aaron to the Levites. The prophet Samuel, by God's direction, anointed David to be king (1Sam 6:13) and the Holy Spirit and leaders of the church in Antioch appointed Paul and Barnabas to the work God called them to do (Acts 13:1-4).

Laying on hands is one of the basic principles or foundational teachings in the church (Heb 6:1-2). In this act, one imparts something to another.

In the sacrificial ceremonies of the Old Covenant one would lay hands on an animal to be sacrificed in order to *transfer* one's own sin onto the animal. In this way, the sin of the person is imputed to the animal and the death which is due because of human sin (the wages of sin is death - Rom 6:23) is paid by the death of the animal sacrificed.

Moses *imparted* wisdom and the Holy Spirit to Joshua when he laid hands on him - Dt 34:9.

Laying on hands is also recognized to impart ...

- *healing* (1Kg 5:11; Mk 16:18; Lk 4:40, 13:13; Acts 28:8, etc)

- *the Holy Spirit* (Acts 8:17-19; 9:12, 17; 19:6)

- or to bestow a *blessing* (Gen. 48:13-20; Mk 10:13, 16; The example of Jesus lifting his hand and blessing the disciples is part of why we ask the congregation to extend hands in prayer, even though there is no physical contact - Lk 24:50-51).

Laying on hands is also part of appointing people to leadership ministry within the church and of commissioning and ordaining pastors to the ministerial office. The examples of Aaron, the Levites, and Joshua have already been mentioned. Note also deacons (Acts 6:1-7), Paul and Barnabas (Acts 13:3) and Timothy's gifting (1Tim 4:14), which was probably preaching and teaching and leading the church (1Tim 4:11-13).

The examples from the Bible clearly show the importance of laying on hands, and it is therefore a vital part of ordination at NWCC. Just as the leadership of the people of Israel was passed on to Joshua through Moses' hands, so we follow the biblical mandate and example, in full faith that God is present and commissions the pastor with an impartation of the power and authority of the Holy Spirit. The pastor accepts the responsibility to lead and understands that without the presence of the Holy Spirit, the pastor cannot guide the congregation. It is of utmost importance to note as well, that laying on hands is not a ritual for the sake of appearances. In the laying on of hands we come in faith, not only believing for, but expecting and anticipating the impartation of the Holy Spirit, spiritual blessing, healing, authority, and power. The commissioning to ministry and ordination to a pastoral office is a spiritual event in the presence of God, not merely a human stamp of approval.

We do make a distinction here between the ordination of a pastor and the appointing of elders and deacons. The essential purpose of ordination is to set apart and anoint for ministry, as were the priests of the Old Testament in their unique role of representing all the people of Israel before God. Perhaps following that OT model, the King James Version, with a strong influence from Roman Catholicism, is the only Bible translation to use the English word *ordain* regarding church leadership (Mk 3:14; Jn 15:16; Acts 6:1-6, 13:1-3, 14:23; 1Tim 4:14; 2Tim 1:6, 2:7; Tit 1:5), whereas other translations use the word *appoint* (RSV, AB, NIV, PME, JB, LB, NEB). In truth, the Greek behind these translations is not one word, translated as ordain, but up to seven different Greek words. So there was not, in New Testament times, a set practice of setting pastors in place, though certainly, prayer and the laying on of hands were part of all such commissionings or appointments.[2] In modern

---

[2] "In view of the fluidity of practice in the early Christian communities and the technical meanings that 'ordain' has [since] acquired, it is

practice, the pastor is accepting a specific call of God and making a commitment of full devotion to nurture and be responsible for the health of the whole congregation, a commitment for which they will have to give an account (Heb 13:17). The elders and deacons are to lead and serve as a group, whereas the pastor has more individual duties and responsibilities. So though we do not ordain elders and deacons, we do see a strong biblical directive to practice the laying on of hands to impart leadership authority and anointing.

THE HOLY SPIRIT

Over the past 25 plus years, North Way Christian Community has been blessed with a theological and practical balance in our understanding of the ministry of the Holy Spirit.

The intent of this brief document is to re-state North Way's position on how the Holy Spirit works in our lives and what we as individuals and as a church should expect the Holy Spirit to do in order to bring about the fullness of life of Jesus in us.

It is necessary that we begin by understanding that

---

probably best to avoid the use of this term in rendering biblical terms that deal with appointments to various types of service. Awareness of this hazard of anachronism should not, on the other hand, prejudice the privilege of each Christian community to adopt such practices and rites as may assist the Church in expressing and discharging its principal responsibility, the proclamation of the gospel." Danker, FW, "Ordain", *The International Standard Bible Encyclopedia*, ed. GW Bromiley, 1986, Vol. 3: 612-613.

everything about the Holy Spirit points us back to Jesus. Conversely, Jesus frequently points us to the Holy Spirit as the source of power to live the life that he calls us to live throughout the Gospels. In fact, I would say that it is

- impossible for the **person** of Jesus to be made visible in our character except by allowing the Holy Spirit to come in and dwell with us, and

- we cannot have the **power** of Jesus flowing through our lives unless the Holy Spirit comes in and overflows us.

Now, of course, the danger of language is that if we use terms like "impossible" or "cannot," it implies that there is absolutely no evidence that the Lord is in a life unless we have defined our terms exactly the same way. This is where I want to urge the reader to be very careful to understand that we're not about trying to define terms to the point where we eliminate the reality that all the work of God's grace in our lives falls within a certain **continuum** and therefore some of the presence and some of the power of Jesus can be manifest in the beginning stages of the Christian life, but should be much more demonstrable and evident as we mature and move toward the other end of the spectrum.

The Holy Spirit dwells within and overflows in believers. One of the clearest and simplest metaphors to understand how the Holy Spirit works in our lives is to see the language that Jesus used in John's gospel.

"The Spring of Water." This is the first expression of the presence of the Holy Spirit that occurs *within* us to satisfy the thirst in *our life.* This happens when we are saved. In John 4:13-14 when Jesus said to the Samaritan woman at the well, *"Everyone who drinks this water will be thirsty again, but whoever drink the water I give him will never thirst. Indeed, the water I give him will become in him a <u>spring of water</u> welling up to eternal life"* (NIV). Clearly, the Holy Spirit is described as an indwelling presence which satisfies the thirst in our own personal hearts. Notice that the word *spring* is singular - it refers to something for our personal need.

"The Streams." The second dynamic of the Holy Spirit flows *outward* to serve the needs of others. The overflow of our lives makes us vessels of Christ's life to satisfy other people's thirst. In John 7:37-39, Jesus says, *"If anyone is thirsty, let him come to me and drink. Whoever believes in me, as the Scripture has said, streams of living water will flow from within him. By this he meant the Spirit, whom those who believed in him were later to receive. Up to that time the Spirit had not been given, since Jesus had not yet been glorified."*

Clearly, the Holy Spirit is described here as empowering the believer to reach out, to serve, to witness, to love, and to give. This is the *flowing* out of God's life into others. Notice that the word *"streams"* is plural in these verses. The one spring of water overflows and becomes many streams as God works through us to minister His love to many others. We are the well of water and God moves the well to the thirsty people. This indicates that we will be equipped for the needs of many people!

And so, it is imperative that we begin by understanding that the Holy Spirit, as a member of the Trinity, both *indwells us* and *empowers us*; he has a two-fold role just as Jesus said he would. It would seem that every believer would desire for both of those experiences in the same way that Jesus fulfilled the experience of **redeemer** and **restorer.** Jesus didn't just forgive us for our sins, he restored us to the fullness of life!

Important Terminology

One of the most frequent comments that we encounter about the Holy Spirit is, "When we receive Christ, don't we receive the Holy Spirit as well?" Or, "When we receive Christ, aren't we baptized in the Holy Spirit?"

This is one of those places where the Greek language is very helpful. It's clear that all who come to Christ are baptized by the Holy Spirit into the body of Christ (1 Cor 12:13a). In other words, the Holy Spirit is the agent that immerses them into the body of Christ and helps them to be fully part of God's family.

It is also accurate to say that when one receives Christ, you receive the Holy Spirit as the presence of God in your heart (Romans 8:9). However, it seems clear that Jesus had something else in mind. He says in Acts 1:5, *"For John baptized with water, but in a few days you will be baptized with the Holy Spirit"* (NIV). Friends, there are six different expressions to describe this same event throughout the remainder of the book of Acts. It is not accurate to say that the "baptism of the Holy Spirit" is the only language that can be used for the experience of the overflow of the Spirit in your life. However, being baptized *with* the Holy Spirit is different than being baptized *by* the Holy Spirit.

Being baptized with the Holy Spirit is the language of "overflow." The word "baptizo" is a picture that is something that is immersed, or sunken, much like a ship would be that has fallen to the bottom of the ocean floor. It is completely immersed and overflowing in the water. Likewise, Jesus is saying that when we are baptized with the Holy Spirit, we are completely immersed and overflowing with His life.

384

APPENDIX FOUR:
PROSE AND PRAISE BY SUSIE MCCABE

"New Wineskin - a prophetic word to leaders"
Matthew 9:17

What God wants to do with us involves a totally new wineskin. This is not news but we are still out searching for a used wineskin that will do and there is none. We must become as a newborn with no preconceived idea of how God is, will work, or will be made known. God wants to build our experience of Him from the foundation up. It is not a remodeling job He is doing but an original work; not a replica, not a print, but an original. We must start with a new tapestry and allow God to paint. Our form has become the veil; God rent the veil but we hold it taut. The things we do keep the veil in place. He would have the veil relax, fall open, separate so that His love can reach and He can usher people into the Holy of Holies. The Holy of Holies is not what you think you have come to know. It is vastly deeper - without limits, without end. It is holy, yes, but it is the depth of the heart of God; His unfathomableness! One can barely speak of it! To be ushered into the heart of the Living God! His hand reaching, ushering we simply ARE with Him, as one, from the depth of His being

He calls out. From the bowels of His Spirit, He utters! That is the Spirit song - Utterance Compelled! That is the song of the Lord!

Worship! The presence of God, ushered by His hand into Himself for He is everything. Into the all-knowing, all-seeing, Omnipotent being of the Lord Most High. Even as the Father, Son, and Spirit are one, we become one with Him. Except by the blood of the Lamb we would be consumed in the presence of Holy God. Only as spotless can we be absorbed into His being and that is only by the spotless sacrifice of a Risen Savior. When that was done, He reached, we met Him, and He waits to take us into Himself. Our directive as leaders is to simply relax the veil so that He can reach. He ushers - He absorbs us - He makes Himself known. We must allow ourselves to be ushered and from the depths or bowels of His heart respond… having seen, having known… say, "Come, Welcome", assist, point toward, God ushers! We have no need to be God, we simply point the way, "See Him," "Come," "Know Him," "Grab His hand," "Go" into the presence of a Holy God! We are ushered into His being and we are saved!

Where does music fit into this? Music (inspired by His Spirit) draws, woos, moves! In the Spirit, in what God has called us to do, He wants to use music - notes shaped in beauty, awe, power, to be used in such a way that people cannot turn away, they are ushered and drawn and the veil falls away and they are drawn by His hand into His being. Music is simply a vehicle of God's reaching, movement toward Him, an instrument of wooing. We can be drawn by His power, by His care, by His gentleness, by His majesty and authority, by His still small voice, by His rushing river, by His quiet stream. We are drawn by His right hand (the place where God dispenses His blessing, purposes, and protection, ultimately revealed in Christ) into His being.

Our RESPONSE-ability then becomes to His vastness, the immensity and depth of His love. Awesomeness takes on a whole new dimension, without end. MAN-i-festation - His revealedness to man, comes from the place of His being - His Spirit revealed to man, a tangible experience or expression of Himself in a visible way is limitless. It simply cannot be defined and will be different for each one, each time. Such is His nature to make Himself known. This is our call to let Him!

"Loss of a Love"
Psalm 65:4, 1 Corinthians 12:12, 27

As I came home after reaching some shattering moments and could not stop the flood of tears, I am realizing I am grieving a grave loss - so I have let myself grieve. I've lost a love - a deep love - love that had grown through the ages, a love that I had held close and treasured, and it has been torn away and I must now put it in the grave - the love of birthing music, the love of giving life to a song through the gift of others; watching, listen to God, hear him give a song, and being part of giving it wings to soar through a voice or voices, through instruments and watching others glow with finding the fulfillment of letting God use their gift to His glory. What joy! Match gift to opportunity, watch life begin in a heart, see it given away, and be part of the "Aha" moment. I miss it so. I miss being used to bring such pleasure to a heart, to nurture insecurity into faith, to see God meet and blossom in an instrument of His glory and see the light of His Spirit bring joy. Oh such grace to see His face in the countenance of discovery of His faithfulness; His hand moving, releasing, birthing; and to know I had a part in His plan. It is amazing being part of the whole, to rejoice with those who rejoice, to watch God use the gift of music to enlighten another heart, to see His tender mercies at work, gently wooing others to Himself through His creative nature; seeing God use something you've chosen through His direction be released into the Spirit to be carried into the heart of others and to see them changed. And Wow! God used my meager offering to transform. How my heart cries and aches to have lost such a love as this. It is as if a light in my soul has been extinguished and I see so much dimmer His glory. Oh how I love the Lord. Oh how I've felt His power and love and mercy in such times. It has been such a treasure to be His handmaiden in such a way! What a love! How do you explain such a loss? It is too deep to comprehend. This releasing of life, injecting life into the lives of others that the glory of God is seen, and you've had the privilege of partaking, drinking of its loveliness, being satisfied with His likeness seen in the lives of others.

Such richness, such awe; the Lord of the universe manifest in feeble human efforts and transformed into beauty; so unexplainable.

Psalm 65:4 Blessed are those you choose and bring near to live in Your courts. We are filled with the good things of Your house, of Your Holy Temple.

Such is His majesty - that it draws and fills

Such is His glory - that it fills and fulfills

Such is His mercy - that He brings us near

Such is His grace - that He chooses us

Such is His love - that we are blessed with His good things.

O for the love of the living God, so immense and full. Spirit of God, take this grieving heart and make it a pathway to Your throne where healing waters flow that I might again be a vessel used by You to quench the thirst of others by helping them find their place in You.

"Sing for Joy" (Journey Through the Veil)
Isaiah 44:23

Sing for joy, O heaven

Exult and shout, O earth

Break forth, O mountain into singing

    For the Lord will be glorified

Sing to the Lord,

    He has redeemed us

Break forth in joy,

    Give glory to the Lord

Sing to the Lord,

    He has redeemed us

And He will be glorified

"Land of the Living" (Journey Through the Veil)
Psalm 27:13-14

I believe that I shall see the goodness of the Lord in the land of
the living

I believe that I shall see the goodness of the Lord in the land of
the living

I believe that I shall see the goodness of the Lord in the land of
the living

Wait for the Lord! Wait for the Lord! Wait for the Lord!

Be strong! Let your heart take courage

Be strong! Let your heart take courage

Be strong! Let your heart take courage

Wait for the Lord!

Be strong! Let your heart take courage

Be strong! Let your heart take courage

Wait for the Lord!

Wait for the Lord!

"Blessed Be Your Name"
Psalm 40:16, Isaiah 25:9

Blessed by Your Name, Most High,

    Risen Lord, triumphant, I will rejoice and be made glad.

Blessed by Your Name, Most High,

    Risen Lord, triumphant, I will rejoice and be made glad.

Lord, You are my righteousness,

      Showing truth and faithfulness,

         I will rejoice and be made glad.

Lord, You are my righteousness,

      Showing truth and faithfulness,

         I will rejoice and be made glad.

"Enter His Gates"
Psalm 100:4, Psalm 116:18-19

I will enter His gates and sing with much thanksgiving

I will enter His gates with a sacrifice of Praise

I will fulfill my vow in the congregation

      acknowledge all His ways

I will enter His gates with thanksgiving in my heart

"Glory to God in the Highest"
1 John 5:11

Glory to God in the highest;

Peace to His people on earth.

Glory to God in the highest;

Let us rejoice at His birth.

God sent His glory among us;

Dwelling with us as a child.

Humbly He took on our nature;

Through Him alone, we are reconciled.

Eternity's gift has been given;

Setting us free from our strife.

Now we are joined with our Maker;

Partakers of His everlasting life.

"Behold the Lamb" (Journey Through the Veil)
John 1:35

Behold the Lamb in the beauty of His Holiness

Behold the Lamb, clothed in majesty

Behold the Lamb, adorned in robes of righteousness

Behold the Lamb of God

    With arms open wide,

        With love in His eyes,

            He's reaching out to me.

"Come Now Behold Your King" (Journey Through the Veil)
Exodus 9:16, Psalm 22:22

Come now behold Your King

  Lift up your voices and sing.

His holy name proclaim

  Jesus is Lord, glorious Lord.

Just past the veil we see

  To worship His majesty.

Held by His glory and grace, His love we embrace.

"We Glorify"
Psalm 86:12, Psalm 71:7

We glorify Your name on high

We celebrate all You create

We magnify and lift You high

Your Name adored, we crown You Lord.

All praise and honor be unto You, Lord.

Send Your Spirit to break the bonds

And set us free to worship Thee.

"Rejoice in the Goodness of the Lord"
Psalm 32:11

Rejoice, rejoice in the goodness of the Lord,

    For His name is to be greatly exalted.

Rejoice, rejoice in the goodness of the Lord,

    His name is worthy of our highest praise.

Life your voice and sing, praise to the great and mighty King,

    Praise the Lord!

Life your voice and sing, praise to the great and mighty King,

    Praise the Lord!

"Make Me Faithful"
Deuteronomy 28:1-6

Lord, make me faithful to all I've been given.

Let me answer the call, give You my all,

    As I search to find my way.

Lord, make me faithful in ev'ry provision.

Let me just know your voice make the right choice

    To trust and obey.

"Wherever You Lead"
John 16:13, Lamentations 3:25

Wherever You lead, there I will follow,

Willing and eager to do what You say;

Open to be used as a vessel,

Flowing abundantly filled with Your power.

"You Are My Lord" (Journey Through the Veil)
Mark 1:10-11

Your Spirit like a dove, is abound with endless love,

As we see You face to face, showing forth amazing grace.

You came to dwell within me and set my spirit free.

All the fullness of Your love released in me.

You give life to my soul, peace to my heart

Light to my feet, joy overflowing,

You give life ever after and love evermore.

My future in You is secure.

You are love, You are peace,

You are joy, You are my Lord,

You give life, You give piece,

You give light and joy overflowing,

You give life, You are love,

You are my Lord.

As a bonus to these dozen favorites by Susie, here is one written by Jay Passavant.

"Most High"

Most High, Most High, O Lord Most High,

We're in this Holy Place.

Most High, Most High, O Lord Most High,

I yearn to see Your face.

Before Your throne, I bow, Most High,

I hear Your Word; Be still.

Reveal to me Your ways, Most High,

I seek to do Your will.

My heart I give to You, Most High,

Please draw me to Your side.

Your will is my desire, Most High,

The height of earth I'll ride.

Most High, Most High, O Lord Most High,

My hands to You I raise.

Most High, Most High, O Lord Most High

Confirm in me Your ways, confirm in me Your ways.

APPENDIX FIVE:
PHOTOS

REV. W. A. PASSAVANT

DINNER AT THE COMMANDANT'S HOUSE
(JAY AND CAROL FAR RIGHT)

FISHERMAN'S UNION OF DEVOTED DISCIPLES
(BRUCE AND KATHY BAIN FAR LEFT)

PRAYER CIRCLES BENEATH BANNER, ST. TERESA'S

JAY AND CAROL WITH BILLY GRAHAM

STARLIGHT PROPERTY AND SURROUNDING LAND

STARLIGHT FOR SALE

410

COMMISSIONING SERVICE WITH ABRAHAM POTHEN, INDIA

JAY AND RICK WARREN

ACKNOWLEDGEMENTS

The stories in this book could not have been written without the gracious willingness of those who shared them with me. In addition to more than 15 interviews with Pastor Jay and one with Carol, I had the privilege of sitting down with Bruce and Kathy Bain, Amy Scheuring, Blaine Workman, Sue Dawson, Roy Thompson, Susie McCabe, Ray and Marcia Speicher, and Scott and Missy McCabe. Michael Geer shared his story over the phone, and Grant and Rosa Lee Smith shared via email. I am thankful for the faithful examples and kind friendships of these saints and for how freely they gave of their time and thoughts.

After years of transcribing interviews and weaving this history together, I have been blessed to have the help of Paul Frank Spencer in bringing it to publication. We owe sincere thanks to a few individuals who have donated funds to get the initial printing into the hands of North Way's families. While publication of this book took only a handful of key contributors who believe in the value of the project, we pray that many more will be inspired by it to believe in all that God has in store for the future of North Way.

ABOUT THE AUTHOR

Alexander Hettinga is a reader, writer, and collector of books. He came to Pittsburgh from Ohio in 2009 to study violin at Carnegie Mellon University. He met his wife Angela at North Way when they were both students at CMU, and he proposed to her on the roof of the North Way Oakland building. In 2019, a year after the birth of Alex and Angela's daughter Hannah, Alex stepped into full-time ministry, starting a program to coach new and expectant fathers in Pittsburgh.

CPSIA information can be obtained
at www.ICGtesting.com
Printed in the USA
BVHW081326231220
596243BV00001B/1